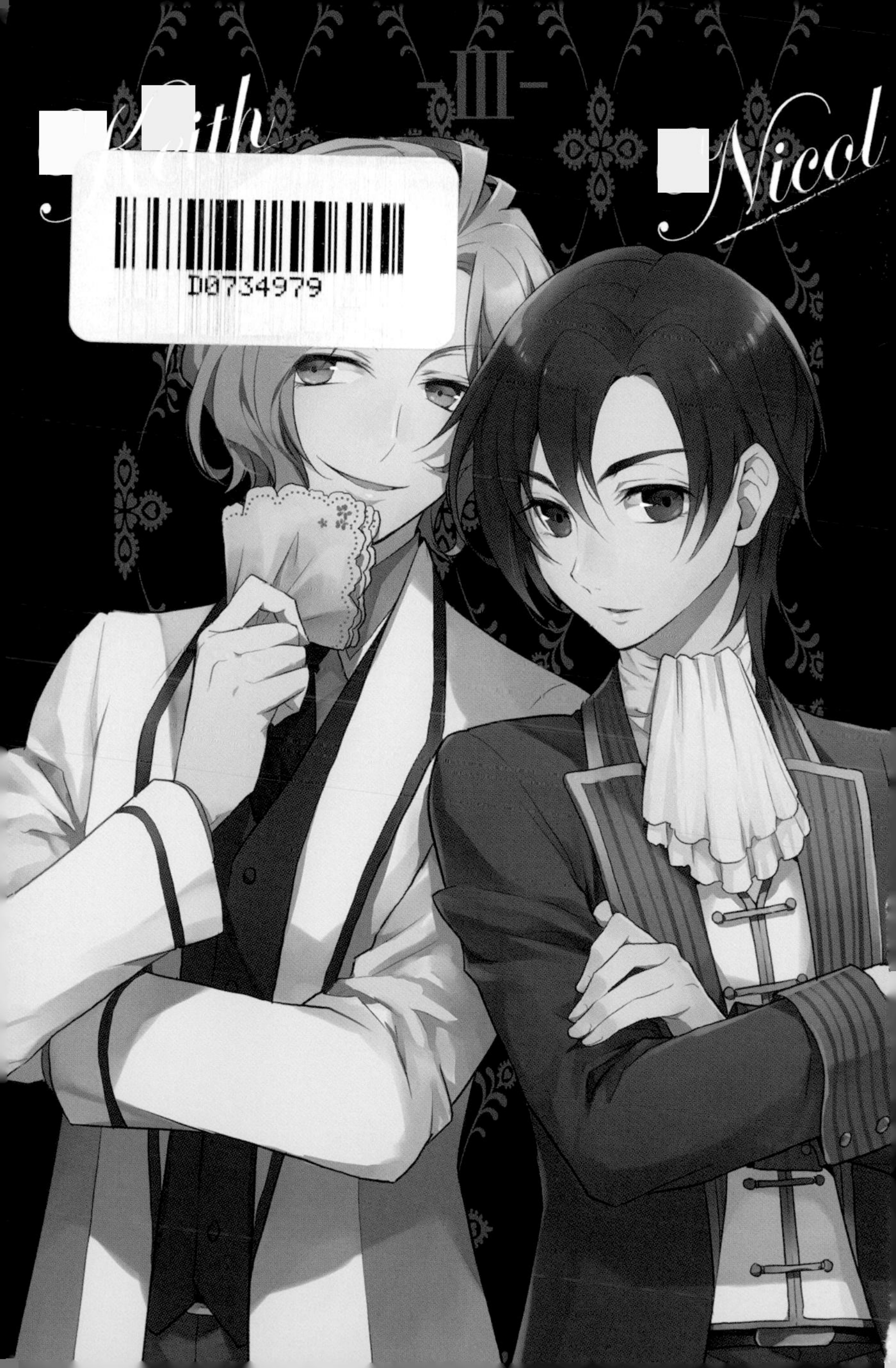
- III -
Nicol

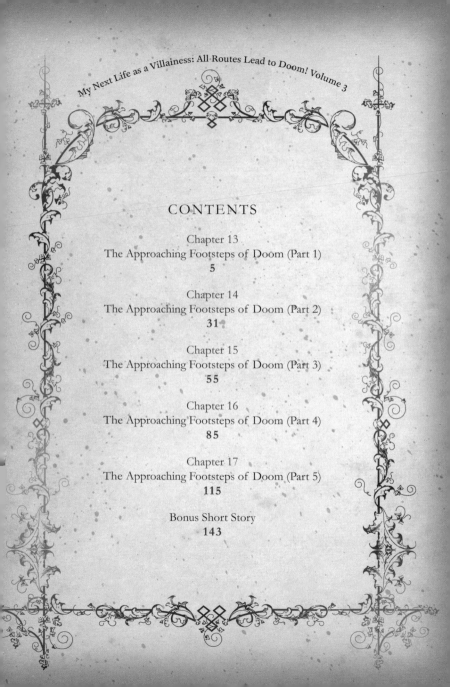

CONTENTS

My Next Life as a Villainess: All Routes Lead to Doom!

Volume 3

Character Design and Art by: Nami Hidaka
Story by: Satoru Yamaguchi

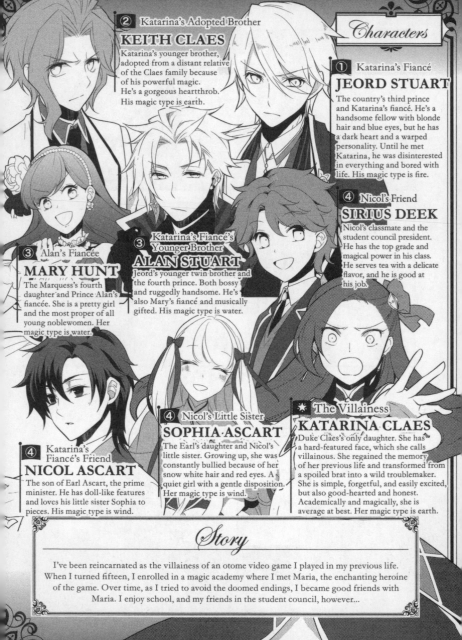

Characters

① Katarina's Fiancé

JEORD STUART

The country's third prince and Katarina's fiancé. He's a handsome fellow with blonde hair and blue eyes, but he has a dark heart and a warped personality. Until he met Katarina, he was disinterested in everything and bored with life. His magic type is fire.

② Katarina's Adopted Brother

KEITH CLAES

Katarina's younger brother, adopted from a distant relative of the Claes family because of his powerful magic. He's a gorgeous heartthrob. His magic type is earth.

③ Katarina's Fiancé's Younger Brother

ALAN STUART

Jeord's younger twin brother and the fourth prince. Both bossy and ruggedly handsome. He's also Mary's fiancé and musically gifted. His magic type is water.

③ Alan's Fiancée

MARY HUNT

The Marquess's fourth daughter and Prince Alan's fiancée. She is a pretty girl and the most proper of all young noblewomen. Her magic type is water.

④ Nicol's Friend

SIRIUS DEEK

Nicol's classmate and the student council president. He has the top grade and magical power in his class. He serves tea with a delicate flavor, and he is good at his job.

④ Katarina's Fiancé's Friend

NICOL ASCART

The son of Earl Ascart, the prime minister. He has doll-like features and loves his little sister Sophia to pieces. His magic type is wind.

④ Nicol's Little Sister

SOPHIA ASCART

The Earl's daughter and Nicol's little sister. Growing up, she was constantly bullied because of her snow white hair and red eyes. A quiet girl with a gentle disposition. Her magic type is wind.

✵ The Villainess

KATARINA CLAES

Duke Claes's only daughter. She has a hard-featured face, which she calls villainous. She regained the memory of her previous life and transformed from a spoiled brat into a wild troublemaker. She is simple, forgetful, and easily excited, but also good-hearted and honest. Academically and magically, she is average at best. Her magic type is earth.

Story

I've been reincarnated as the villainess of an otome video game I played in my previous life. When I turned fifteen, I enrolled in a magic academy where I met Maria, the enchanting heroine of the game. Over time, as I tried to avoid the doomed endings, I became good friends with Maria. I enjoy school, and my friends in the student council, however...

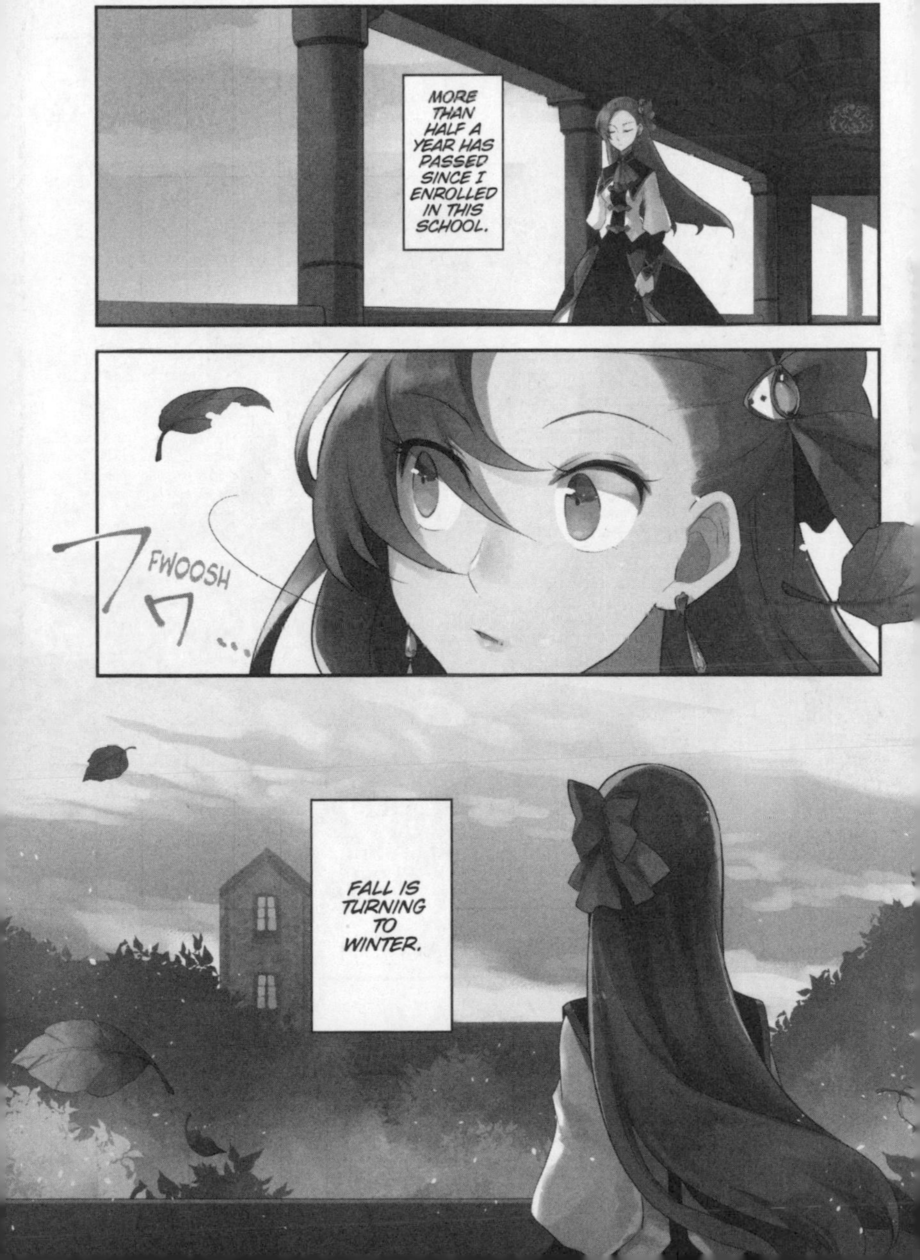
MORE THAN HALF A YEAR HAS PASSED SINCE I ENROLLED IN THIS SCHOOL.
FWOOSH
FALL IS TURNING TO WINTER.

Chapter 13: The Approaching Footsteps of Doom (Part 1)

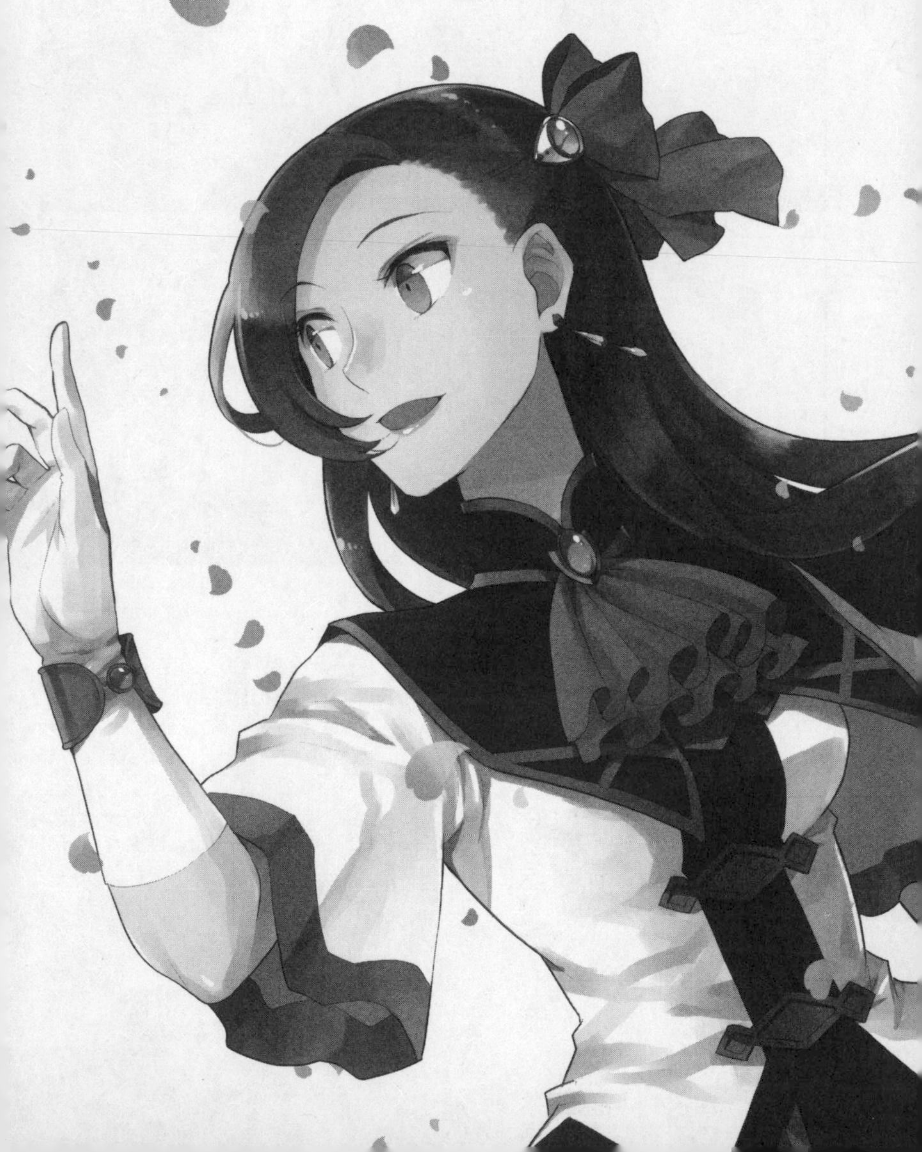

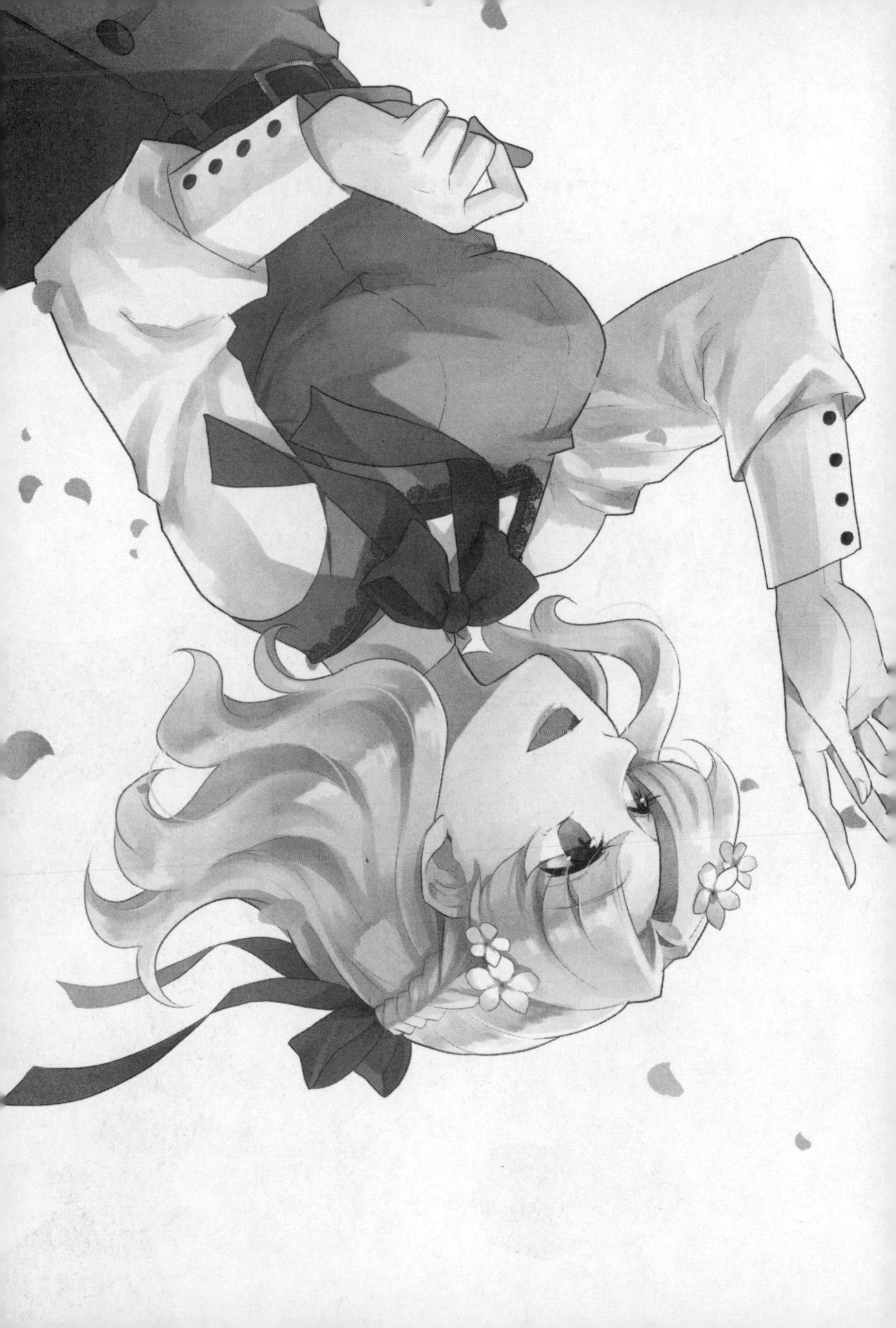

My Next Life
as a **VILLAINESS:**
ALL ROUTES
LEAD
TO **DOOM!**

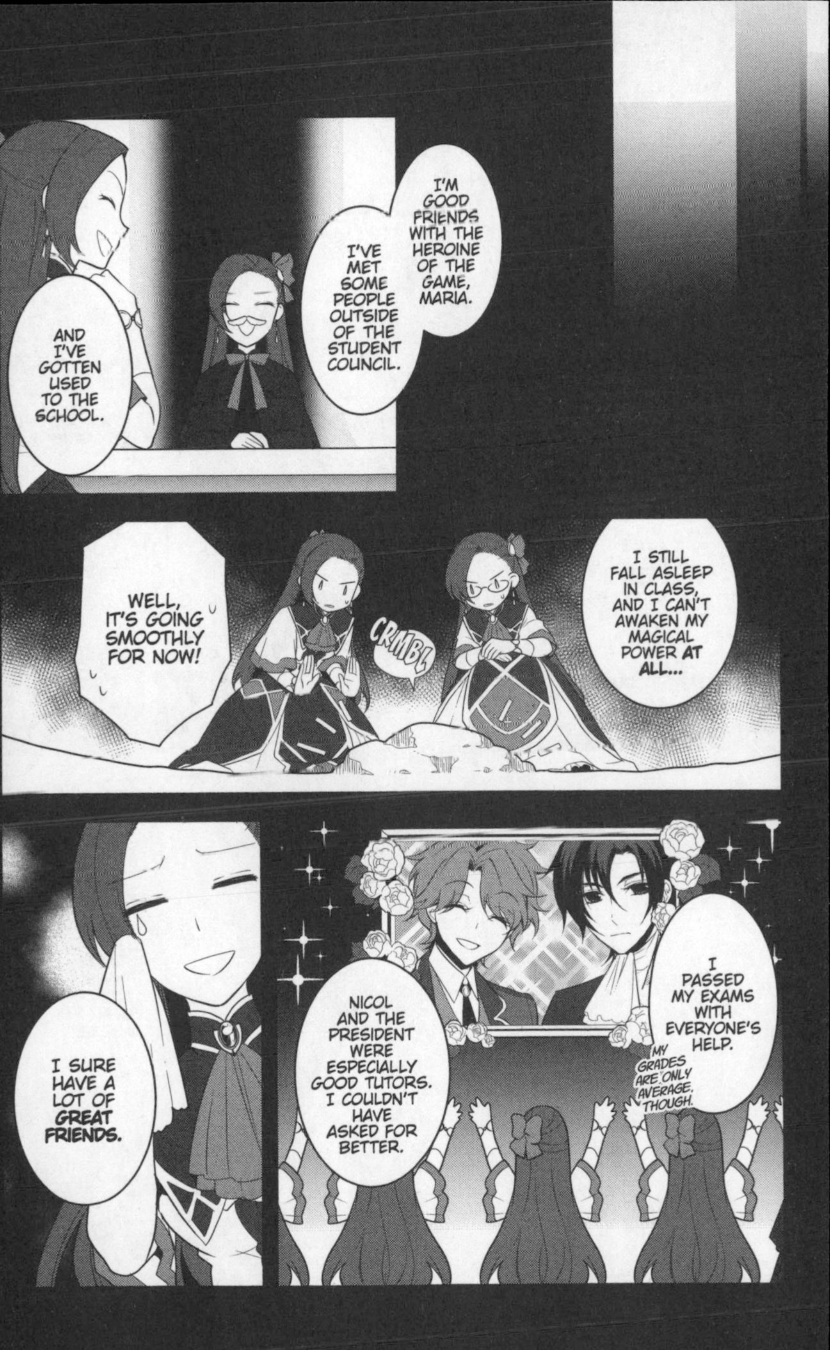
I'M GOOD FRIENDS WITH THE HEROINE OF THE GAME, MARIA.
I'VE MET SOME PEOPLE OUTSIDE OF THE STUDENT COUNCIL.
AND I'VE GOTTEN USED TO THE SCHOOL.
I STILL FALL ASLEEP IN CLASS, AND I CAN'T AWAKEN MY MAGICAL POWER AT ALL...
CRMBL
WELL, IT'S GOING SMOOTHLY FOR NOW!
I PASSED MY EXAMS WITH EVERYONE'S HELP.
MY GRADES ARE ONLY AVERAGE, THOUGH.
NICOL AND THE PRESIDENT WERE ESPECIALLY GOOD TUTORS. I COULDN'T HAVE ASKED FOR BETTER.
I SURE HAVE A LOT OF GREAT FRIENDS.

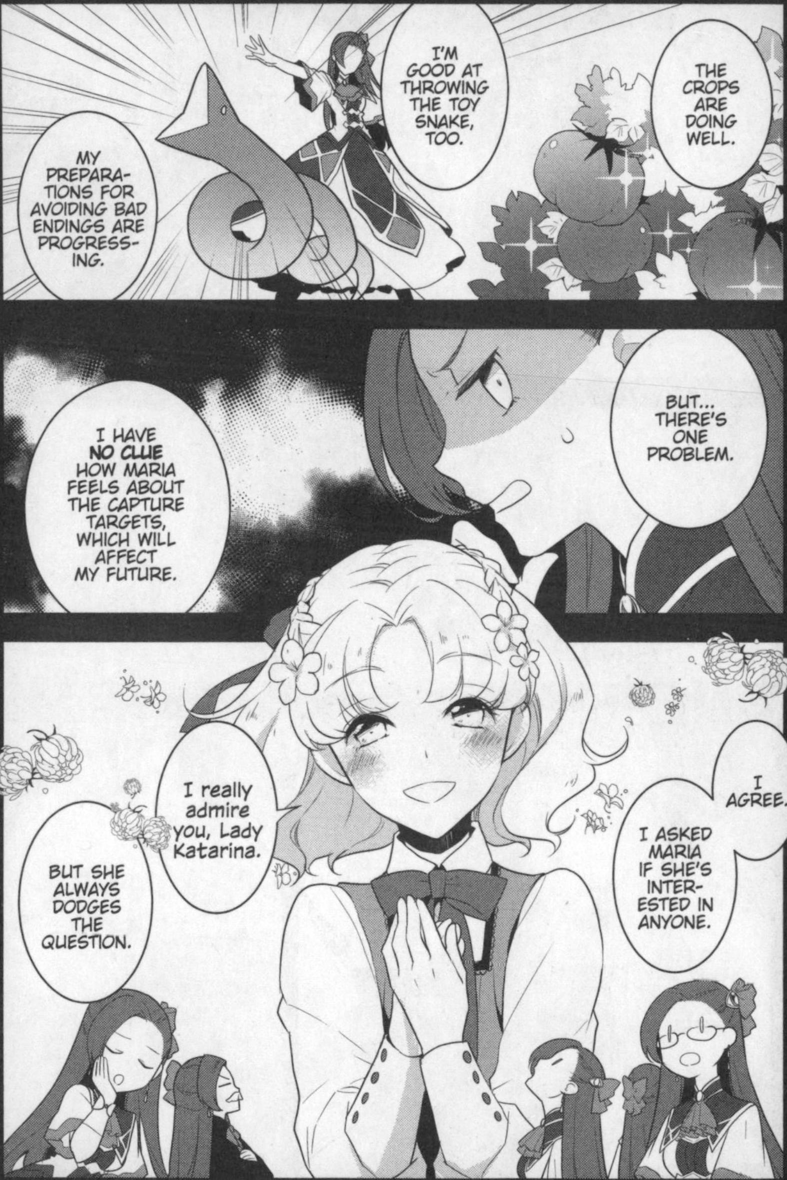
THE CROPS ARE DOING WELL.
I'M GOOD AT THROWING THE TOY SNAKE, TOO.
MY PREPARATIONS FOR AVOIDING BAD ENDINGS ARE PROGRESSING.
BUT... THERE'S ONE PROBLEM.
I HAVE **NO CLUE** HOW MARIA FEELS ABOUT THE CAPTURE TARGETS, WHICH WILL AFFECT MY FUTURE.
I AGREE.
I really admire you, Lady Katarina.
I ASKED MARIA IF SHE'S INTERESTED IN ANYONE.
BUT SHE ALWAYS DODGES THE QUESTION.

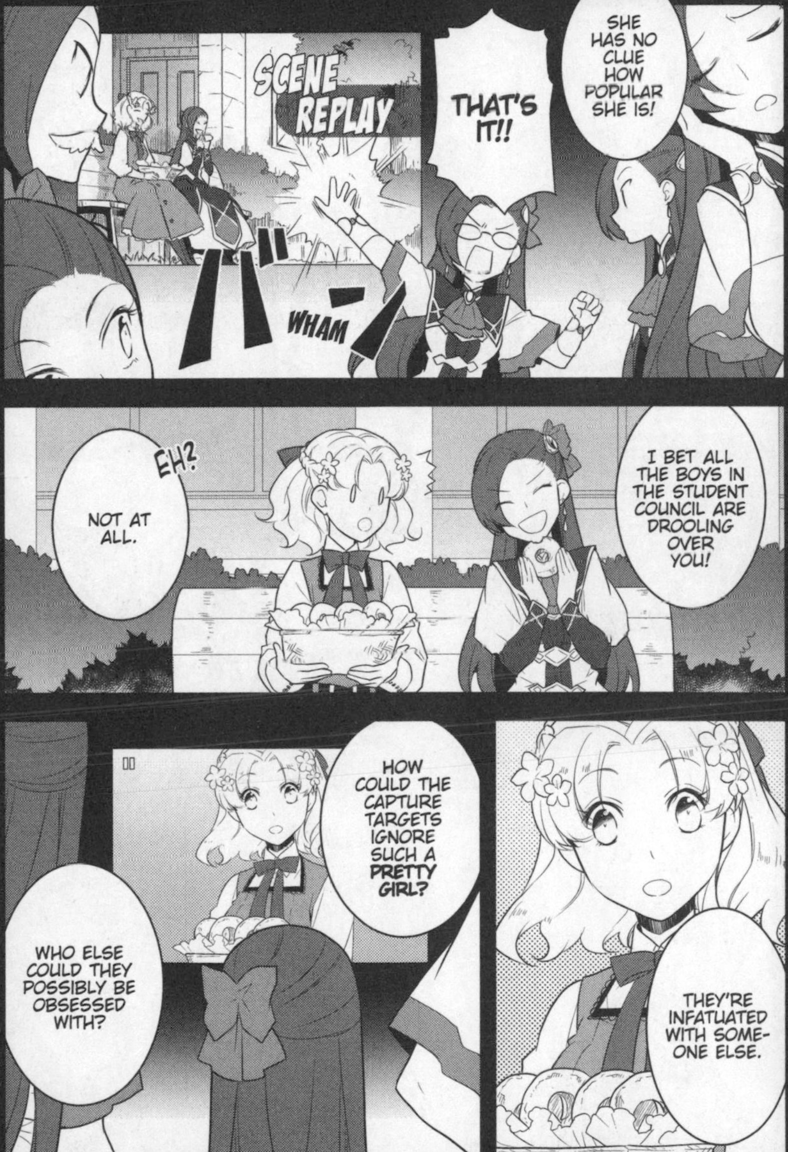
SHE HAS NO CLUE HOW POPULAR SHE IS!
THAT'S IT!!
SCENE REPLAY
WHAM
I BET ALL THE BOYS IN THE STUDENT COUNCIL ARE DROOLING OVER YOU!
EH?
NOT AT ALL.
THEY'RE INFATUATED WITH SOME-ONE ELSE.
HOW COULD THE CAPTURE TARGETS IGNORE SUCH A PRETTY GIRL?
WHO ELSE COULD THEY POSSIBLY BE OBSESSED WITH?

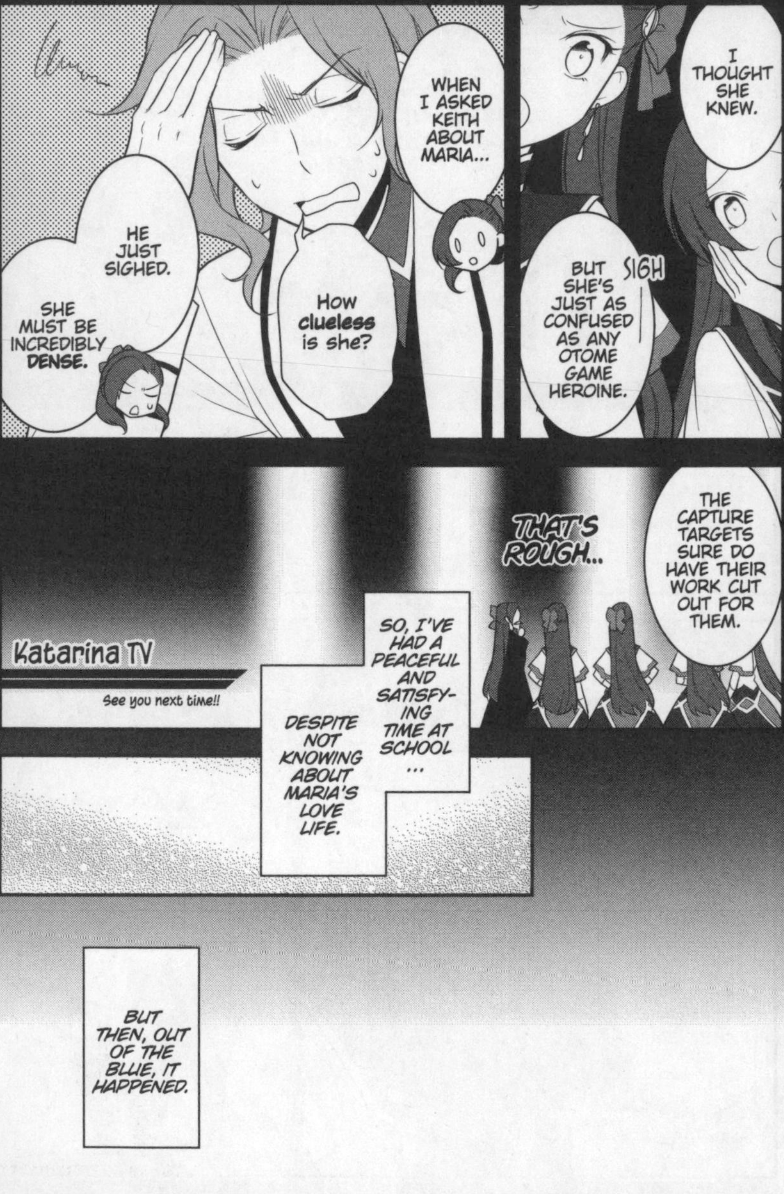
I THOUGHT SHE KNEW.
BUT SHE'S JUST AS CONFUSED AS ANY OTOME GAME HEROINE.
SIGH
WHEN I ASKED KEITH ABOUT MARIA...
HE JUST SIGHED.
How clueless is she?
SHE MUST BE INCREDIBLY DENSE.
THE CAPTURE TARGETS SURE DO HAVE THEIR WORK CUT OUT FOR THEM.
THAT'S ROUGH...
Katarina TV
See you next time!!
SO, I'VE HAD A PEACEFUL AND SATISFYING TIME AT SCHOOL...
DESPITE NOT KNOWING ABOUT MARIA'S LOVE LIFE.
BUT THEN, OUT OF THE BLUE, IT HAPPENED.

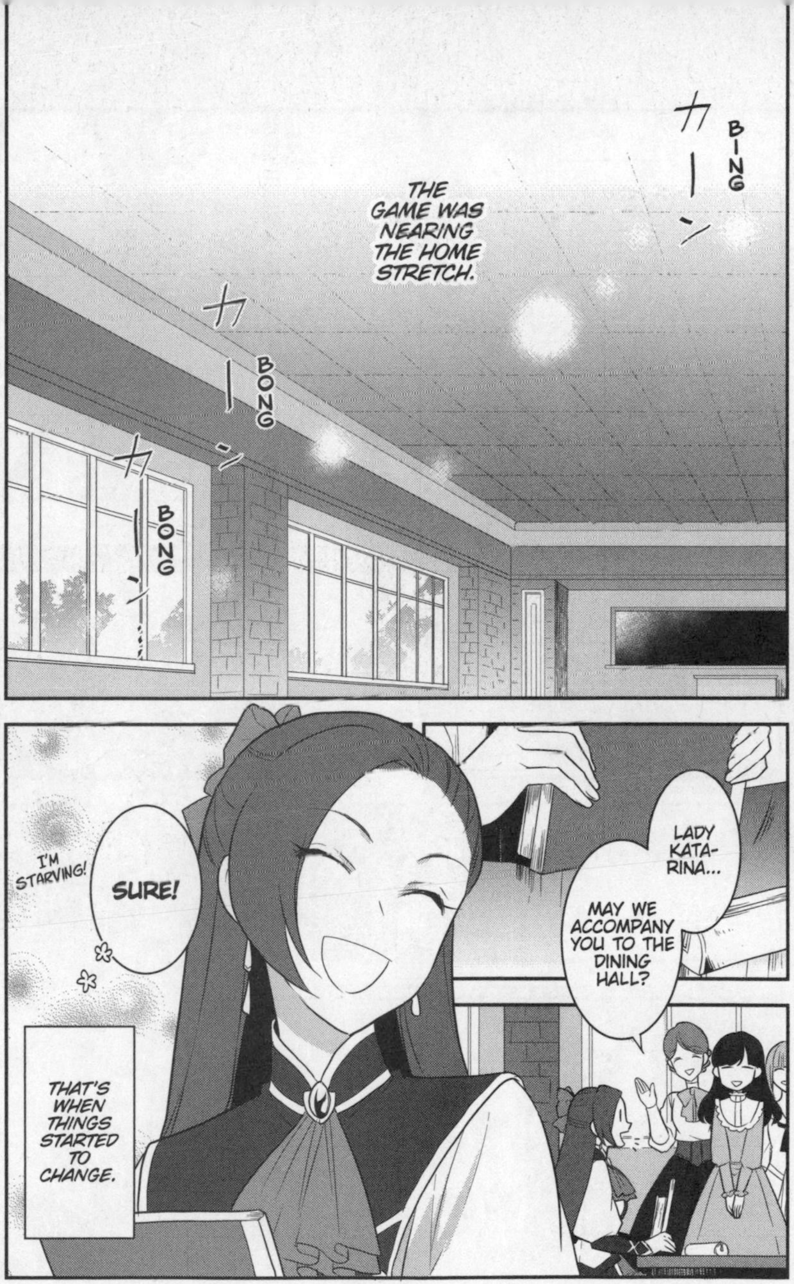
カーン
BING
THE GAME WAS NEARING THE HOME STRETCH.
カーン
BONG
カーン
BONG
LADY KATARINA...
MAY WE ACCOMPANY YOU TO THE DINING HALL?
SURE!
I'M STARVING!
THAT'S WHEN THINGS STARTED TO CHANGE.

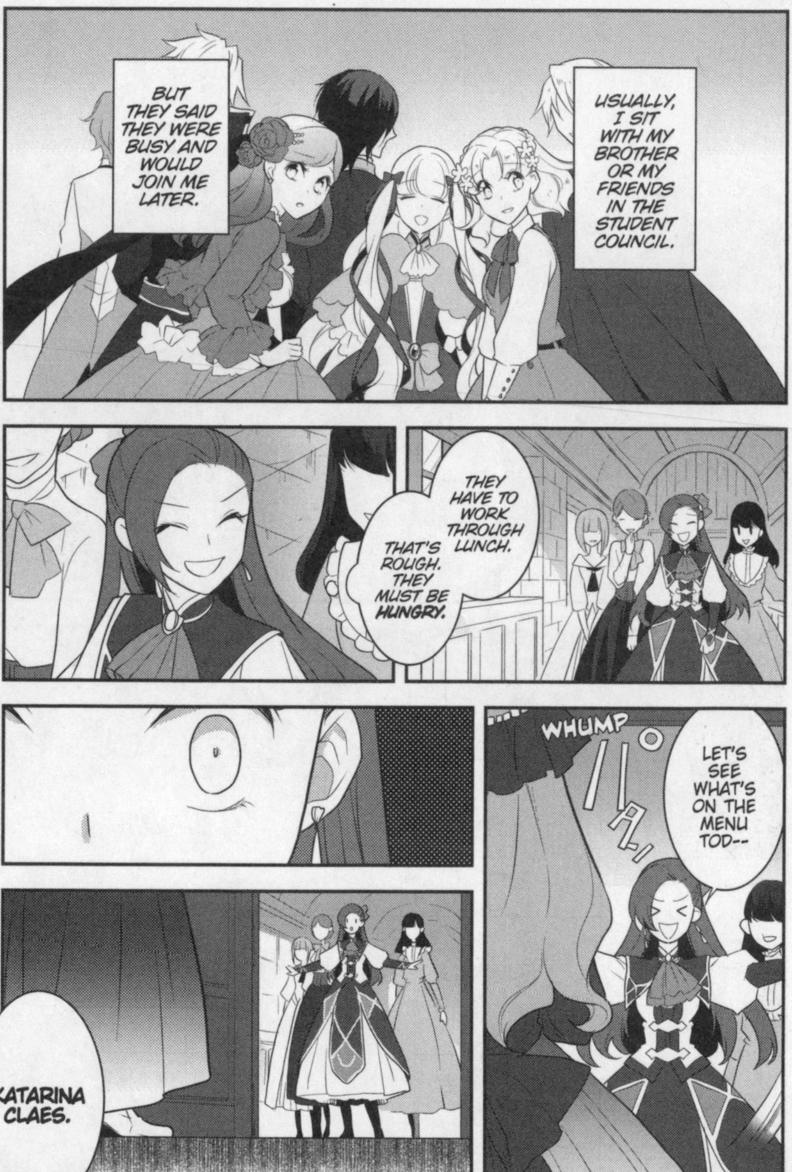
USUALLY, I SIT WITH MY BROTHER OR MY FRIENDS IN THE STUDENT COUNCIL.
BUT THEY SAID THEY WERE BUSY AND WOULD JOIN ME LATER.
THEY HAVE TO WORK THROUGH LUNCH.
THAT'S ROUGH. THEY MUST BE HUNGRY.
WHUMP
LET'S SEE WHAT'S ON THE MENU TOD--
KATARINA CLAES.

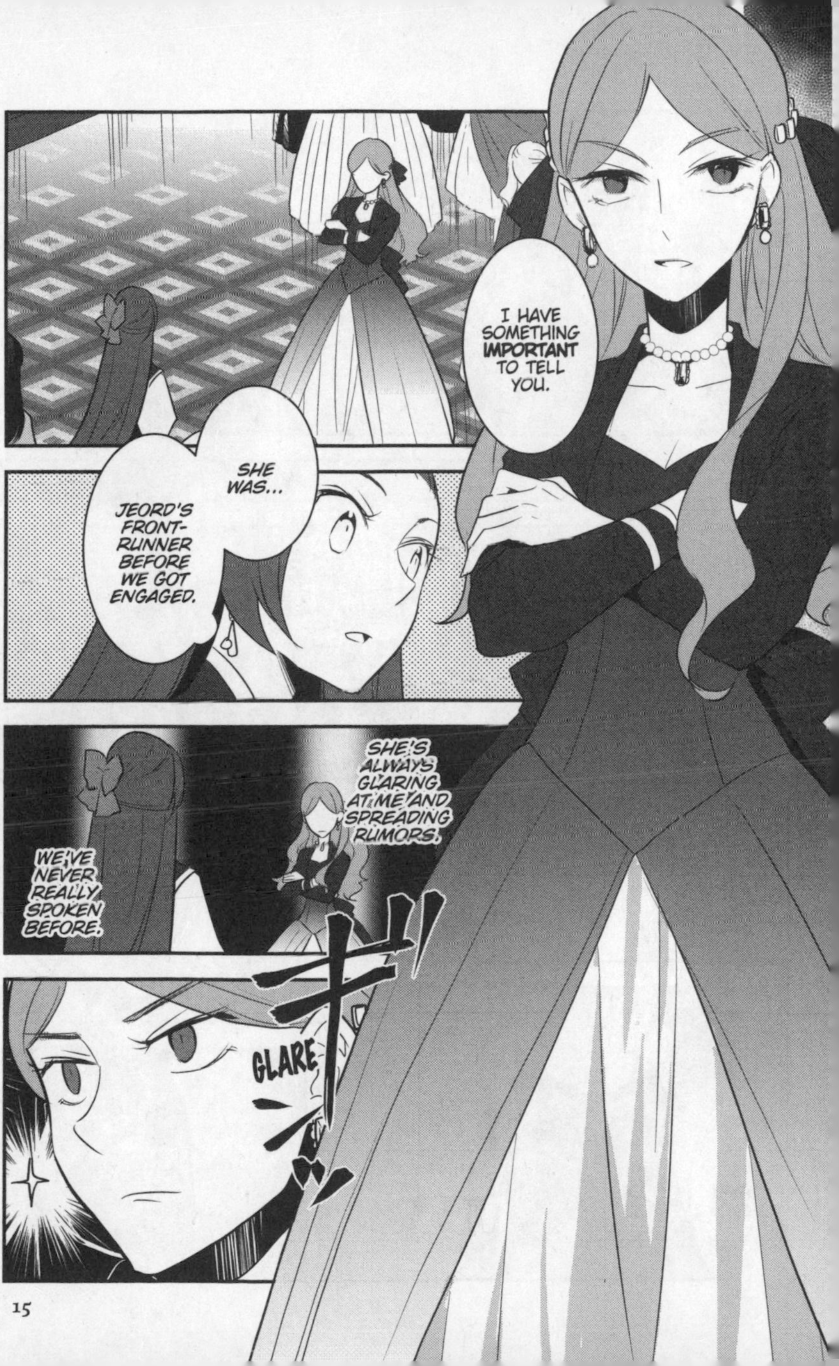
I HAVE SOMETHING **IMPORTANT** TO TELL YOU.
SHE WAS...
JEORD'S FRONT-RUNNER BEFORE WE GOT ENGAGED.
SHE'S ALWAYS GLARING AT ME AND SPREADING RUMORS.
WE'VE NEVER REALLY SPOKEN BEFORE.
GLARE

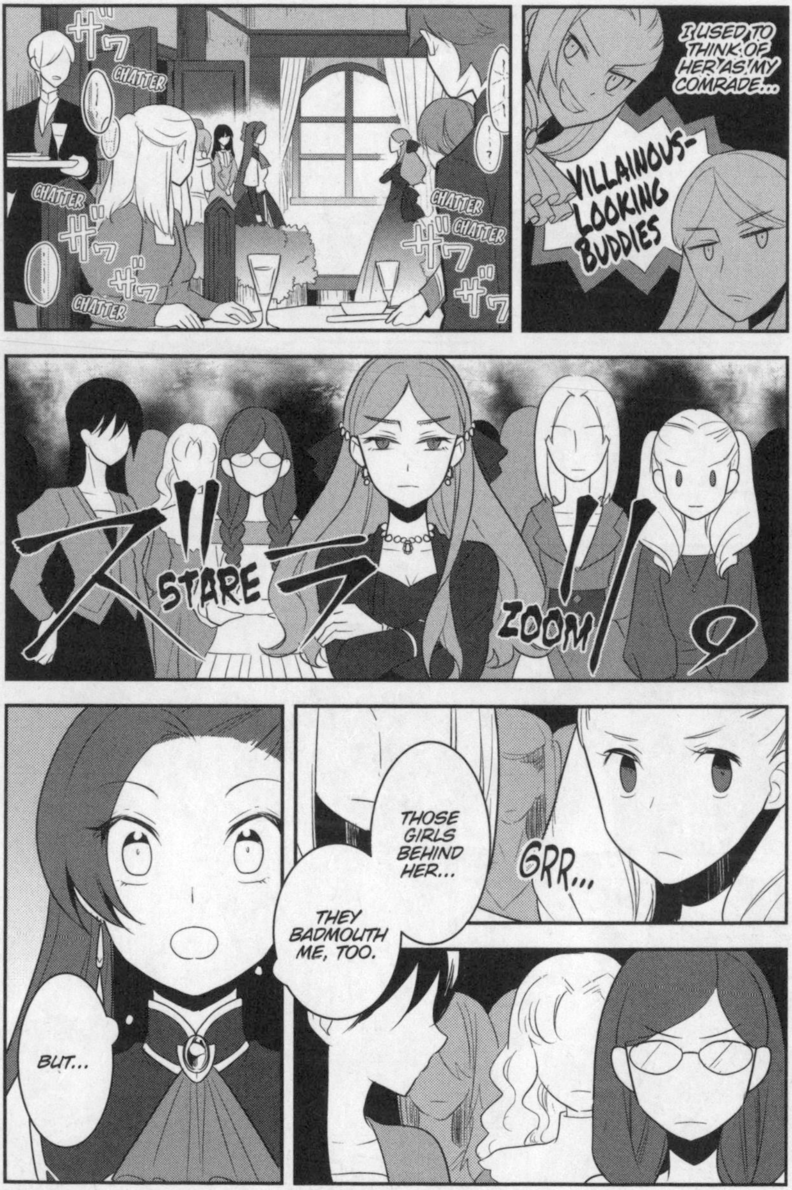
I USED TO THINK OF HER AS MY COMRADE...
VILLAINOUS-LOOKING BUDDIES
ザワ
CHATTER
...!?
...?
CHATTER
CHATTER
ザワ ザワ
CHATTER
ザワ ザワ
CHATTER
ZOOM
STARE
THOSE GIRLS BEHIND HER...
GRR...
THEY BADMOUTH ME, TOO.
BUT...

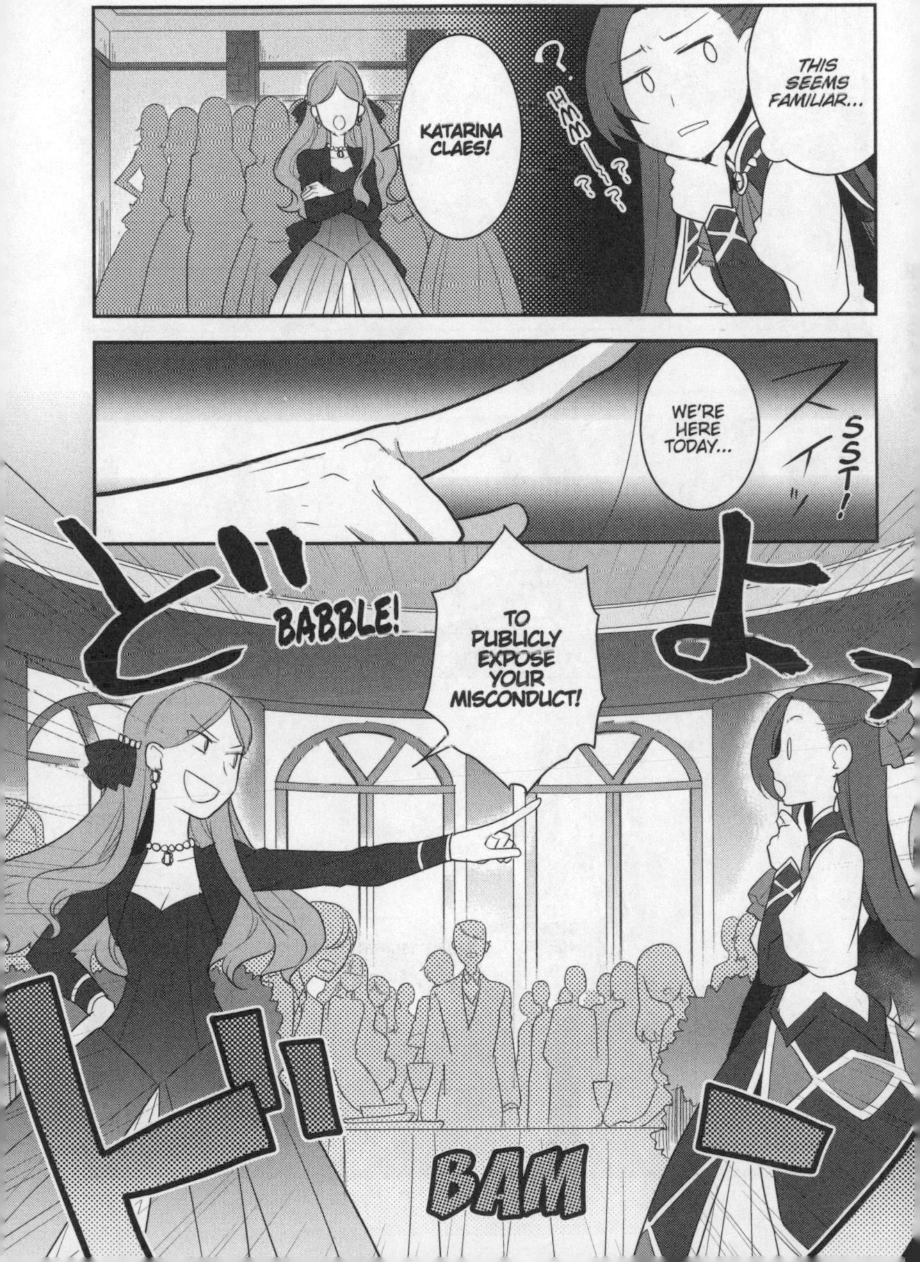
THIS SEEMS FAMILIAR...
? HMMM—???
KATARINA CLAES!
SST!
WE'RE HERE TODAY...
TO PUBLICLY EXPOSE YOUR MISCONDUCT!
BABBLE!
BAM

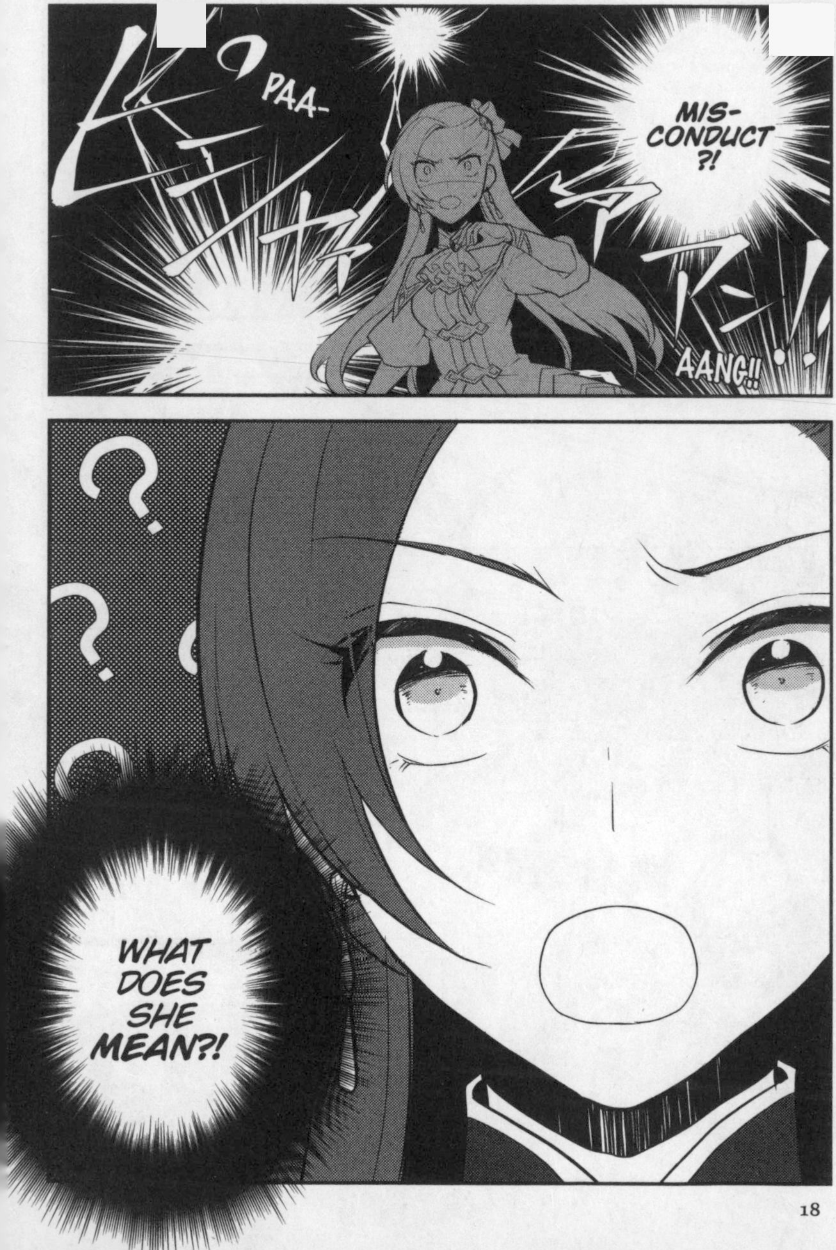
MIS-CONDUCT?!
PAA-
AANG!!
WHAT DOES SHE MEAN?!

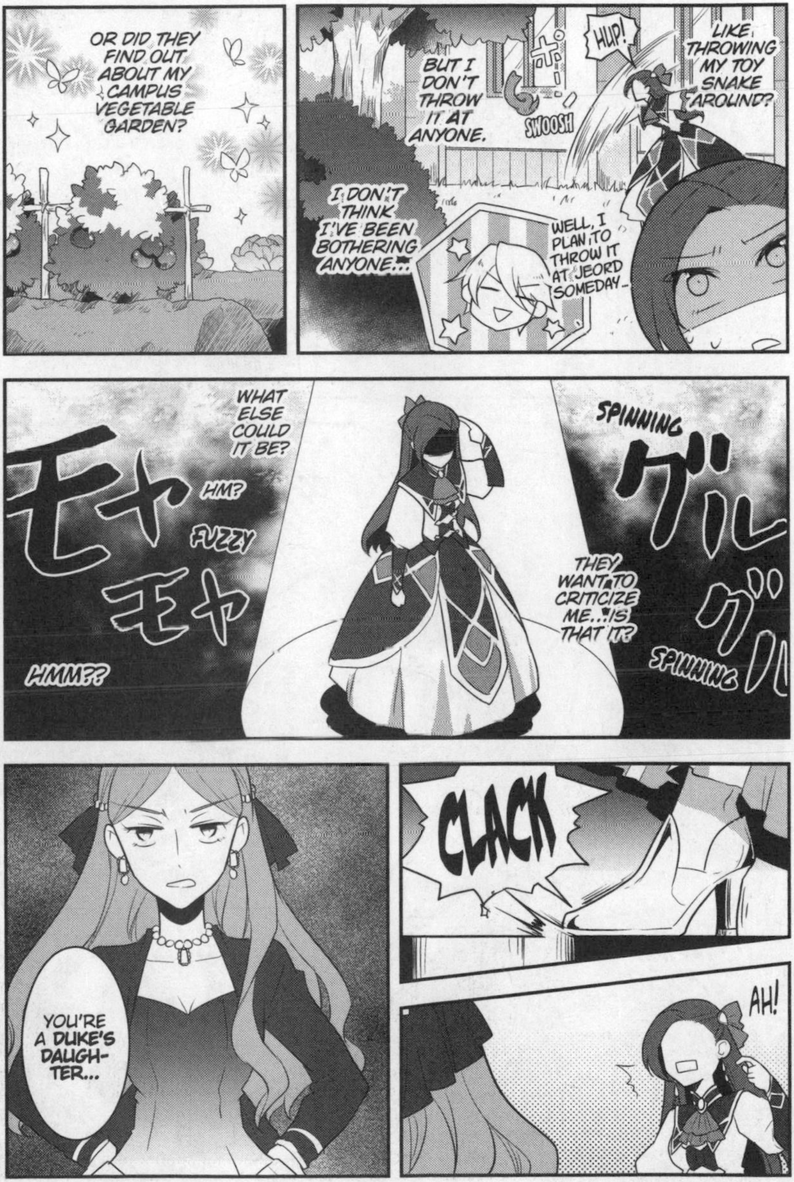
LIKE THROWING MY TOY SNAKE AROUND?
HUP!
BUT I DON'T THROW IT AT ANYONE.
SWOOSH
WELL, I PLAN TO THROW IT AT JEORD SOMEDAY...
I DON'T THINK I'VE BEEN BOTHERING ANYONE...
OR DID THEY FIND OUT ABOUT MY CAMPUS VEGETABLE GARDEN?
SPINNING
グルグル
THEY WANT TO CRITICIZE ME...IS THAT IT?
SPINNING
WHAT ELSE COULD IT BE?
モヤモヤ
HM?
FUZZY
HMM??
CLACK
AH!
YOU'RE A DUKE'S DAUGHTER...

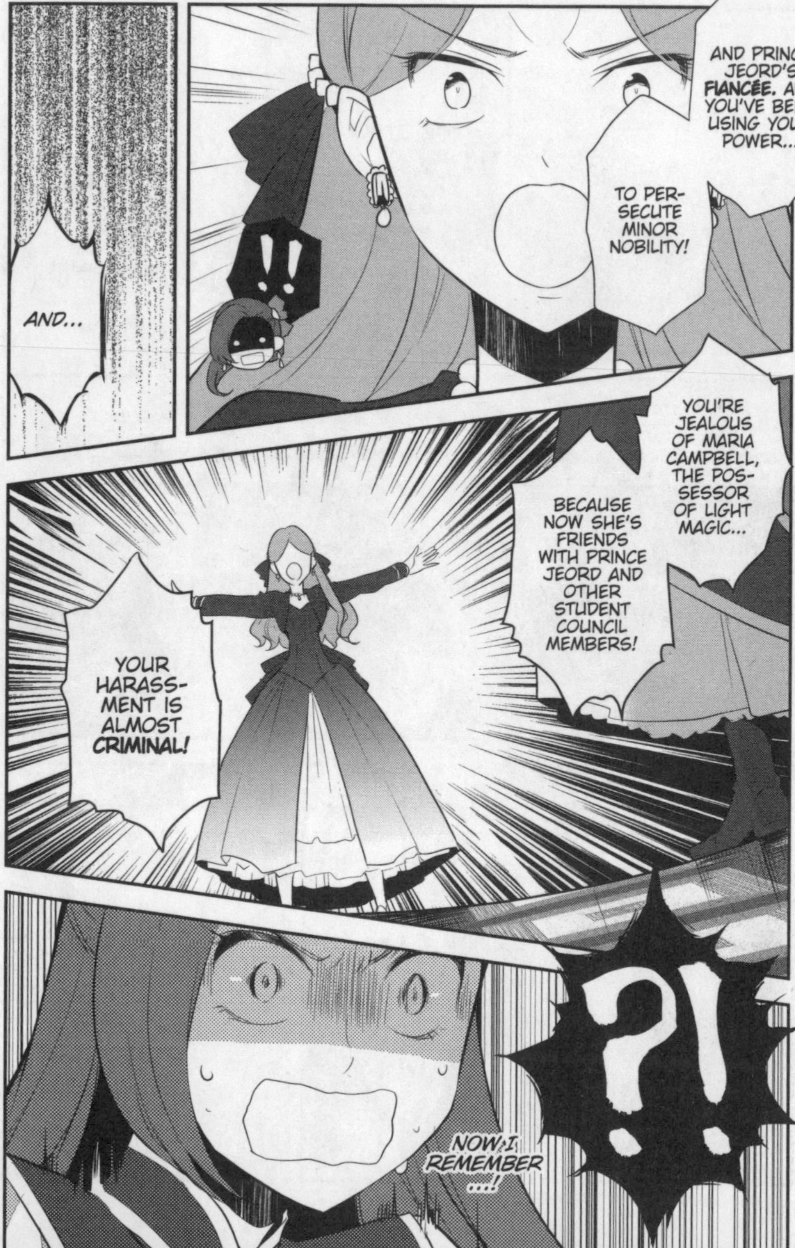
AND PRINCE JEORD'S FIANCÉE. AND YOU'VE BEEN USING YOUR POWER...
TO PERSECUTE MINOR NOBILITY!
AND...
YOU'RE JEALOUS OF MARIA CAMPBELL, THE POSSESSOR OF LIGHT MAGIC...
BECAUSE NOW SHE'S FRIENDS WITH PRINCE JEORD AND OTHER STUDENT COUNCIL MEMBERS!
YOUR HARASSMENT IS ALMOST CRIMINAL!
?!
NOW I REMEMBER ...!

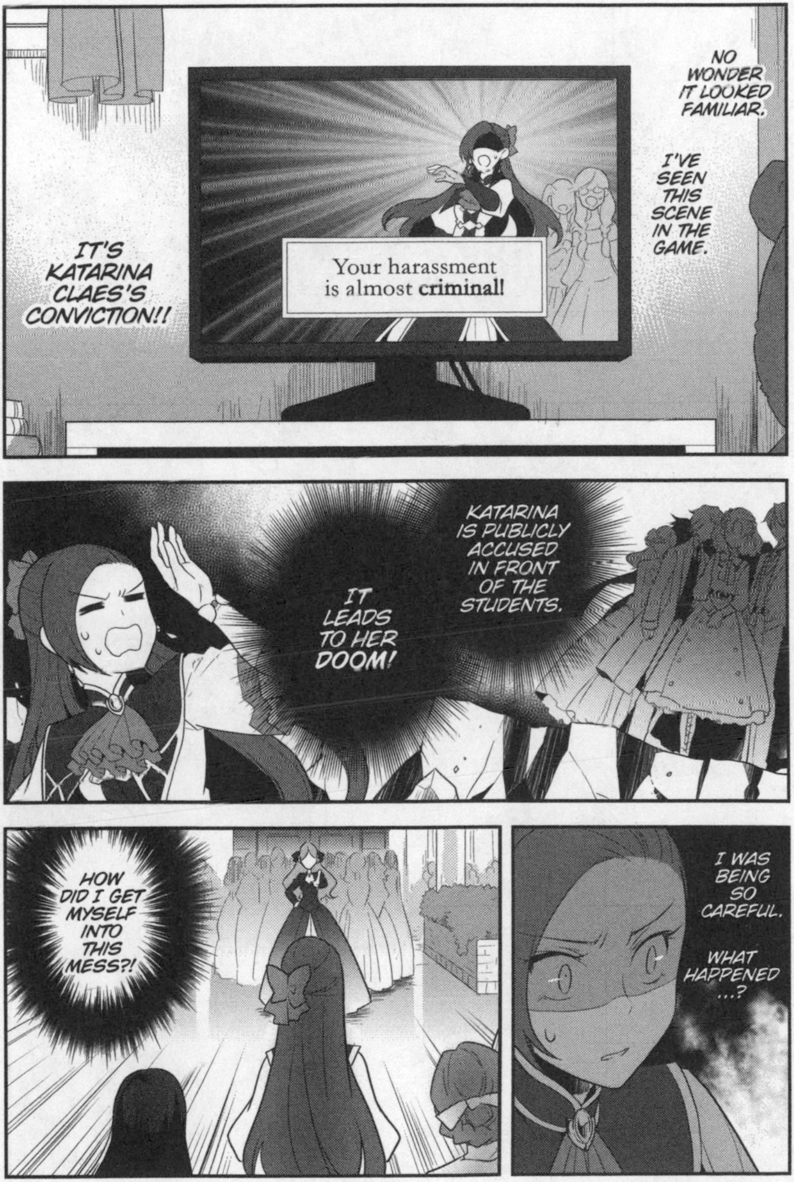
NO WONDER IT LOOKED FAMILIAR.
I'VE SEEN THIS SCENE IN THE GAME.
Your harassment is almost **criminal**!
IT'S KATARINA CLAES'S CONVICTION!!
KATARINA IS PUBLICLY ACCUSED IN FRONT OF THE STUDENTS.
IT LEADS TO HER DOOM!
I WAS BEING SO CAREFUL.
WHAT HAPPENED ...?
HOW DID I GET MYSELF INTO THIS MESS?!

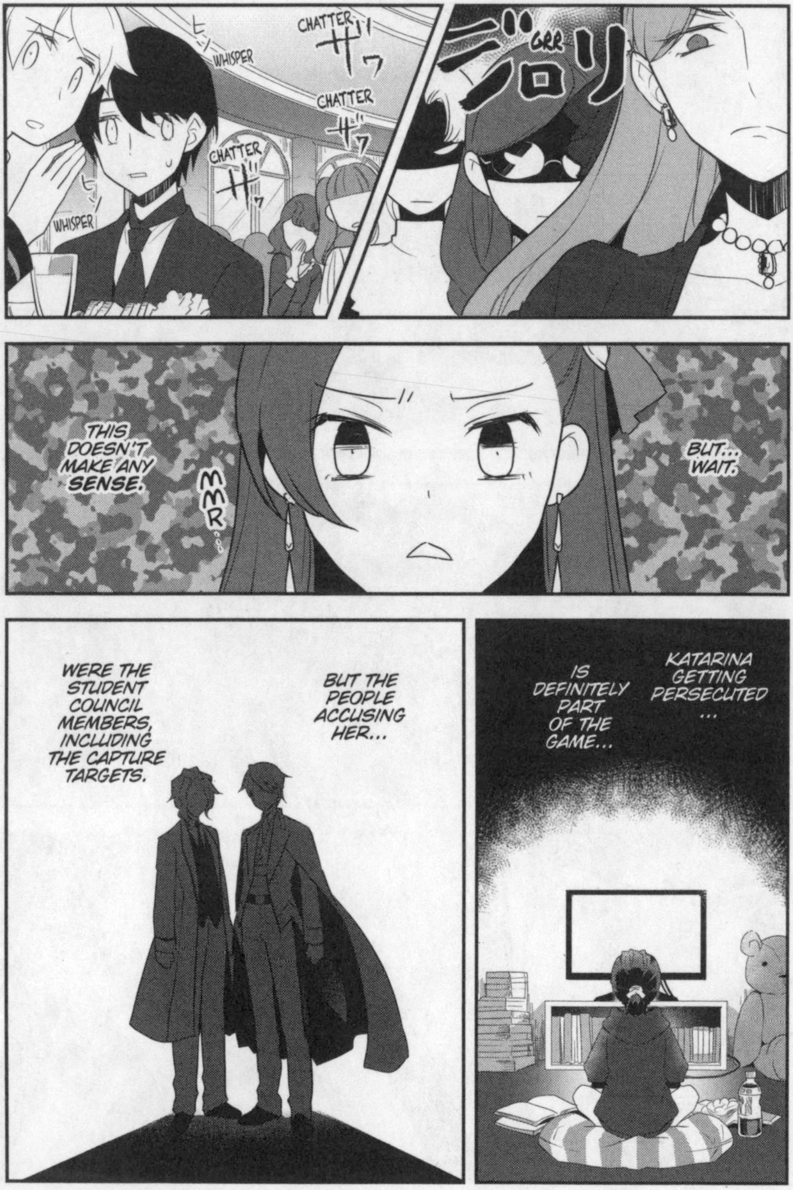
ジロリ
GRR
CHATTER
CHATTER
CHATTER
WHISPER
WHISPER
BUT... WAIT.
MMR
THIS DOESN'T MAKE ANY SENSE.
KATARINA GETTING PERSECUTED...
IS DEFINITELY PART OF THE GAME...
BUT THE PEOPLE ACCUSING HER...
WERE THE STUDENT COUNCIL MEMBERS, INCLUDING THE CAPTURE TARGETS.

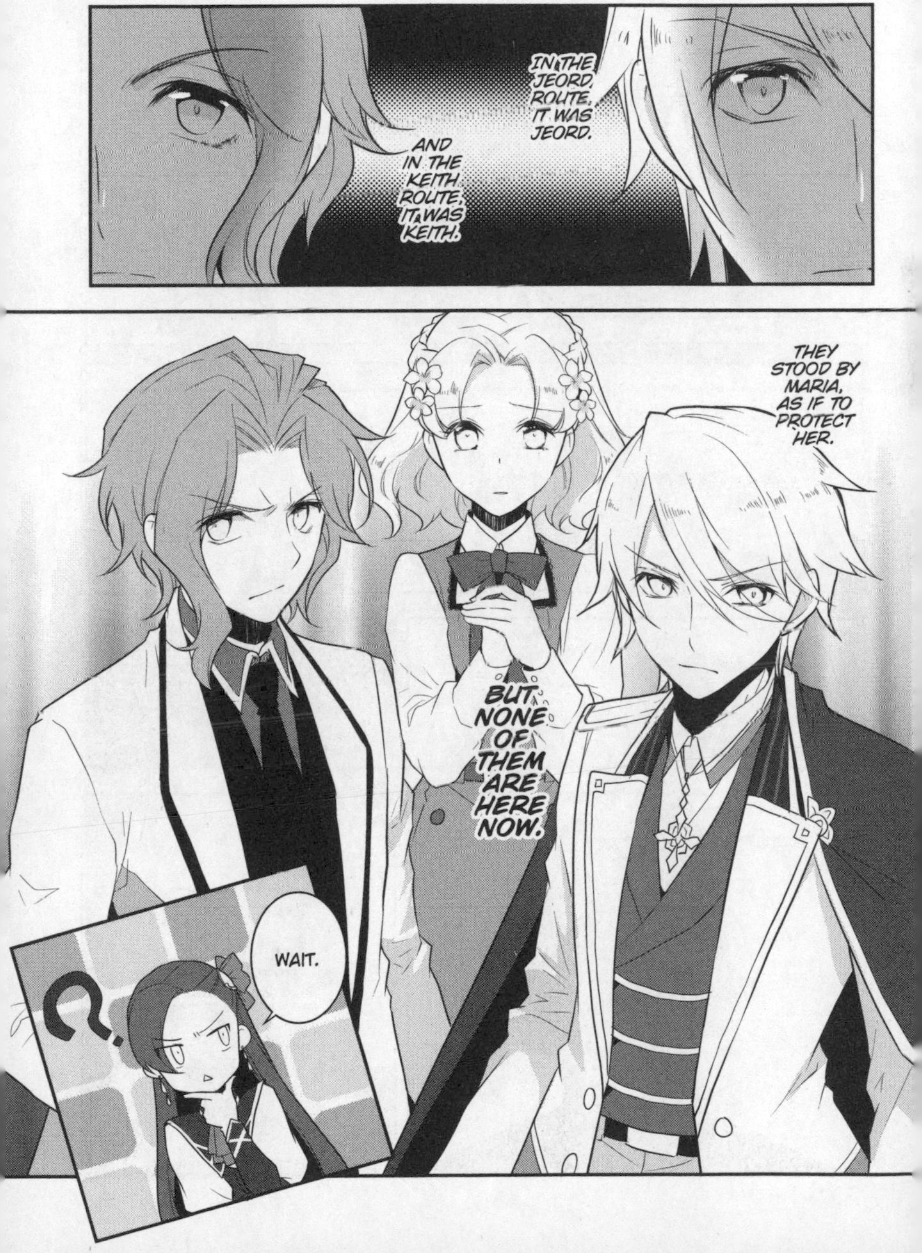
IN THE JEORD ROUTE, IT WAS JEORD.
AND IN THE KEITH ROUTE, IT WAS KEITH.
THEY STOOD BY MARIA, AS IF TO PROTECT HER.
BUT NONE OF THEM ARE HERE NOW.
WAIT.
?

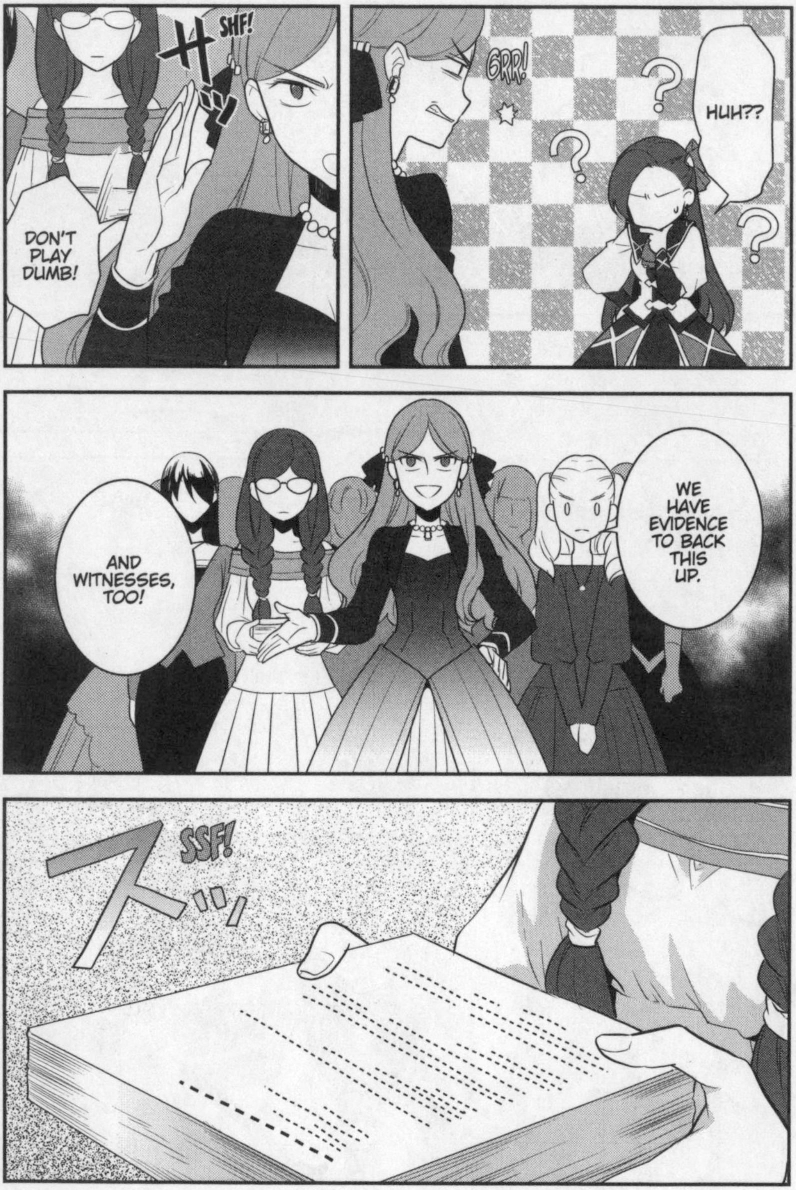
GRR!
HUH??
SHF!
DON'T PLAY DUMB!
WE HAVE EVIDENCE TO BACK THIS UP.
AND WITNESSES, TOO!
SSF!

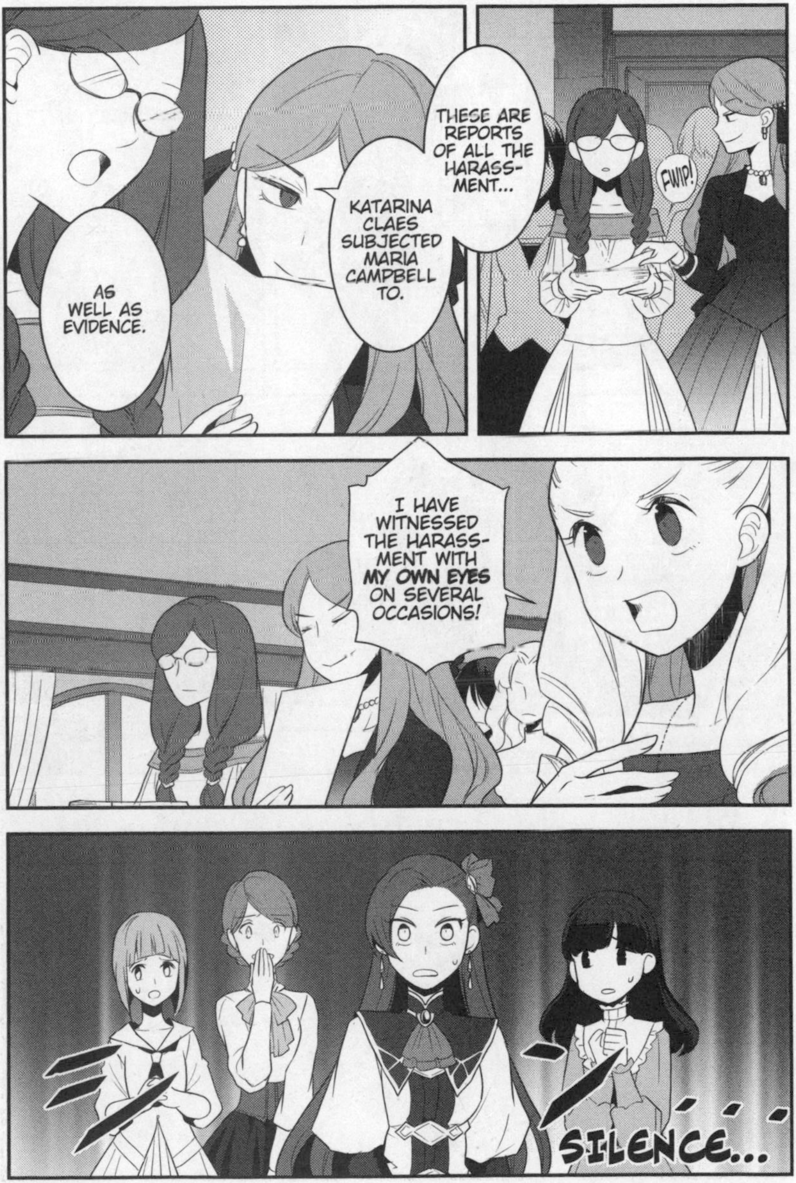
THESE ARE REPORTS OF ALL THE HARASS-MENT...
FWIP!
KATARINA CLAES SUBJECTED MARIA CAMPBELL TO.
AS WELL AS EVIDENCE.
I HAVE WITNESSED THE HARASS-MENT WITH **MY OWN EYES** ON SEVERAL OCCASIONS!
SILENCE...

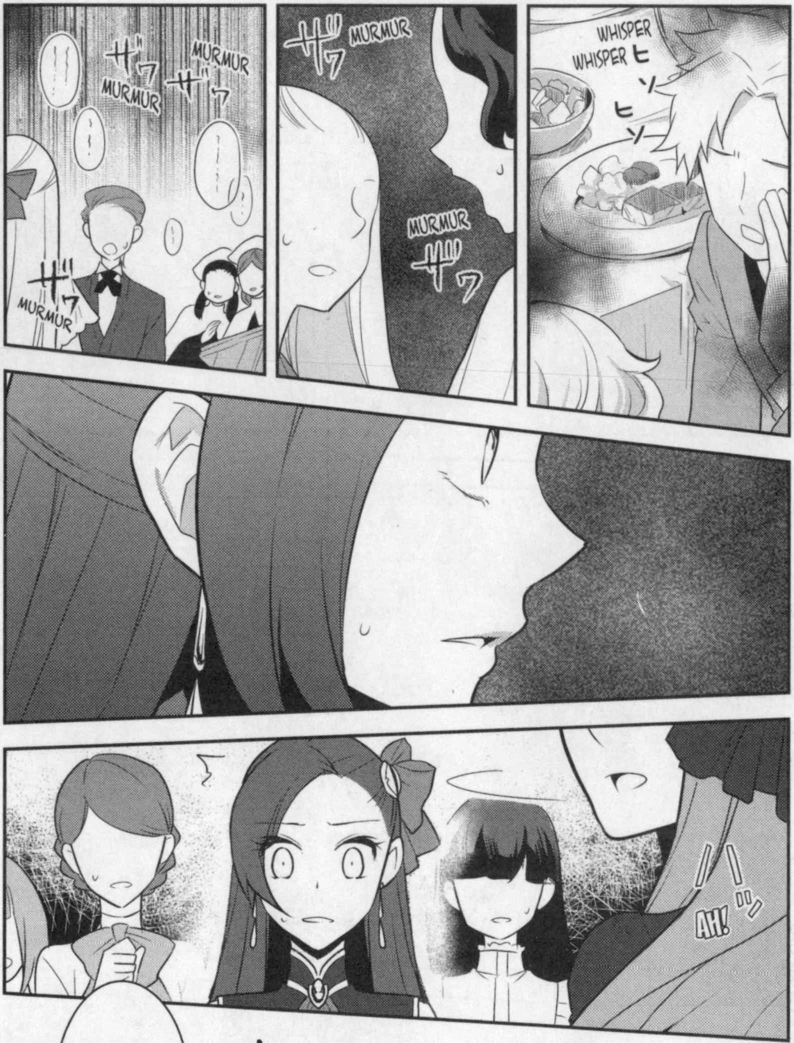
WHISPER WHISPER
ヒソヒソ
ザワ MURMUR
MURMUR ザワ
MURMUR ザワ
MURMUR ザワ
ザワ MURMUR
AH!
WHAT IS GOING ON HERE?
ギィ CREAK

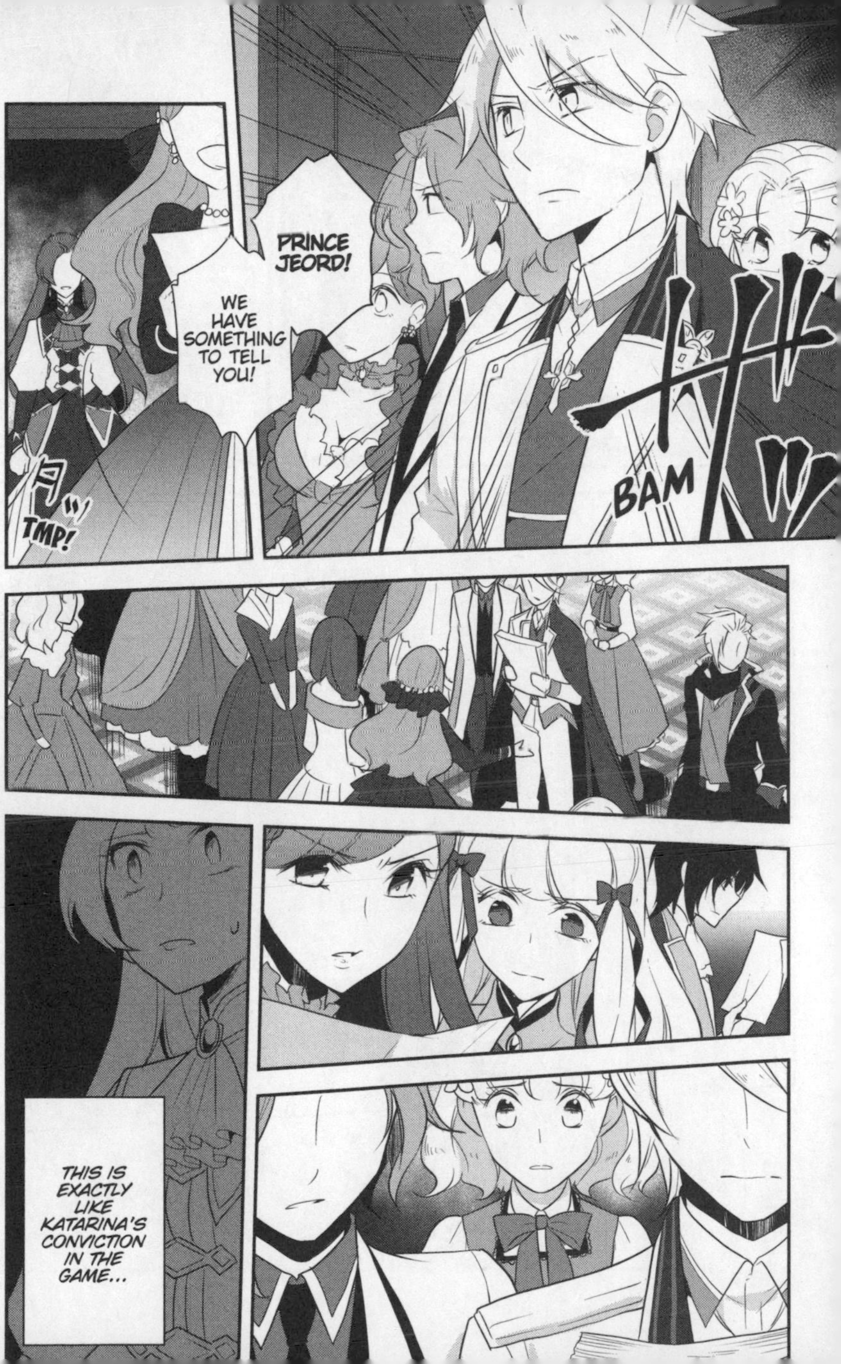
BAM
PRINCE JEORD!
WE HAVE SOMETHING TO TELL YOU!
TMP!
THIS IS EXACTLY LIKE KATARINA'S CONVICTION IN THE GAME...

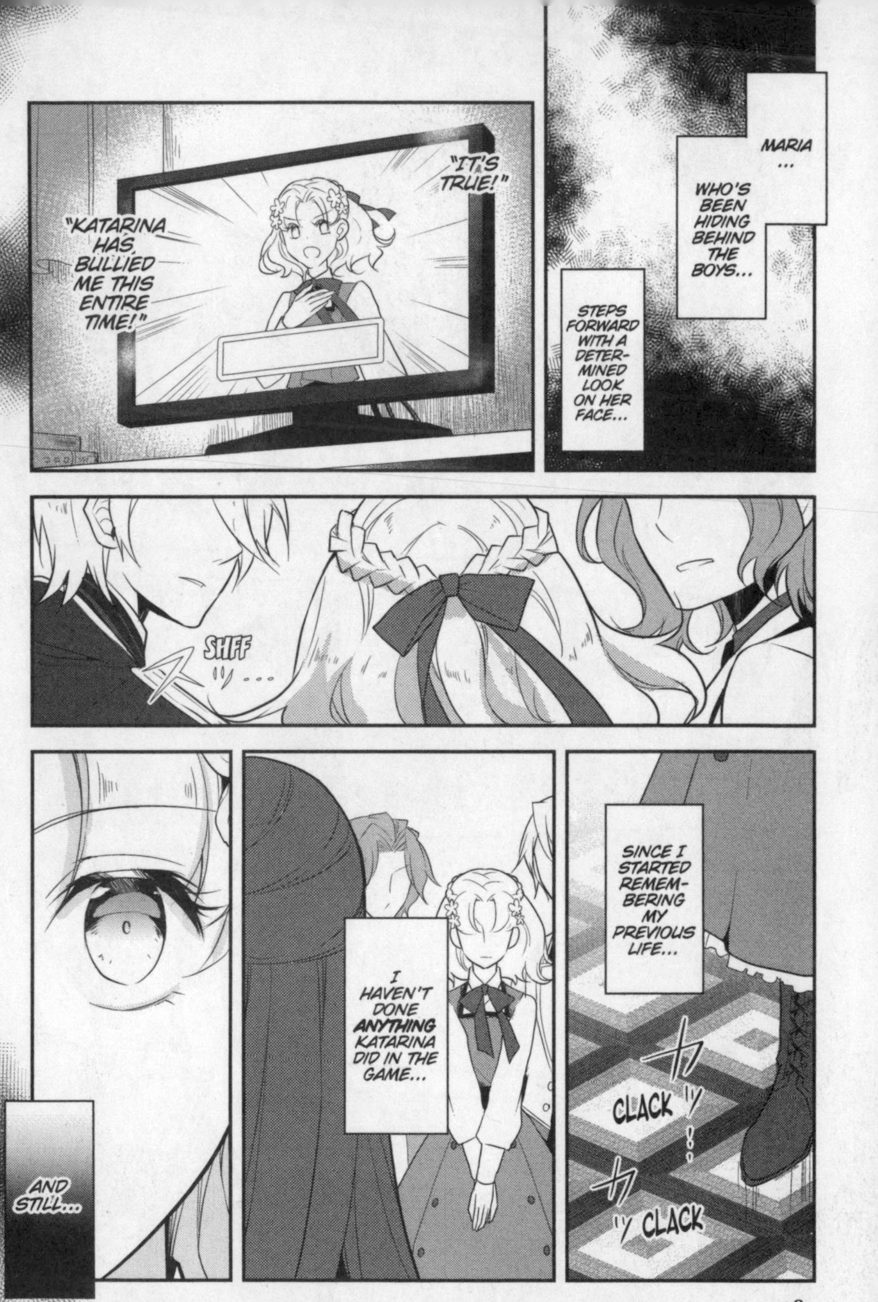
MARIA ...
WHO'S BEEN HIDING BEHIND THE BOYS...
STEPS FORWARD WITH A DETER-MINED LOOK ON HER FACE...
"IT'S TRUE!"
"KATARINA HAS BULLIED ME THIS ENTIRE TIME!"
SHFF
...
SINCE I STARTED REMEM-BERING MY PREVIOUS LIFE...
CLACK
CLACK
I HAVEN'T DONE **ANYTHING** KATARINA DID IN THE GAME...
AND STILL...

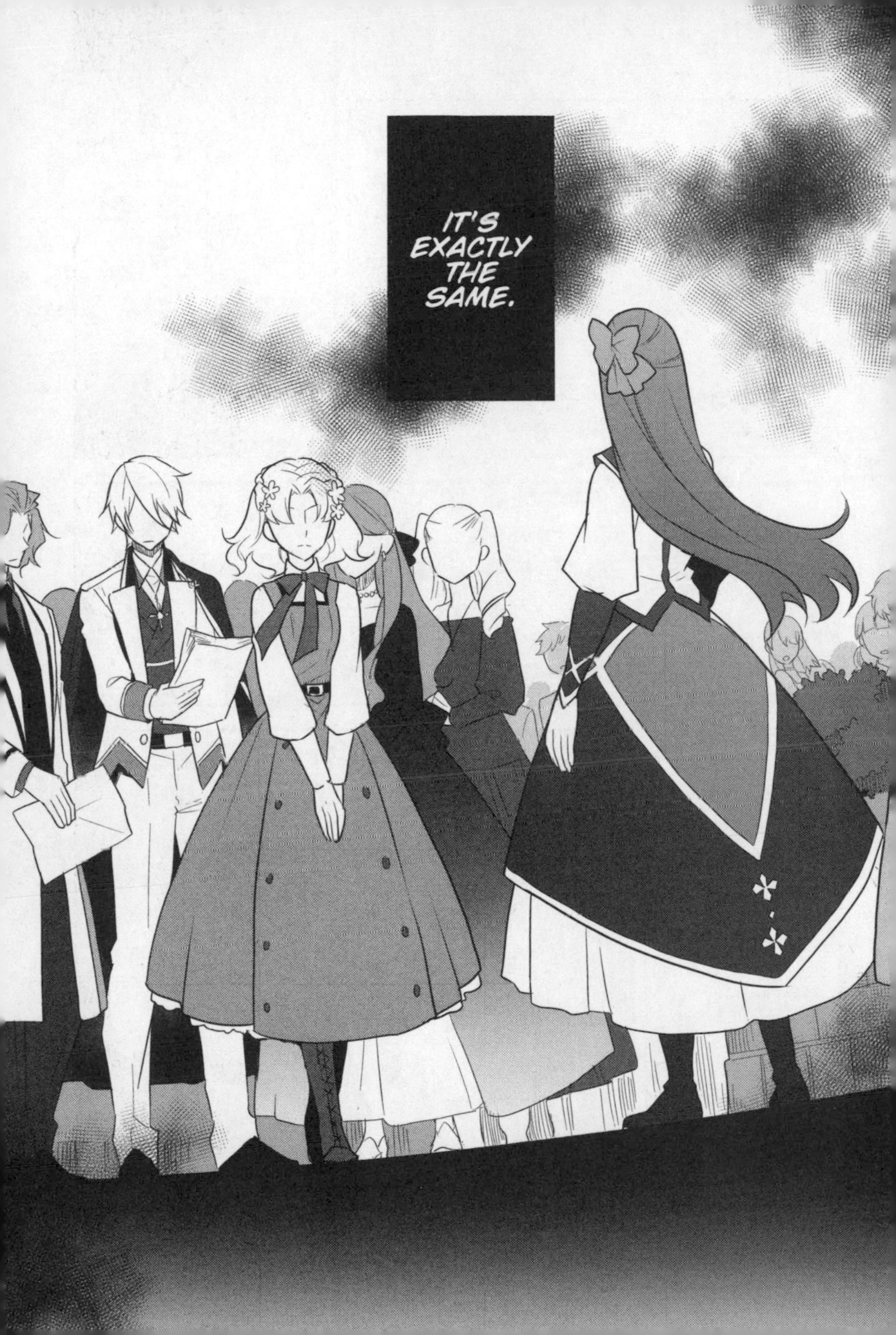
IT'S EXACTLY THE SAME.

My Next Life as a VILLAINESS: ALL ROUTES LEAD TO DOOM!

Chapter 14

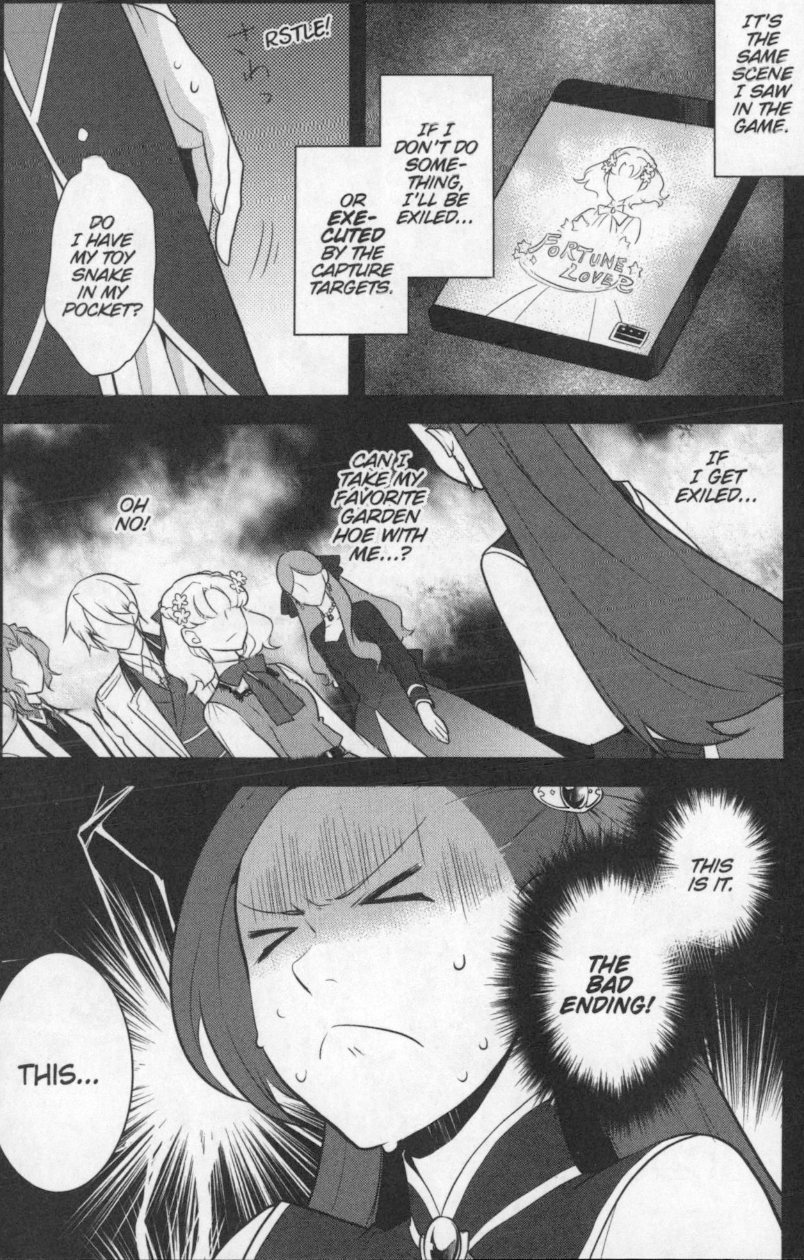
IT'S THE SAME SCENE I SAW IN THE GAME.
FORTUNE LOVER
IF I DON'T DO SOME-THING, I'LL BE EXILED...
OR EXE-CUTED BY THE CAPTURE TARGETS.
RSTLE!
DO I HAVE MY TOY SNAKE IN MY POCKET?
IF I GET EXILED...
CAN I TAKE MY FAVORITE GARDEN HOE WITH ME...?
OH NO!
THIS IS IT.
THE BAD ENDING!
THIS...

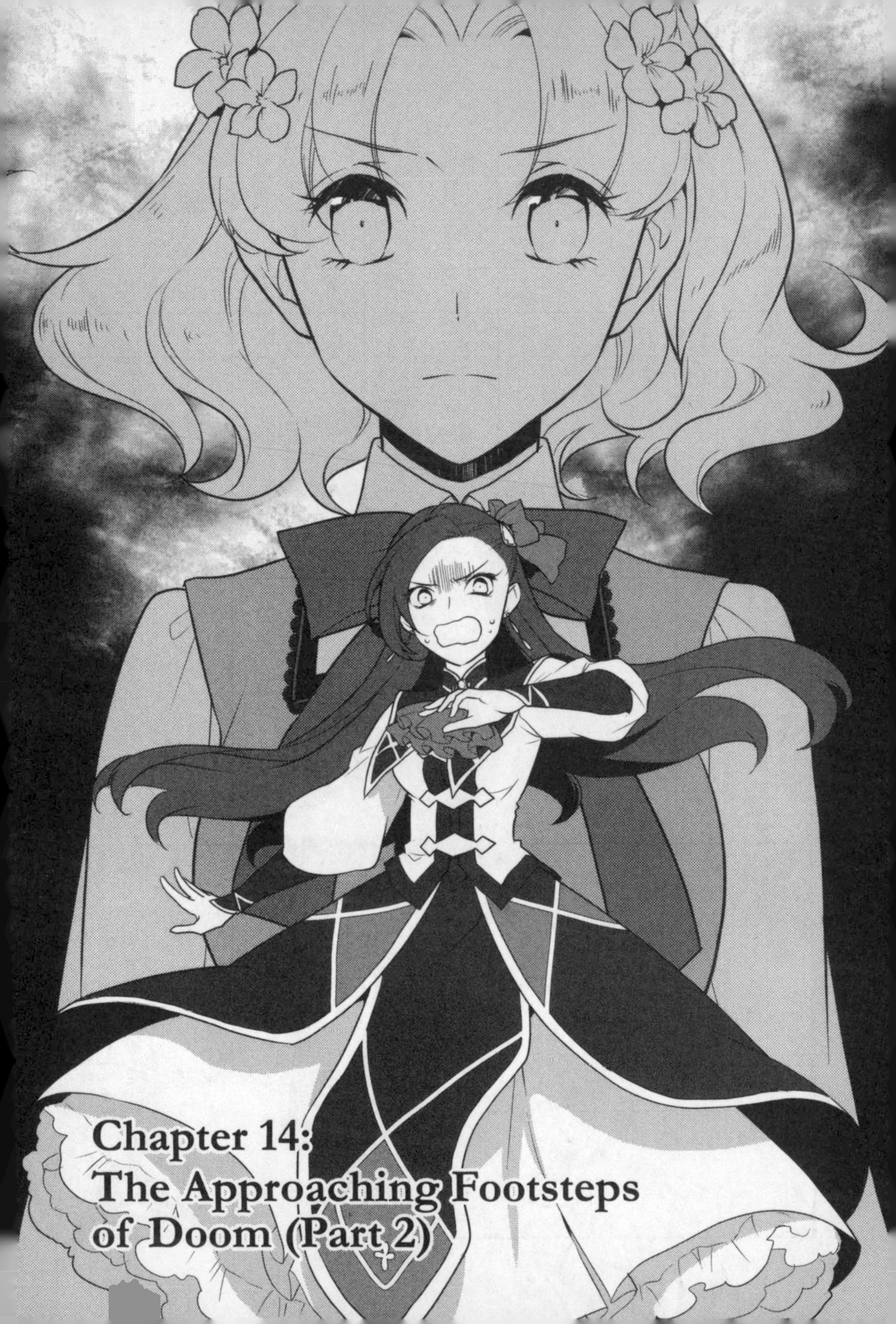

Chapter 14: The Approaching Footsteps of Doom (Part 2)

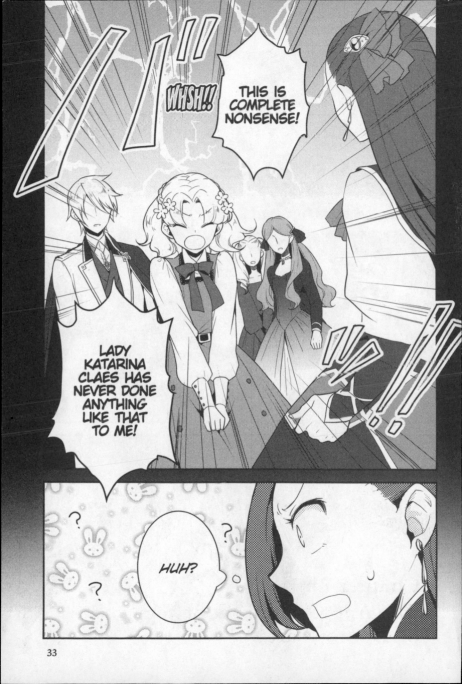

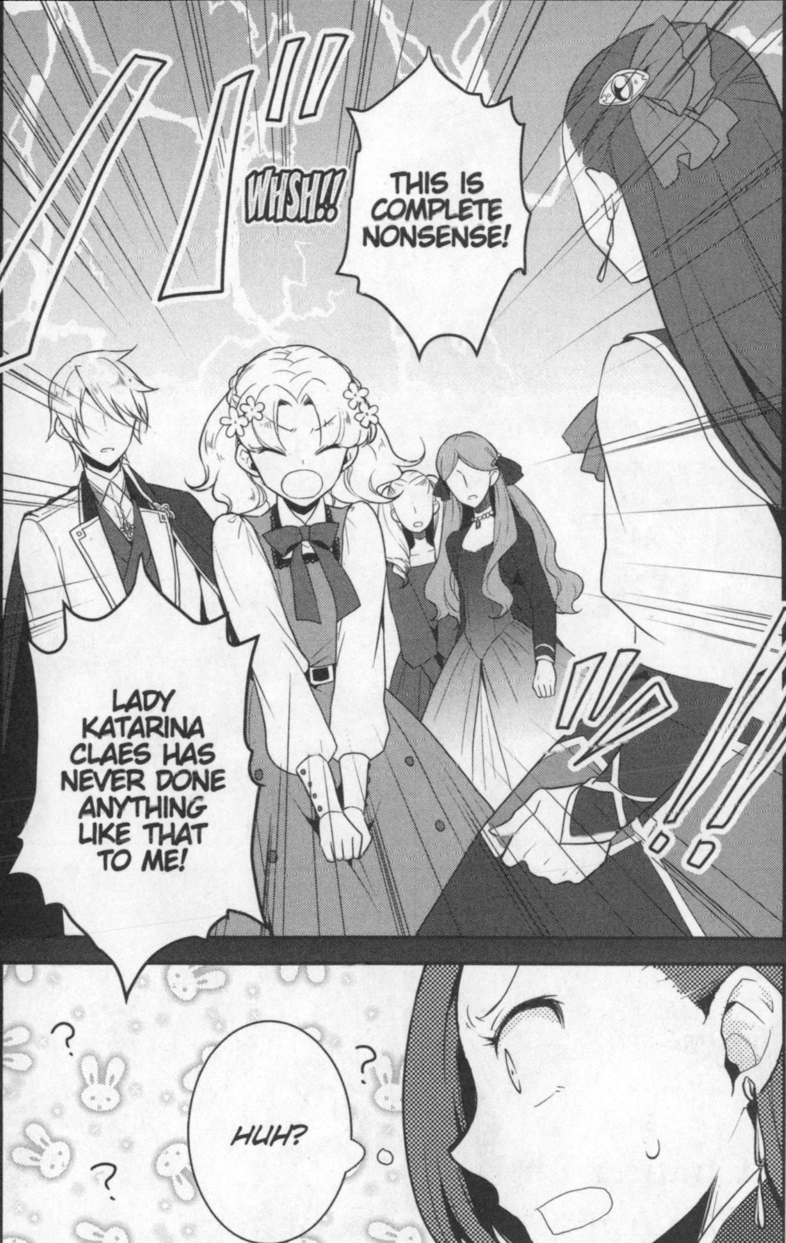
THIS IS COMPLETE NONSENSE!
WHSH!!
LADY KATARINA CLAES HAS NEVER DONE ANYTHING LIKE THAT TO ME!
HUH?
?
?
?

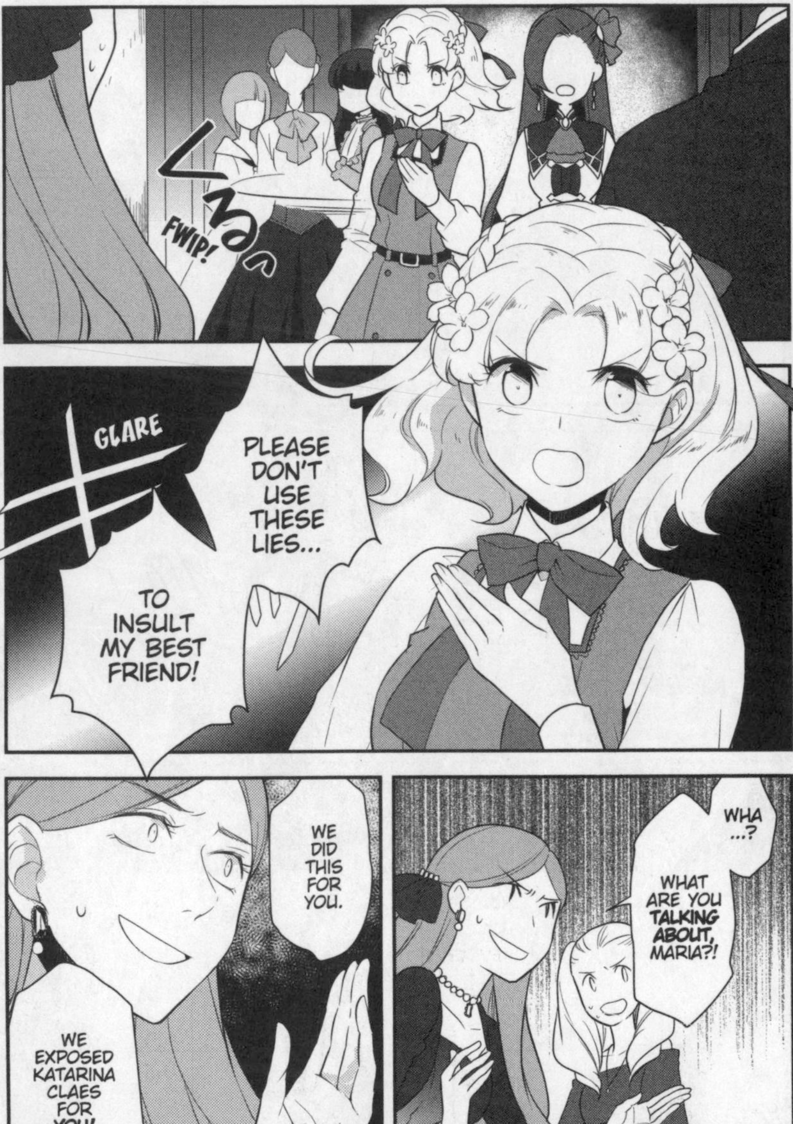

FWIP!
GLARE
PLEASE DON'T USE THESE LIES...
TO INSULT MY BEST FRIEND!
WHA ...?
WHAT ARE YOU TALKING ABOUT, MARIA?!
WE DID THIS FOR YOU.
WE EXPOSED KATARINA CLAES FOR YOU!

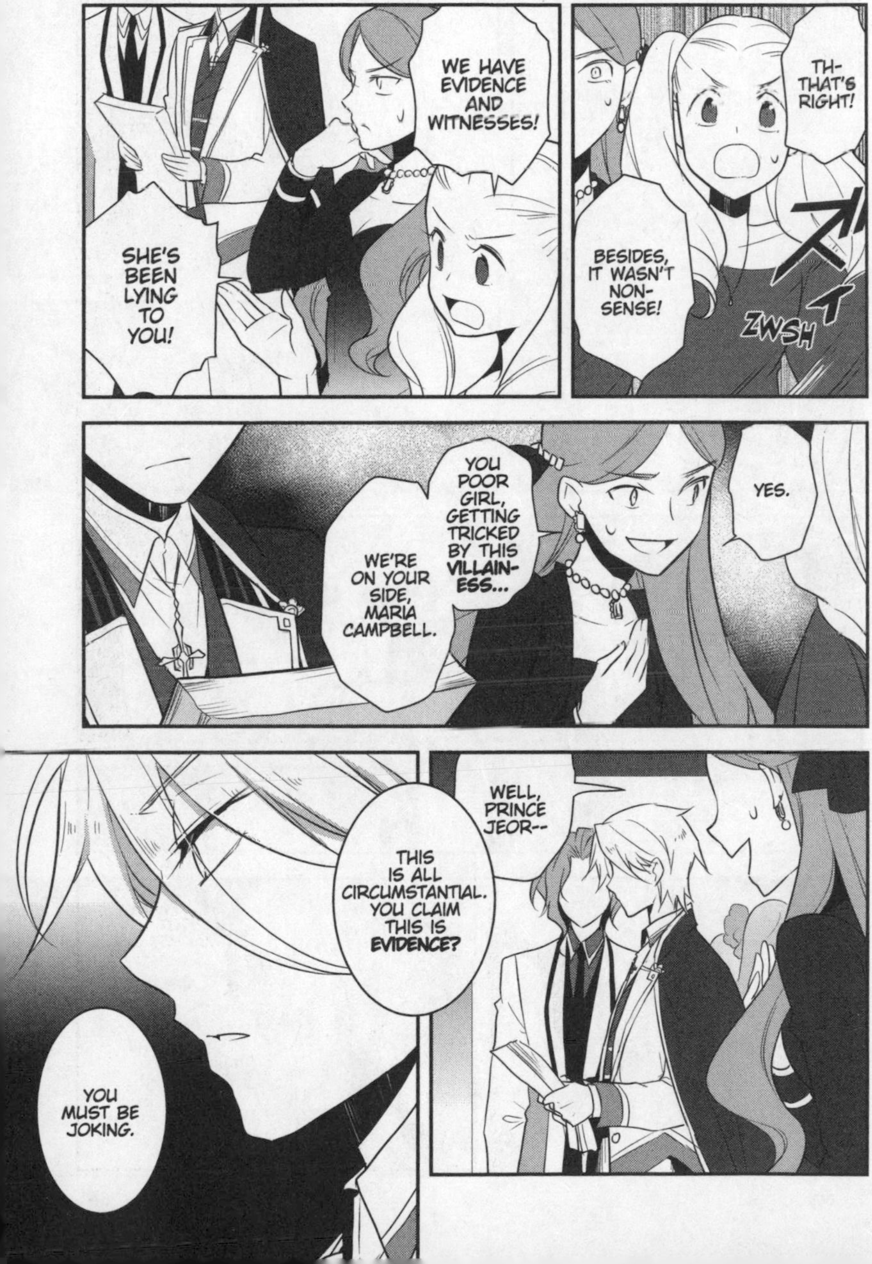
TH- THAT'S RIGHT!
BESIDES, IT WASN'T NON-SENSE!
ZWSH
WE HAVE EVIDENCE AND WITNESSES!
SHE'S BEEN LYING TO YOU!
YES.
YOU POOR GIRL, GETTING TRICKED BY THIS **VILLAIN-ESS...**
WE'RE ON YOUR SIDE, MARIA CAMPBELL.
WELL, PRINCE JEOR--
THIS IS ALL CIRCUMSTANTIAL. YOU CLAIM THIS IS **EVIDENCE?**
YOU MUST BE JOKING.

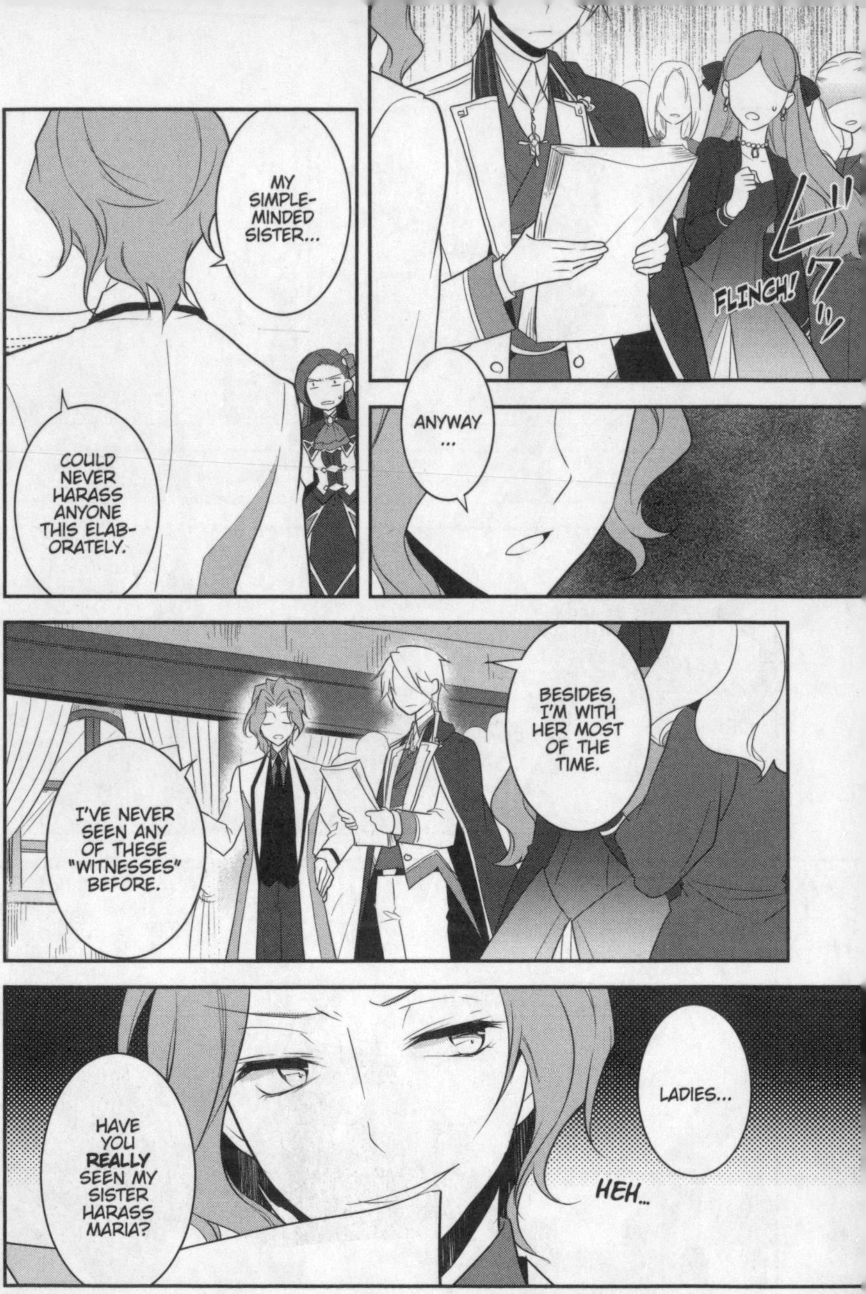
FLINCH!
ANYWAY...
MY SIMPLE-MINDED SISTER...
COULD NEVER HARASS ANYONE THIS ELABORATELY.
BESIDES, I'M WITH HER MOST OF THE TIME.
I'VE NEVER SEEN ANY OF THESE "WITNESSES" BEFORE.
LADIES...
HEH...
HAVE YOU **REALLY** SEEN MY SISTER HARASS MARIA?

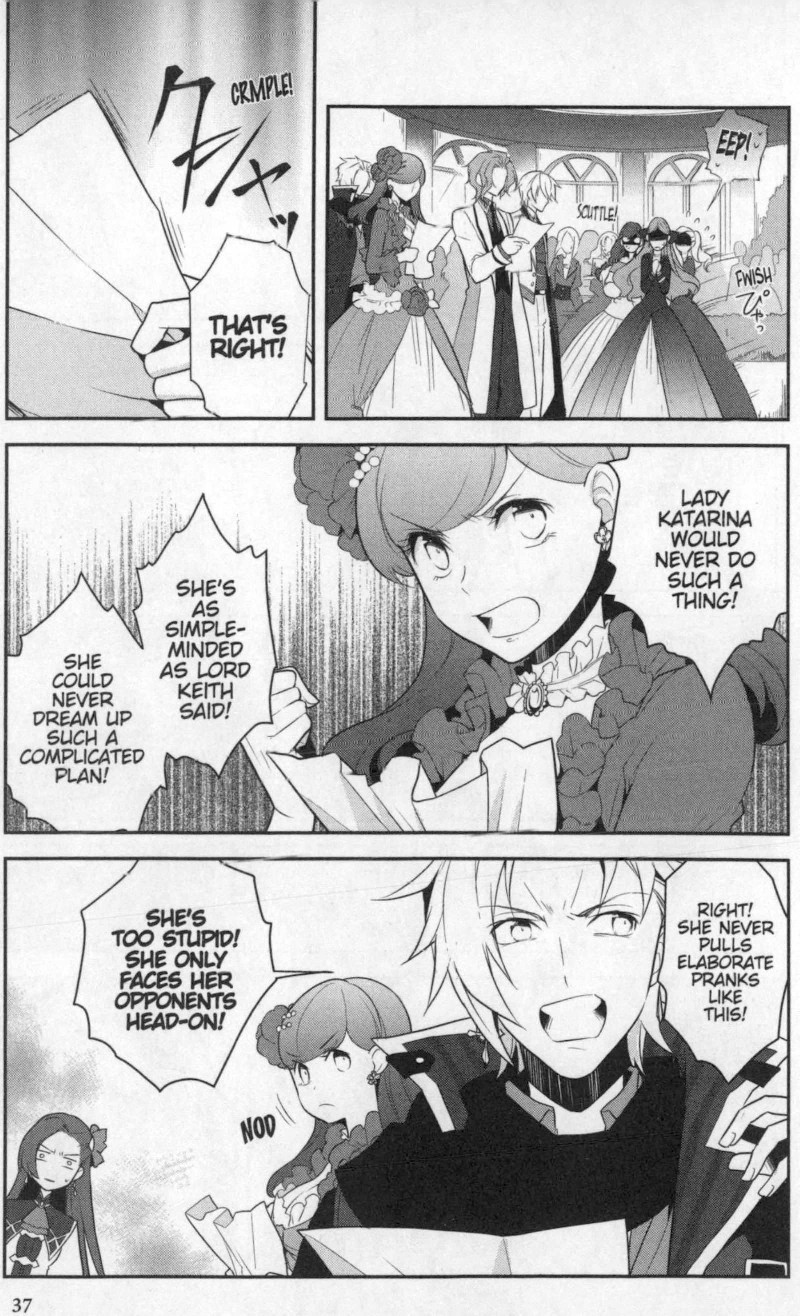
EEP!
SCUTTLE!
FWISH
ぴゃっ
CRMPLE!
クシャッ
THAT'S RIGHT!
LADY KATARINA WOULD NEVER DO SUCH A THING!
SHE'S AS SIMPLE-MINDED AS LORD KEITH SAID!
SHE COULD NEVER DREAM UP SUCH A COMPLICATED PLAN!
RIGHT! SHE NEVER PULLS ELABORATE PRANKS LIKE THIS!
SHE'S TOO STUPID! SHE ONLY FACES HER OPPONENTS HEAD-ON!
NOD

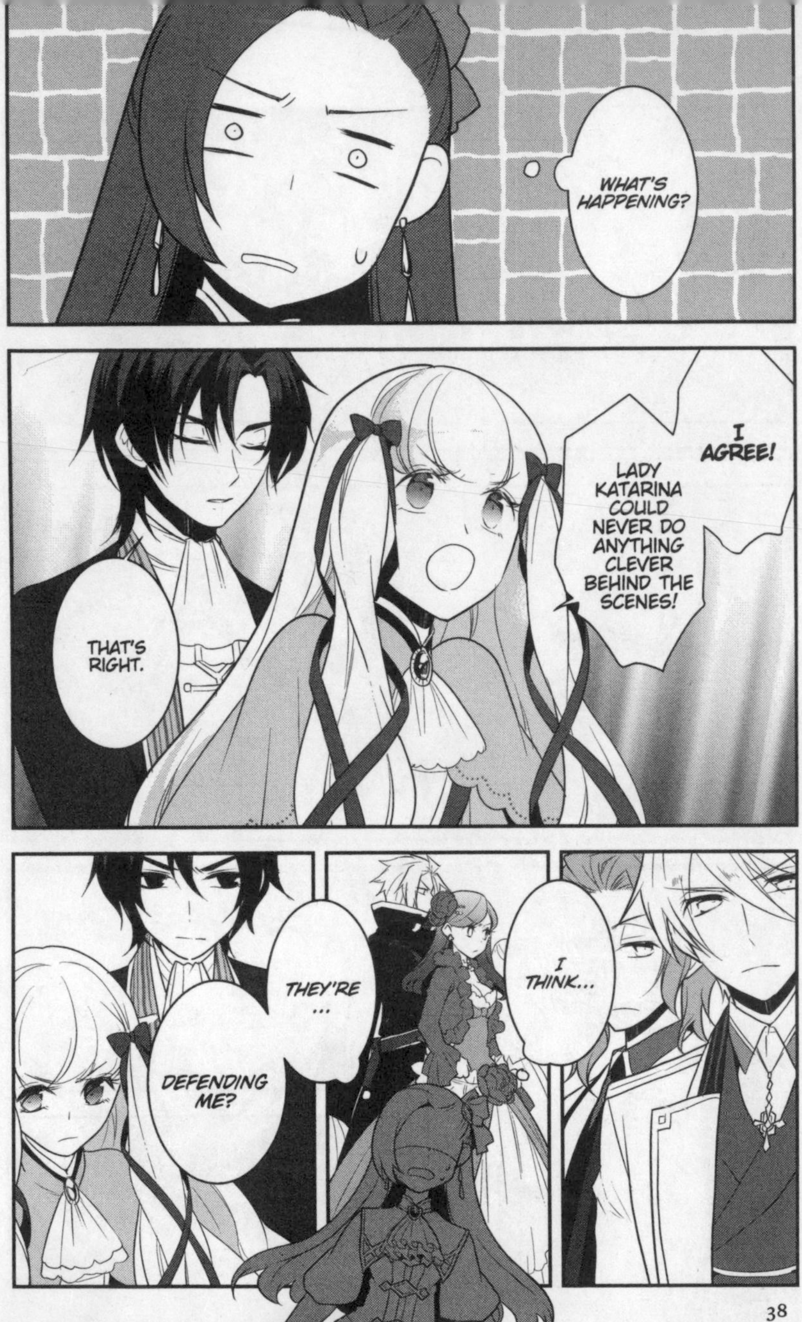
WHAT'S HAPPENING?
I AGREE!
LADY KATARINA COULD NEVER DO ANYTHING CLEVER BEHIND THE SCENES!
THAT'S RIGHT.
I THINK...
THEY'RE ...
DEFENDING ME?

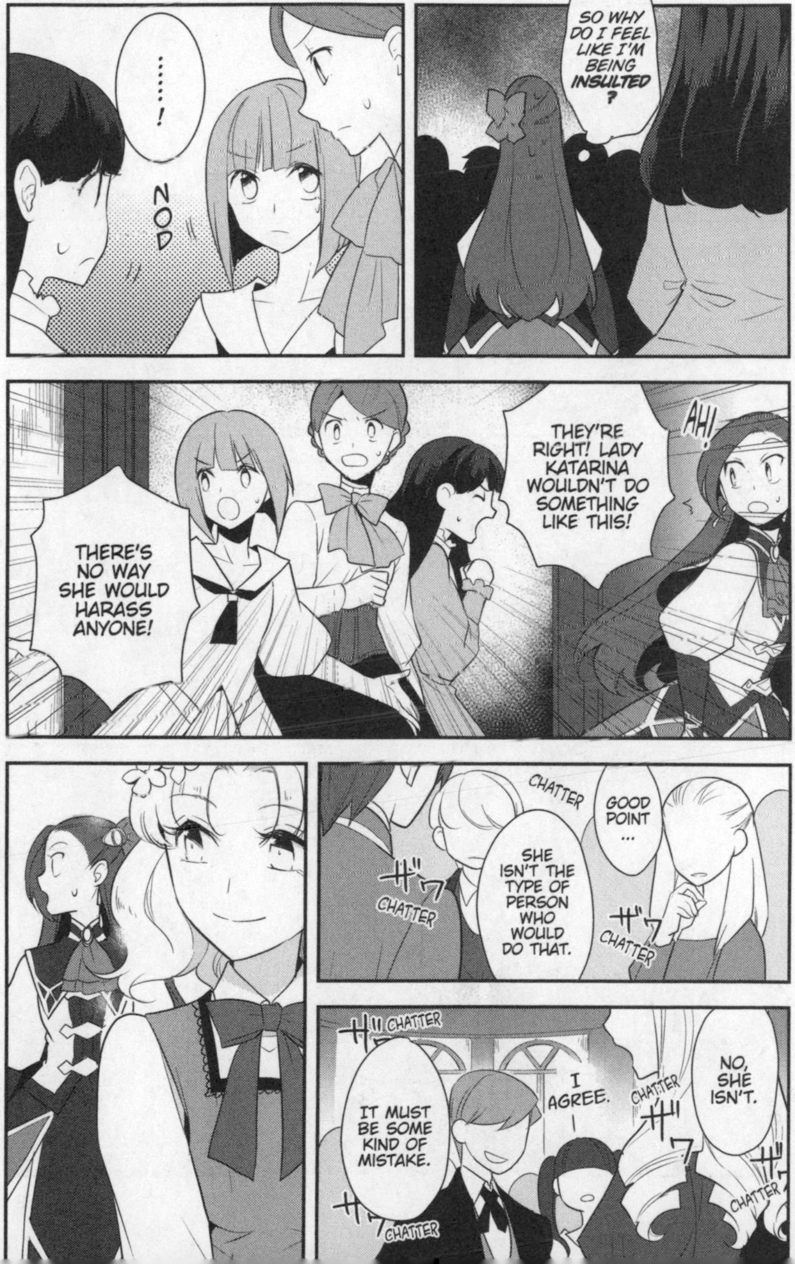
SO WHY DO I FEEL LIKE I'M BEING INSULTED?
......!
NOD
AH!
THEY'RE RIGHT! LADY KATARINA WOULDN'T DO SOMETHING LIKE THIS!
THERE'S NO WAY SHE WOULD HARASS ANYONE!
CHATTER
GOOD POINT...
SHE ISN'T THE TYPE OF PERSON WHO WOULD DO THAT.
ザワ CHATTER
ザワ CHATTER
ザワ CHATTER
NO, SHE ISN'T.
ザワ CHATTER
I AGREE.
ザワ CHATTER
IT MUST BE SOME KIND OF MISTAKE.
ザワ CHATTER

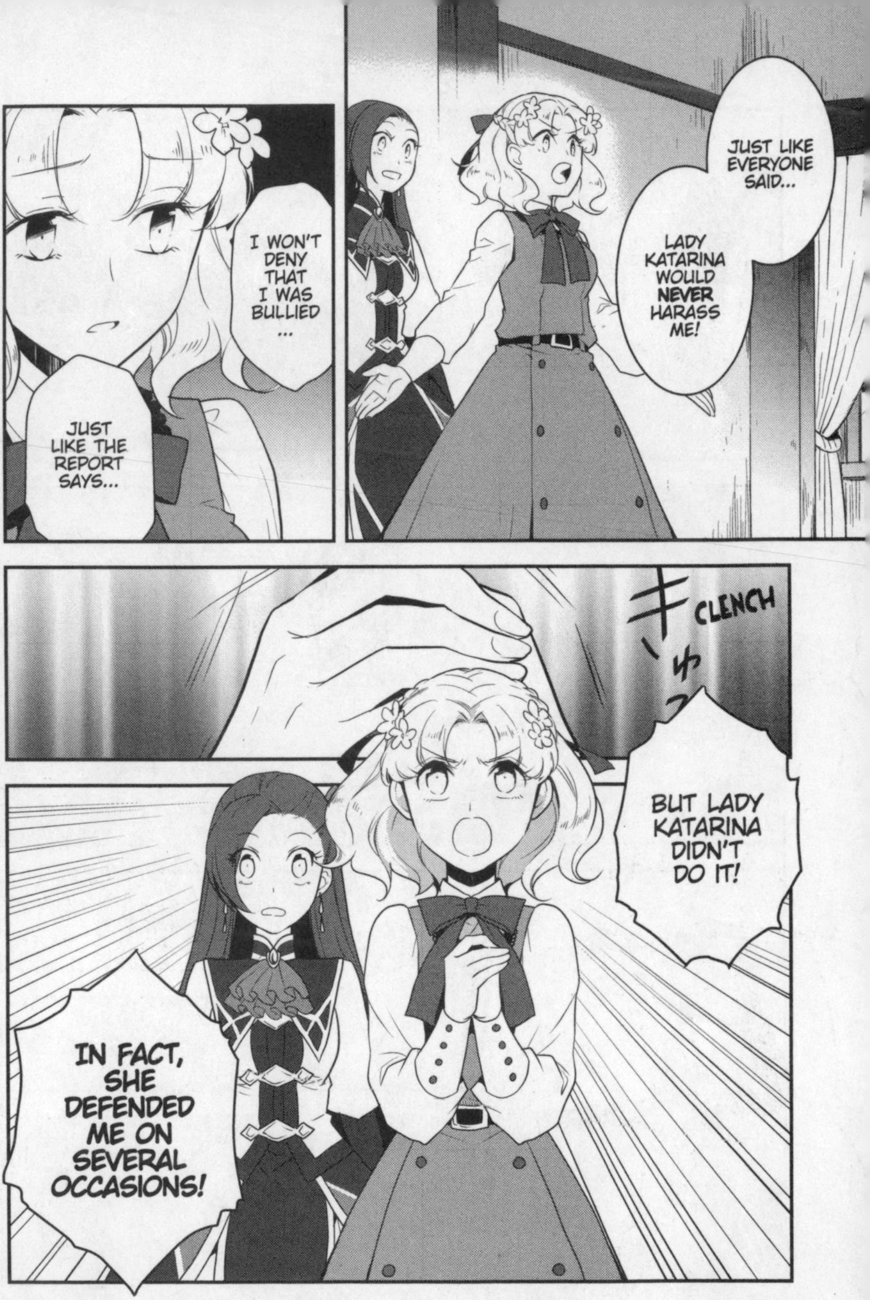
JUST LIKE EVERYONE SAID...
LADY KATARINA WOULD NEVER HARASS ME!
I WON'T DENY THAT I WAS BULLIED ...
JUST LIKE THE REPORT SAYS...
CLENCH
BUT LADY KATARINA DIDN'T DO IT!
IN FACT, SHE DEFENDED ME ON SEVERAL OCCASIONS!

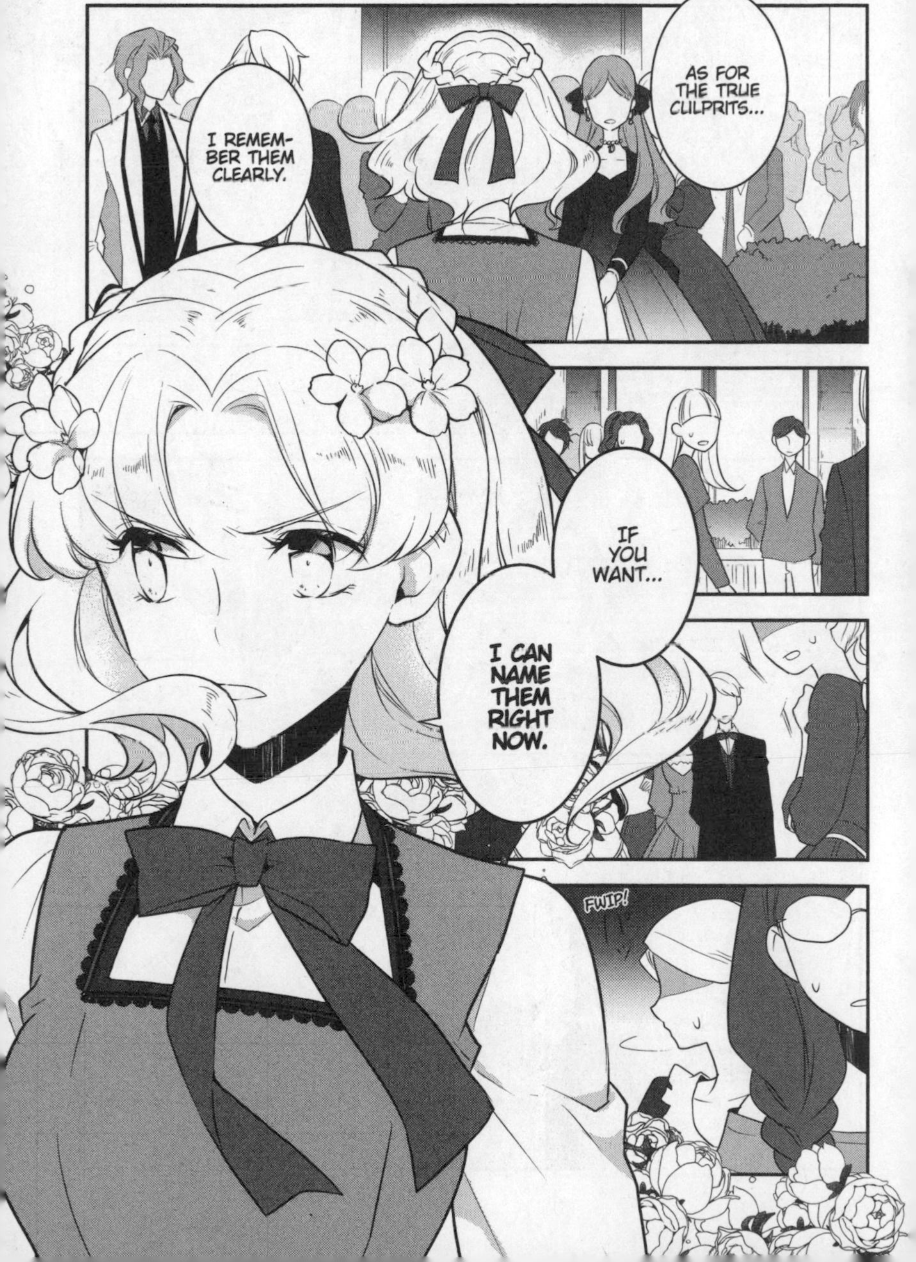
AS FOR THE TRUE CULPRITS...
I REMEMBER THEM CLEARLY.
IF YOU WANT...
I CAN NAME THEM RIGHT NOW.
FWIP!

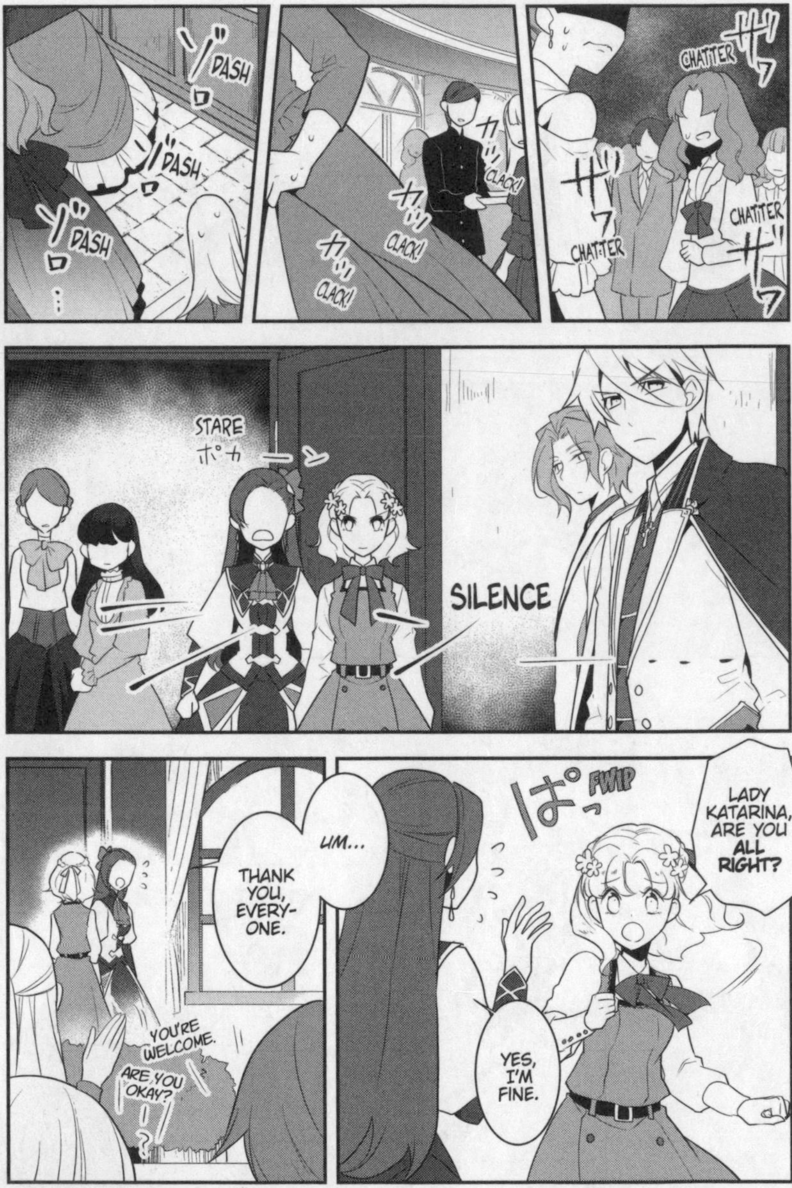
CHATTER
ザワ
CHATTER
ザワ
CHATTER
ザワ
CLACK!
カッ
CLACK!
カッ
CLACK!
カッ
DASH
ゾロ
DASH
ゾロ
DASH
ゾロ
SILENCE
STARE
ポカーン
ぱっ
FWIP
LADY KATARINA, ARE YOU ALL RIGHT?
UM...
THANK YOU, EVERY-ONE.
YES, I'M FINE.
YOU'RE WELCOME.
ARE YOU OKAY?

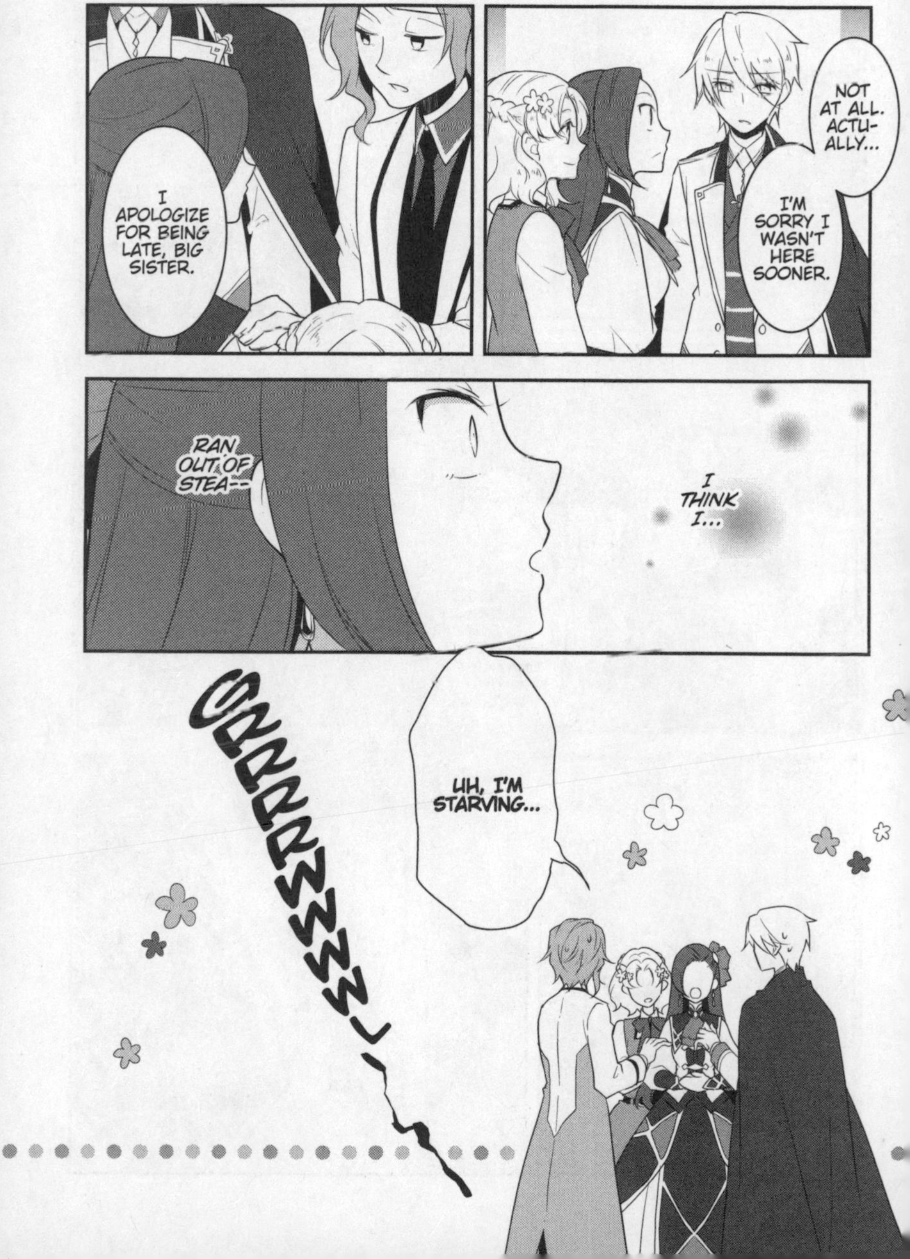
NOT AT ALL. ACTUALLY...
I'M SORRY I WASN'T HERE SOONER.
I APOLOGIZE FOR BEING LATE, BIG SISTER.
I THINK I...
RAN OUT OF STEA--
UH, I'M STARVING...
GRRRRWWWWL

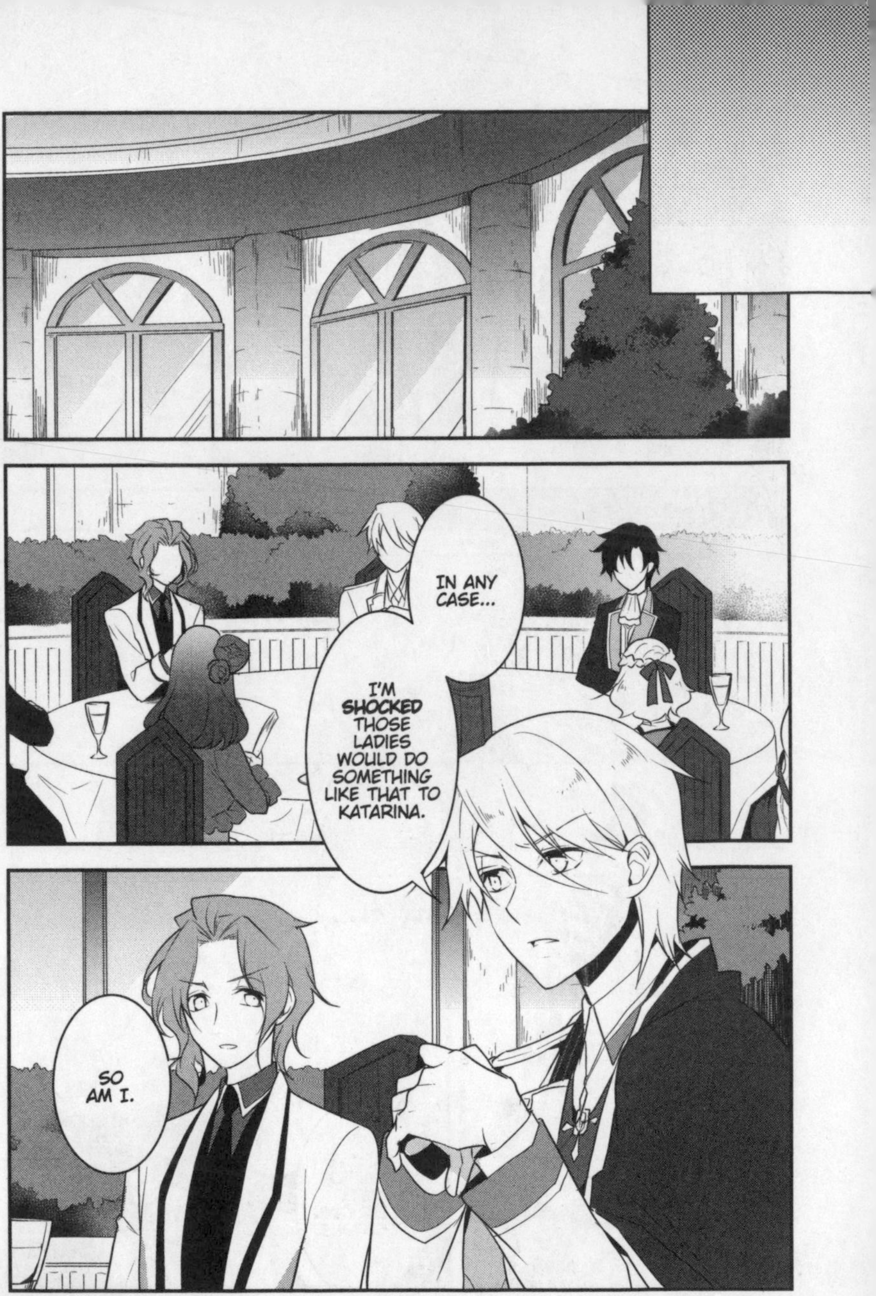
IN ANY CASE...
I'M **SHOCKED** THOSE LADIES WOULD DO SOMETHING LIKE THAT TO KATARINA.
SO AM I.

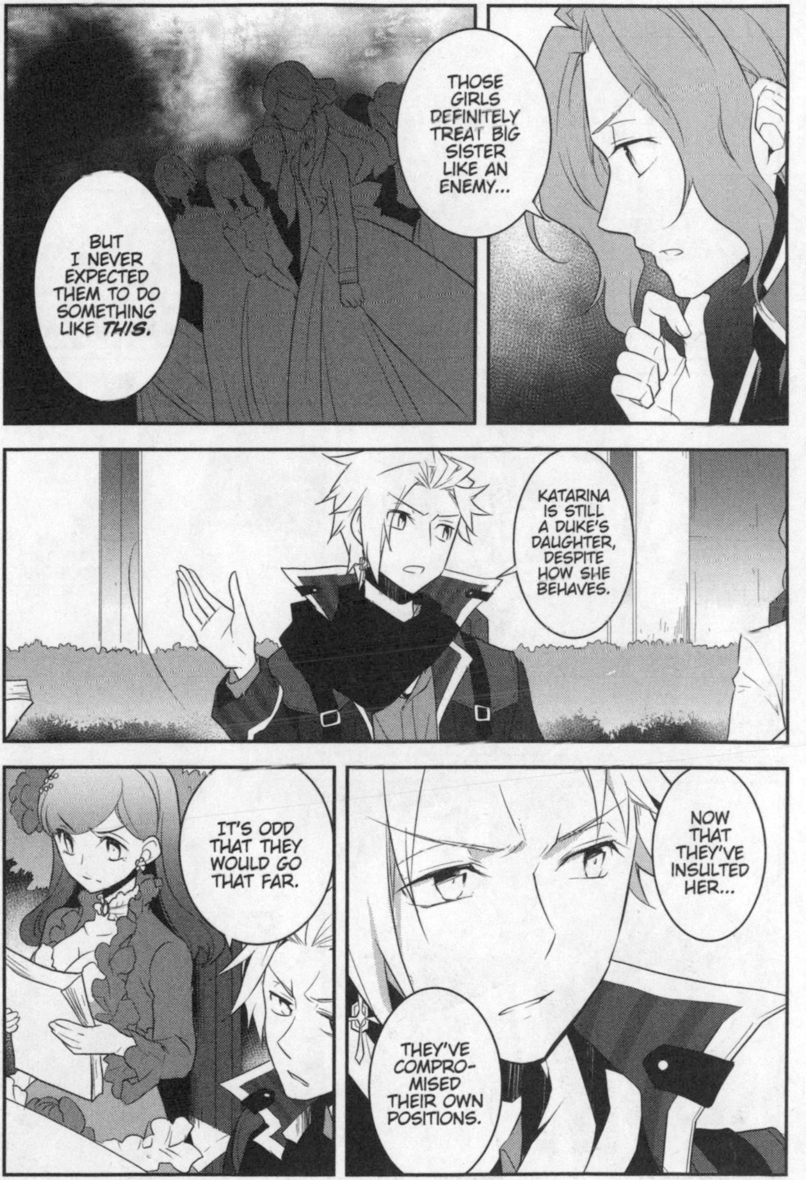
THOSE GIRLS DEFINITELY TREAT BIG SISTER LIKE AN ENEMY...
BUT I NEVER EXPECTED THEM TO DO SOMETHING LIKE *THIS*.
KATARINA IS STILL A DUKE'S DAUGHTER, DESPITE HOW SHE BEHAVES.
NOW THAT THEY'VE INSULTED HER...
THEY'VE COMPRO-MISED THEIR OWN POSITIONS.
IT'S ODD THAT THEY WOULD GO THAT FAR.

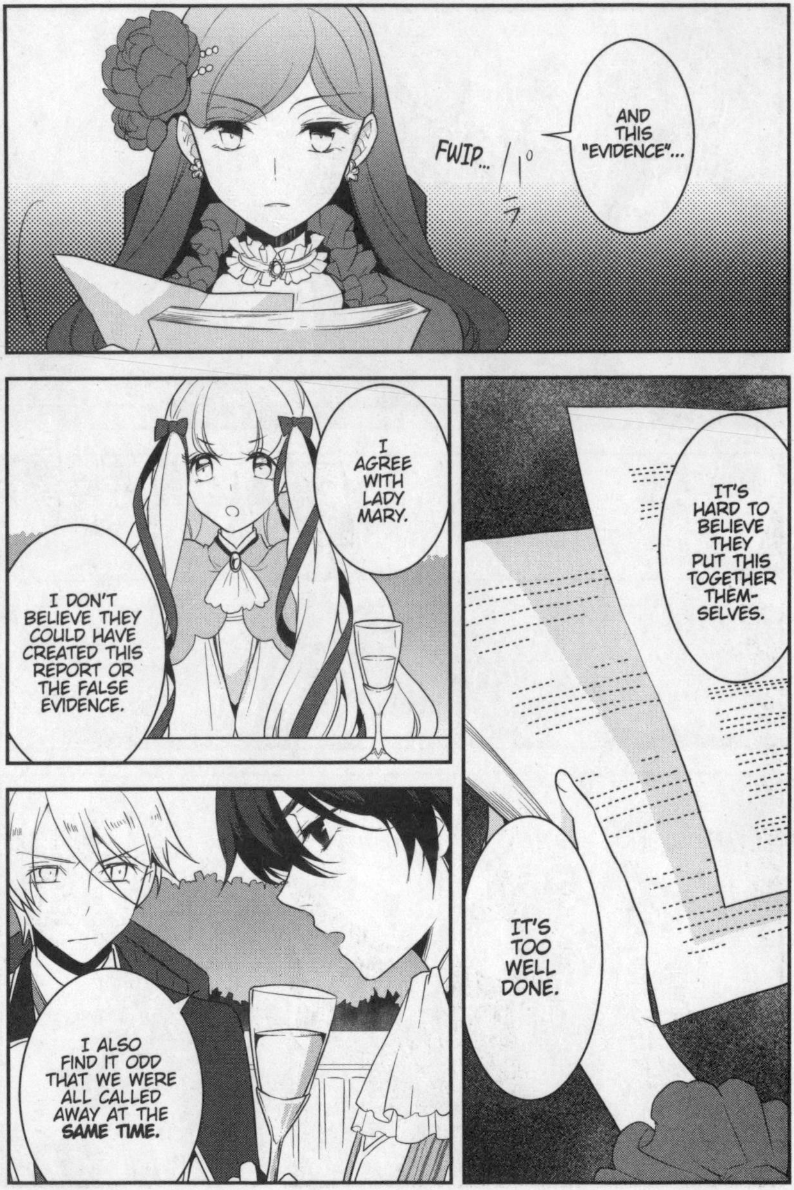
AND THIS "EVIDENCE"...
FWIP...
IT'S HARD TO BELIEVE THEY PUT THIS TOGETHER THEM-SELVES.
IT'S TOO WELL DONE.
I AGREE WITH LADY MARY.
I DON'T BELIEVE THEY COULD HAVE CREATED THIS REPORT OR THE FALSE EVIDENCE.
I ALSO FIND IT ODD THAT WE WERE ALL CALLED AWAY AT THE **SAME TIME.**

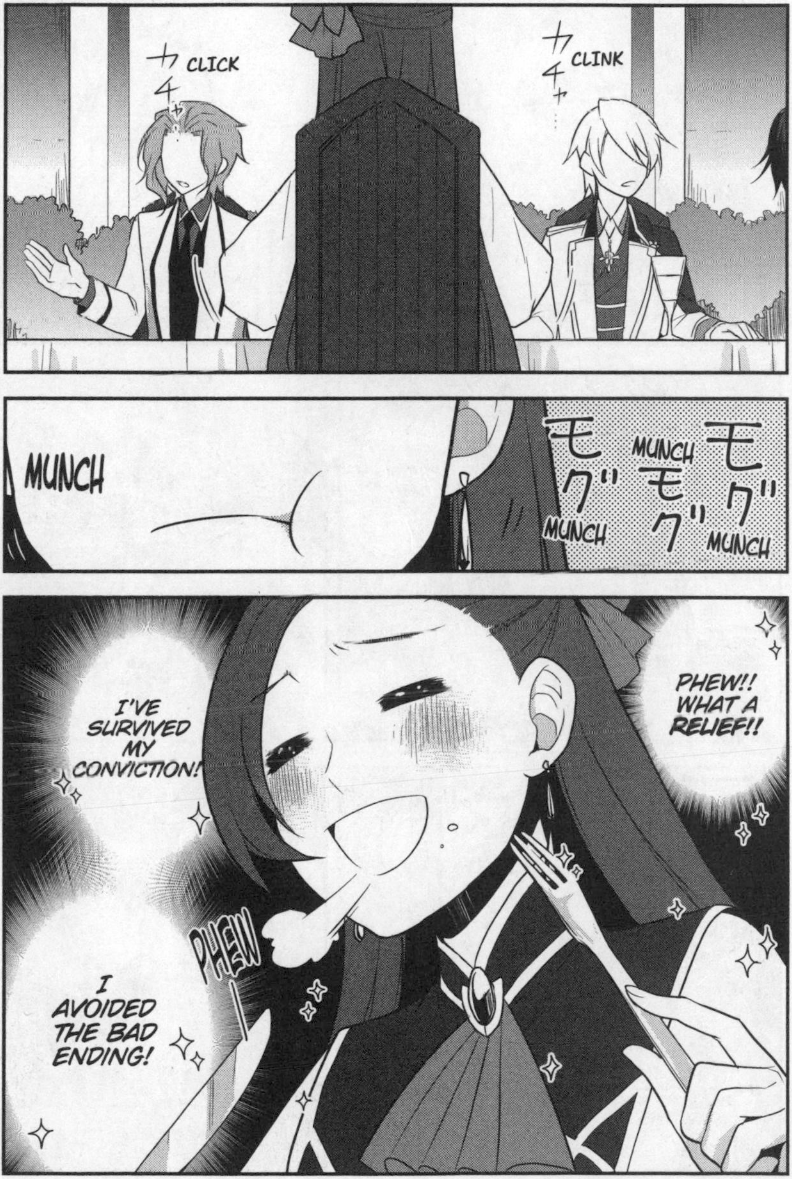
カチャ…
CLINK
カチャ
CLICK
モグ
MUNCH
モグ
MUNCH
モグ
MUNCH
MUNCH
PHEW!! WHAT A RELIEF!!
I'VE SURVIVED MY CONVICTION!
PHEW
I AVOIDED THE BAD ENDING!

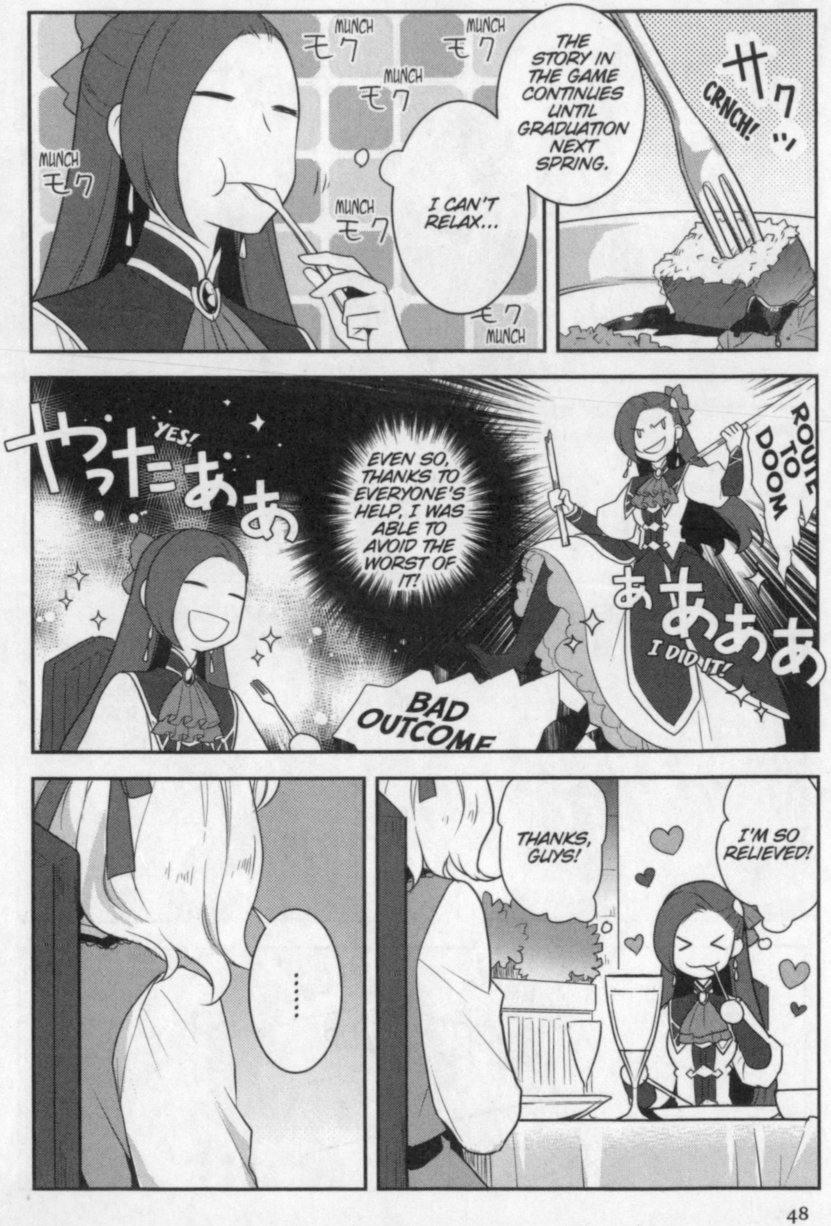
サクッ
CRNCH!
THE STORY IN THE GAME CONTINUES UNTIL GRADUATION NEXT SPRING.
I CAN'T RELAX...
モク MUNCH
モク MUNCH
モク MUNCH
モク MUNCH
モク MUNCH
モク MUNCH
ROUTE TO DOOM
ああああ
I DID IT!
EVEN SO, THANKS TO EVERYONE'S HELP, I WAS ABLE TO AVOID THE WORST OF IT!
BAD OUTCOME
やったあぁ
YES!
I'M SO RELIEVED!
THANKS, GUYS!
......

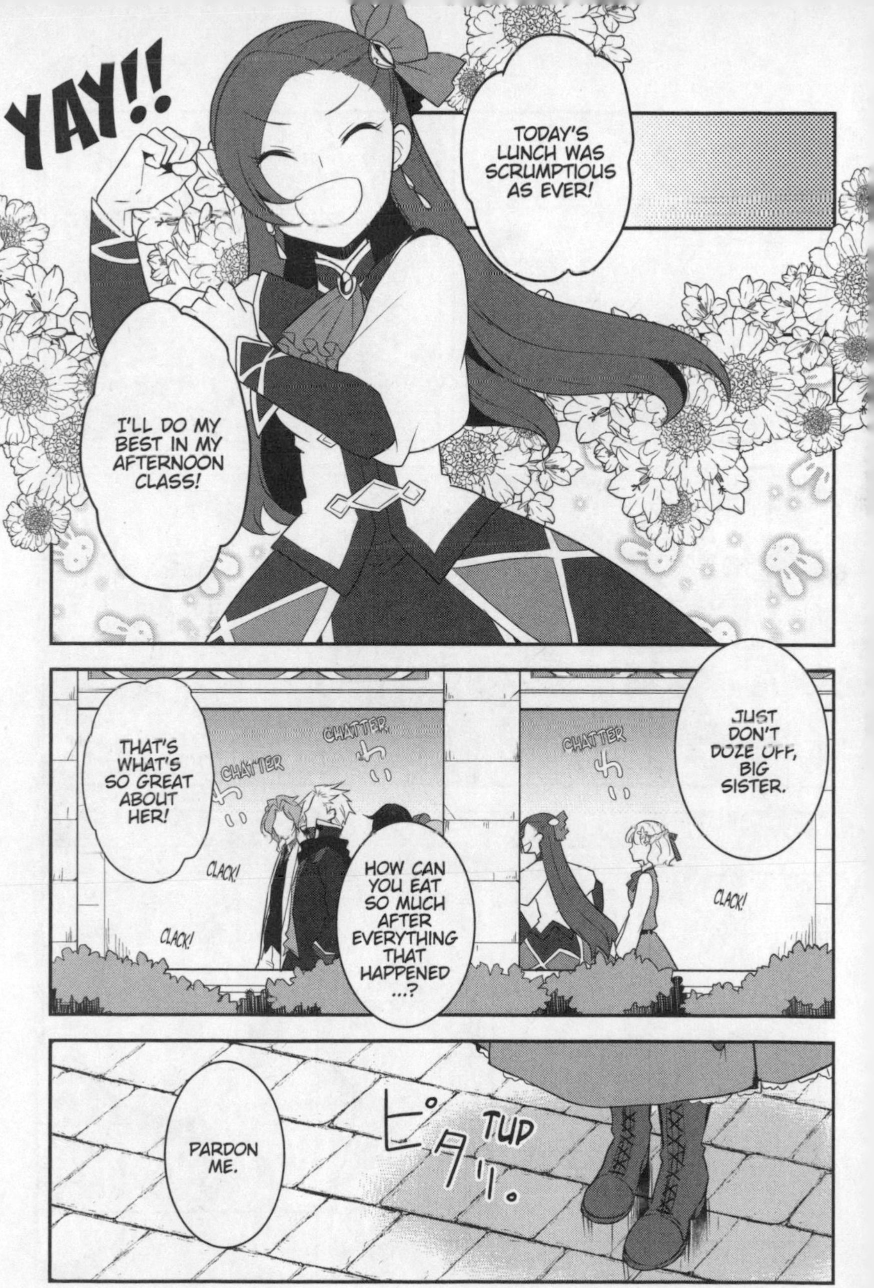
TODAY'S LUNCH WAS SCRUMPTIOUS AS EVER!
YAY!!
I'LL DO MY BEST IN MY AFTERNOON CLASS!
JUST DON'T DOZE OFF, BIG SISTER.
CHATTER
CLACK!
CHATTER
HOW CAN YOU EAT SO MUCH AFTER EVERYTHING THAT HAPPENED ...?
CHATTER
THAT'S WHAT'S SO GREAT ABOUT HER!
CLACK!
CLACK!
TUP
ピタリ。
PARDON ME.

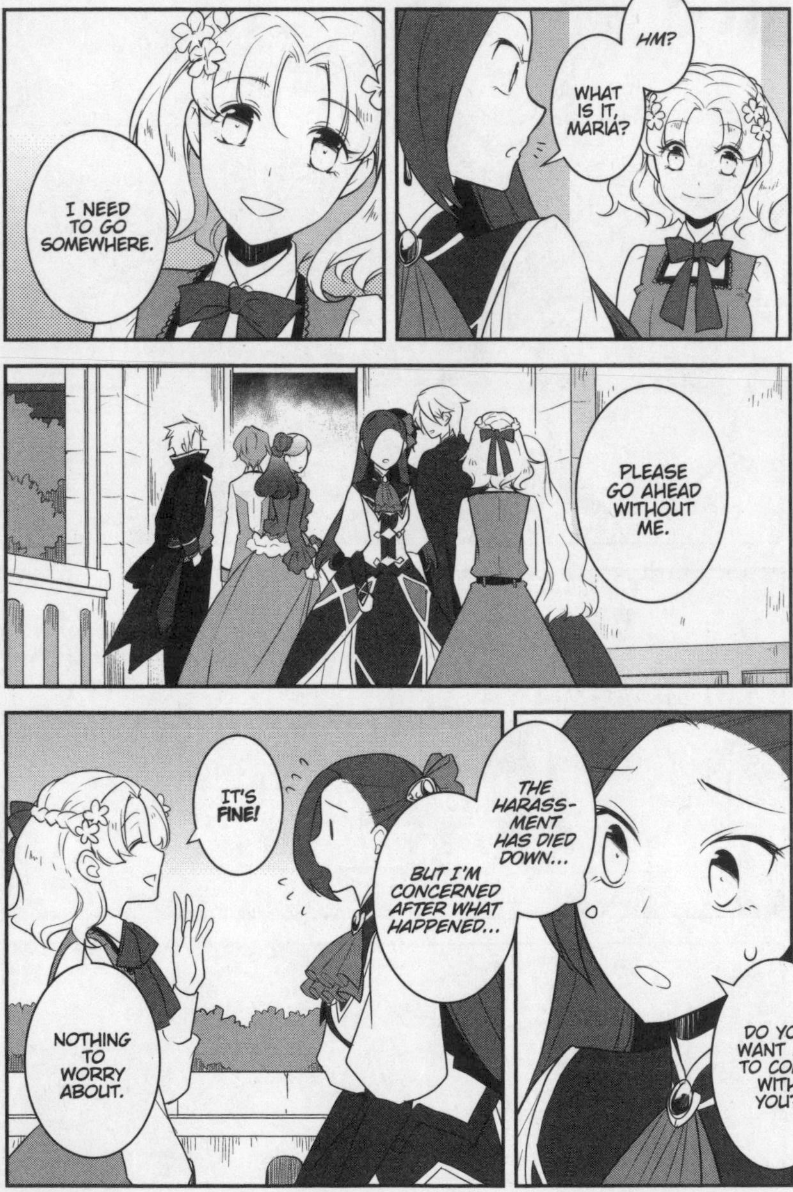
HM?
WHAT IS IT, MARIA?
I NEED TO GO SOMEWHERE.
PLEASE GO AHEAD WITHOUT ME.
THE HARASS-MENT HAS DIED DOWN...
BUT I'M CONCERNED AFTER WHAT HAPPENED...
DO YOU WANT ME TO COME WITH YOU?
IT'S FINE!
NOTHING TO WORRY ABOUT.

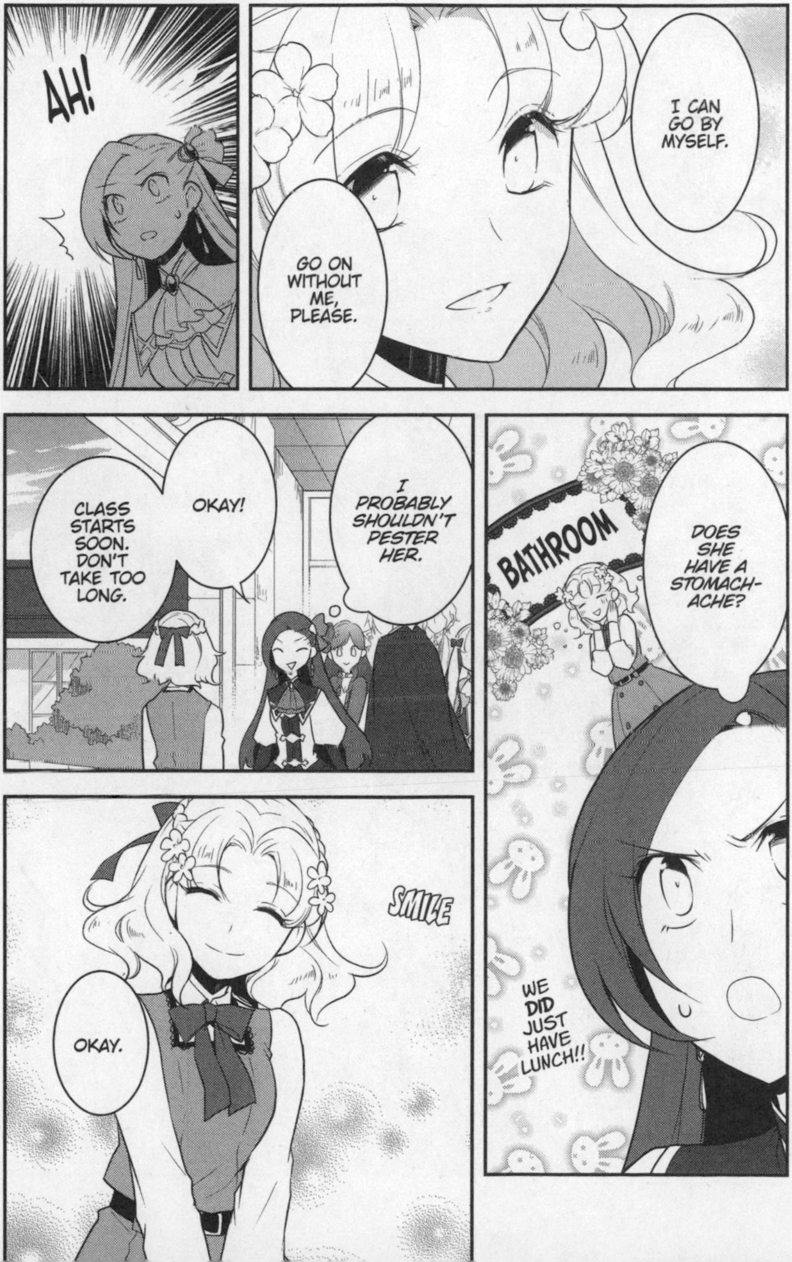
I CAN GO BY MYSELF.
GO ON WITHOUT ME, PLEASE.
AH!
BATHROOM
DOES SHE HAVE A STOMACH-ACHE?
WE **DID** JUST HAVE LUNCH!!
I PROBABLY SHOULDN'T PESTER HER.
OKAY!
CLASS STARTS SOON. DON'T TAKE TOO LONG.
SMILE
OKAY.

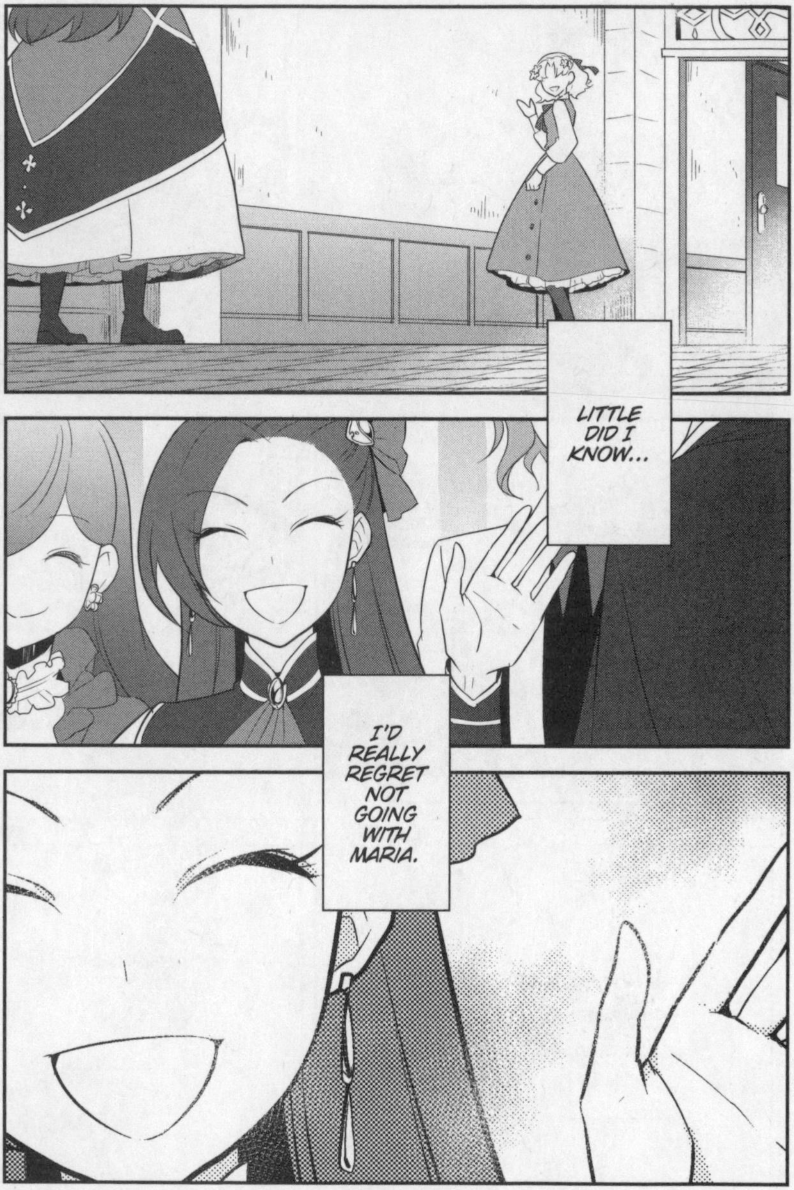
LITTLE DID I KNOW...
I'D REALLY REGRET NOT GOING WITH MARIA.

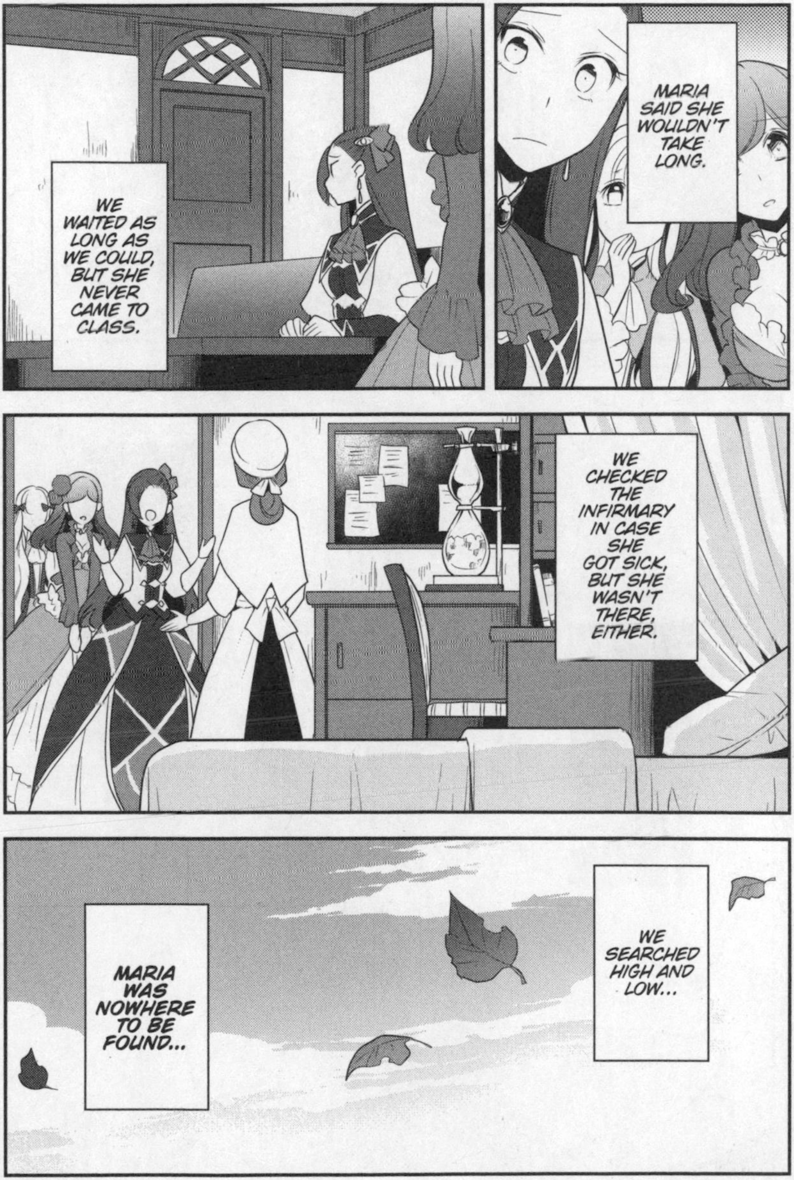
MARIA SAID SHE WOULDN'T TAKE LONG.
WE WAITED AS LONG AS WE COULD, BUT SHE NEVER CAME TO CLASS.
WE CHECKED THE INFIRMARY IN CASE SHE GOT SICK, BUT SHE WASN'T THERE, EITHER.
WE SEARCHED HIGH AND LOW...
MARIA WAS NOWHERE TO BE FOUND...

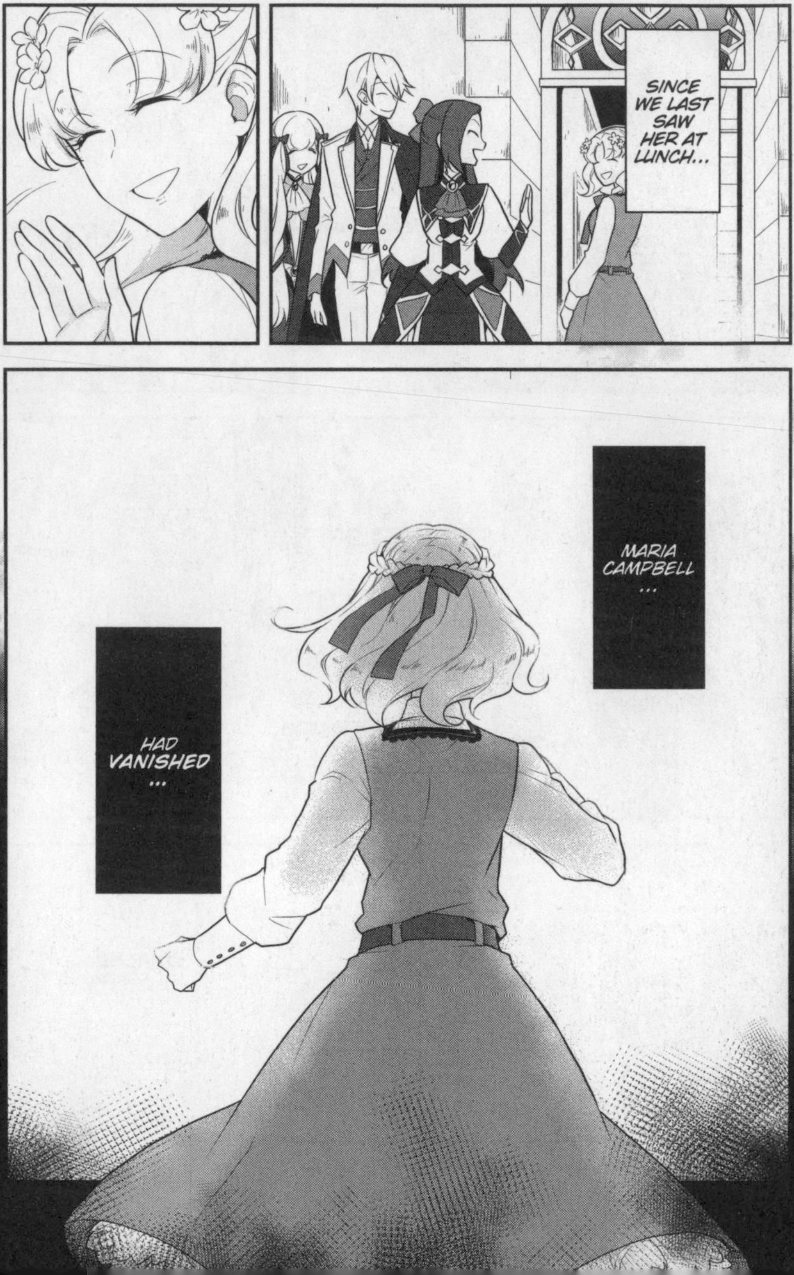
SINCE WE LAST SAW HER AT LUNCH...
MARIA CAMPBELL ...
HAD VANISHED ...

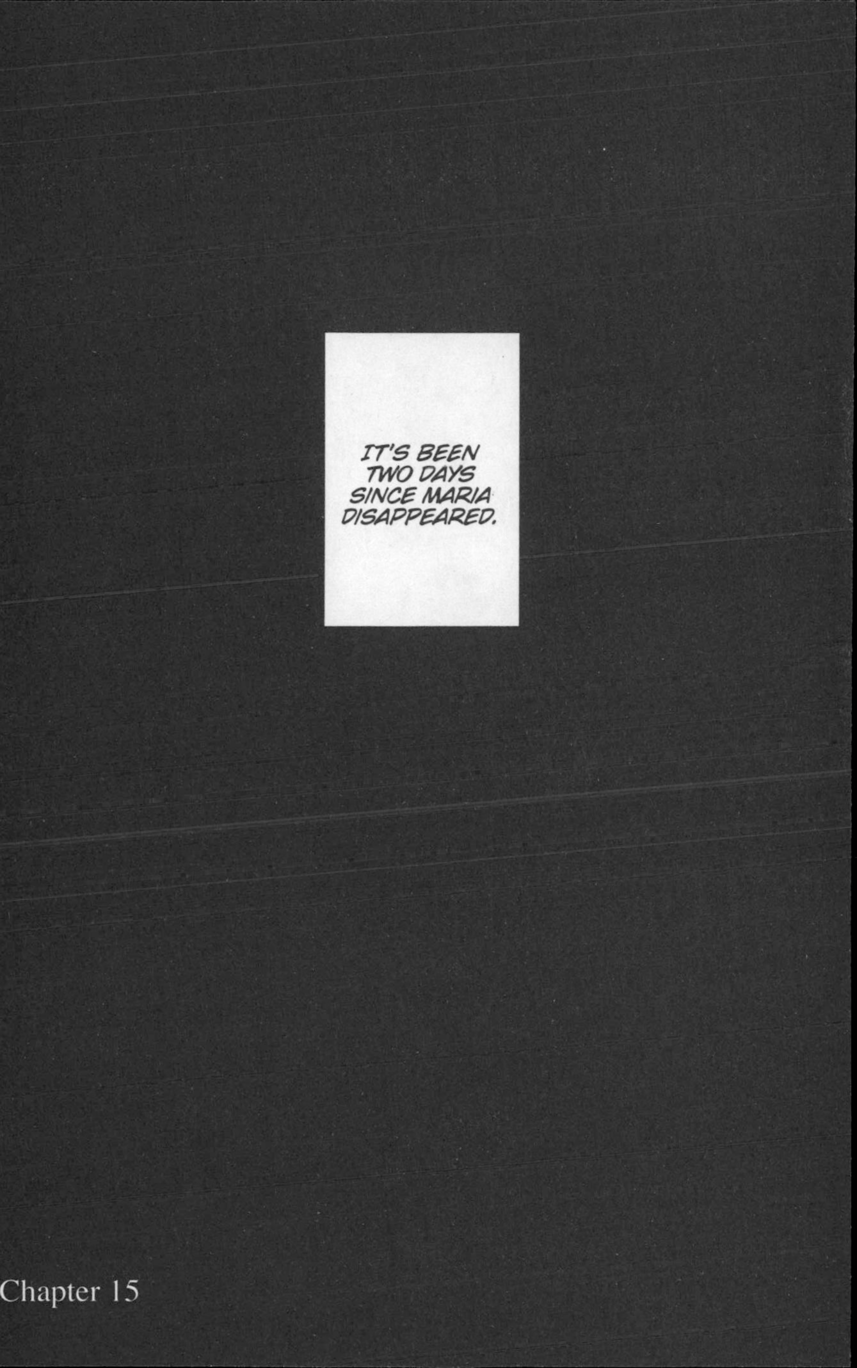
IT'S BEEN TWO DAYS SINCE MARIA DISAPPEARED.

Chapter 15

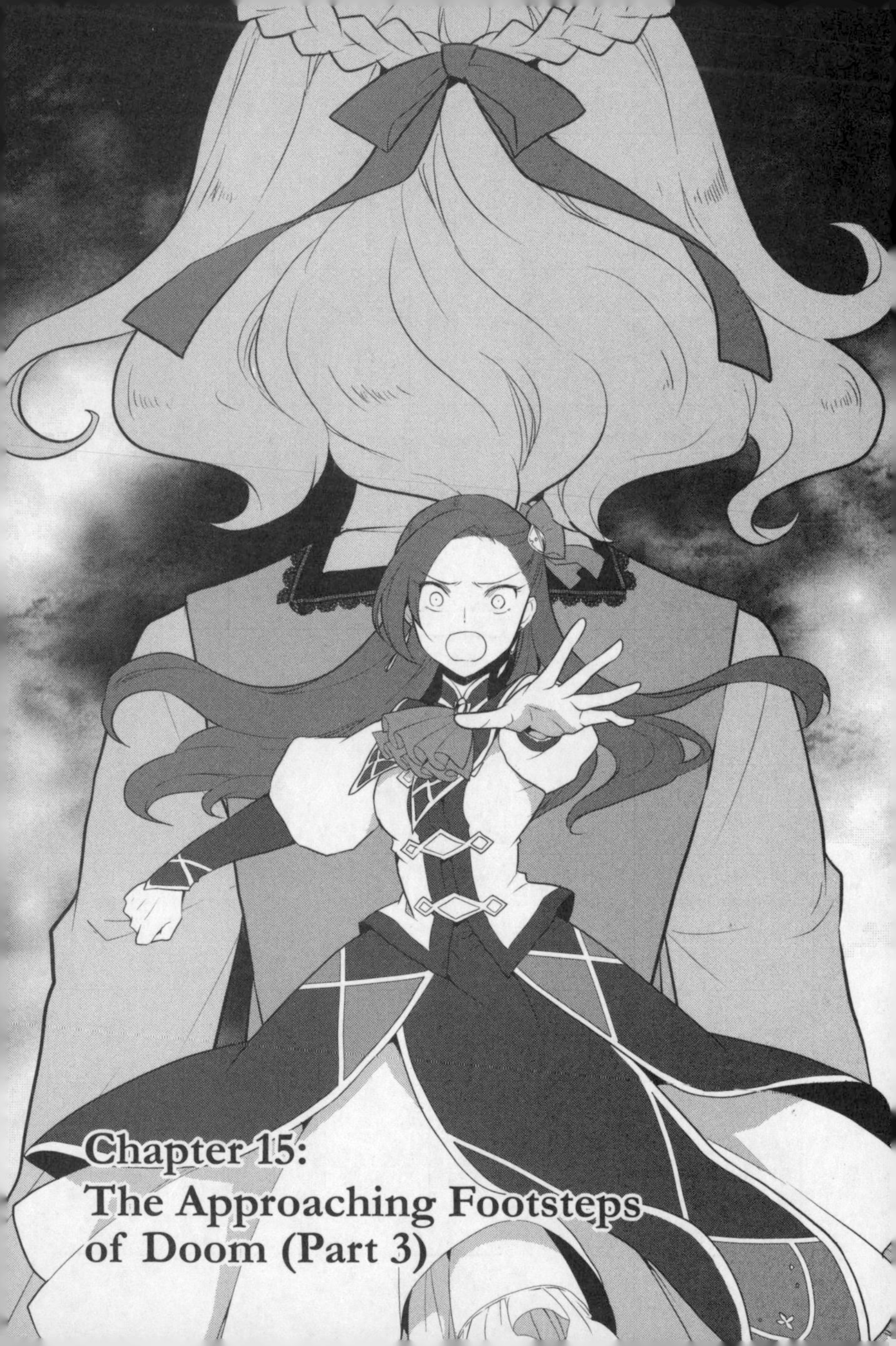

Chapter 15: The Approaching Footsteps of Doom (Part 3)

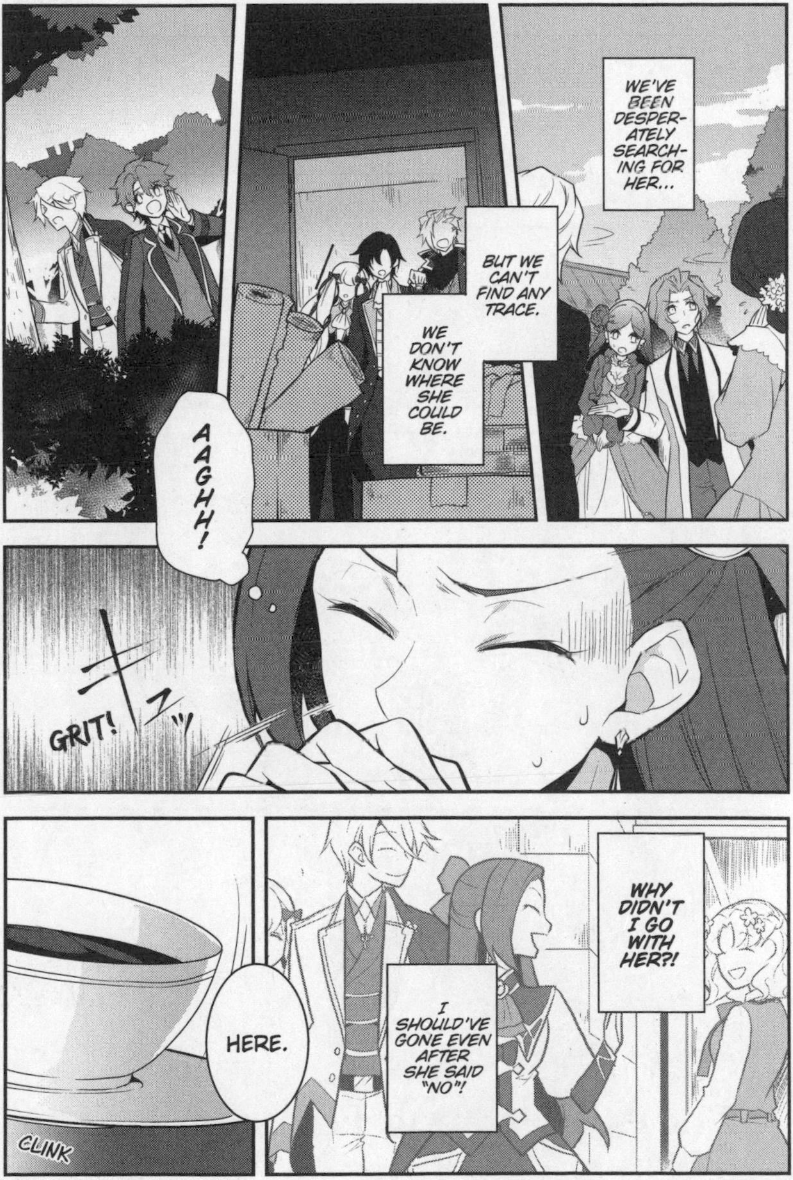
WE'VE BEEN DESPERATELY SEARCHING FOR HER...
BUT WE CAN'T FIND ANY TRACE.
WE DON'T KNOW WHERE SHE COULD BE.
AAGHH!
GRIT!
WHY DIDN'T I GO WITH HER?!
I SHOULD'VE GONE EVEN AFTER SHE SAID "NO"!
HERE.
CLINK

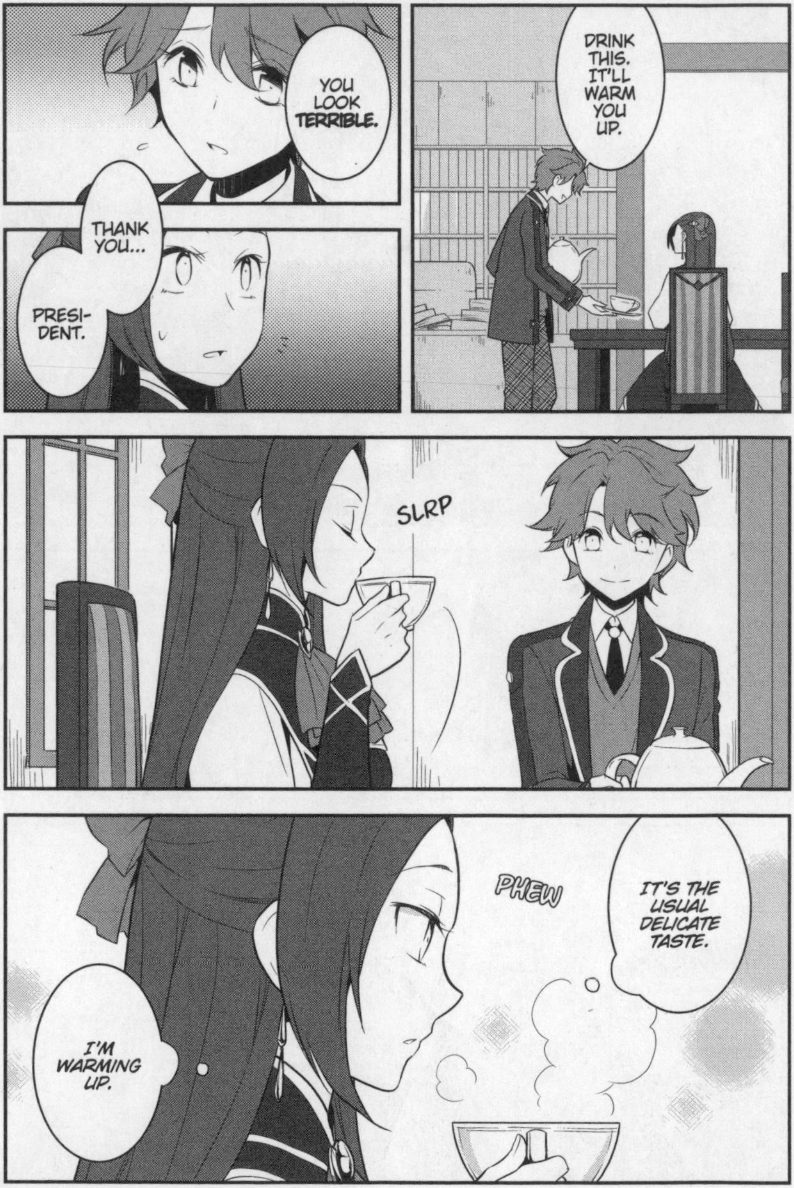

DRINK THIS. IT'LL WARM YOU UP.
YOU LOOK TERRIBLE.
THANK YOU...
PRESIDENT.
SLRP
PHEW
IT'S THE USUAL DELICATE TASTE.
I'M WARMING UP.

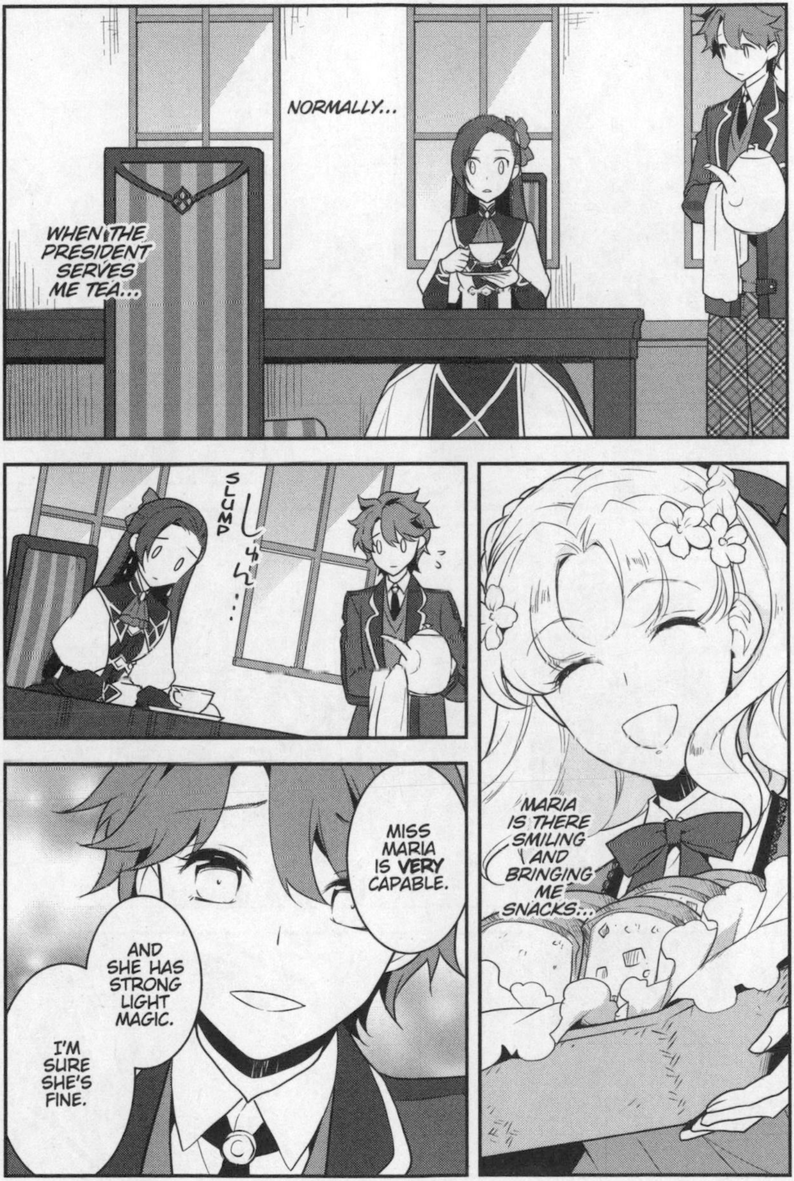
NORMALLY...
WHEN THE PRESIDENT SERVES ME TEA...
MARIA IS THERE SMILING AND BRINGING ME SNACKS...
SLUMP
しゅん...
MISS MARIA IS VERY CAPABLE.
AND SHE HAS STRONG LIGHT MAGIC.
I'M SURE SHE'S FINE.

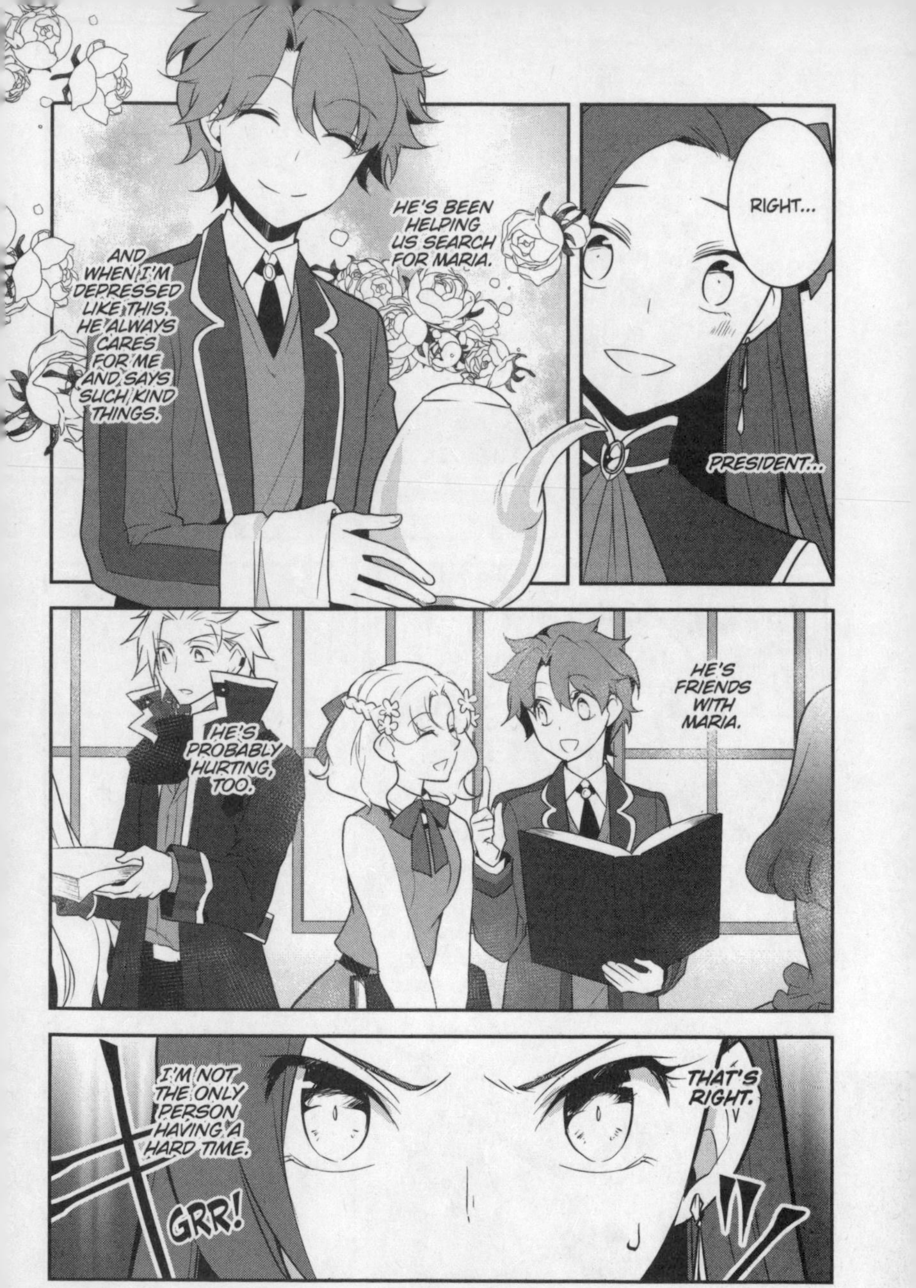
RIGHT...
PRESIDENT...
HE'S BEEN HELPING US SEARCH FOR MARIA.
AND WHEN I'M DEPRESSED LIKE THIS, HE ALWAYS CARES FOR ME AND SAYS SUCH KIND THINGS.
HE'S FRIENDS WITH MARIA.
HE'S PROBABLY HURTING, TOO.
THAT'S RIGHT.
I'M NOT THE ONLY PERSON HAVING A HARD TIME.
GRR!

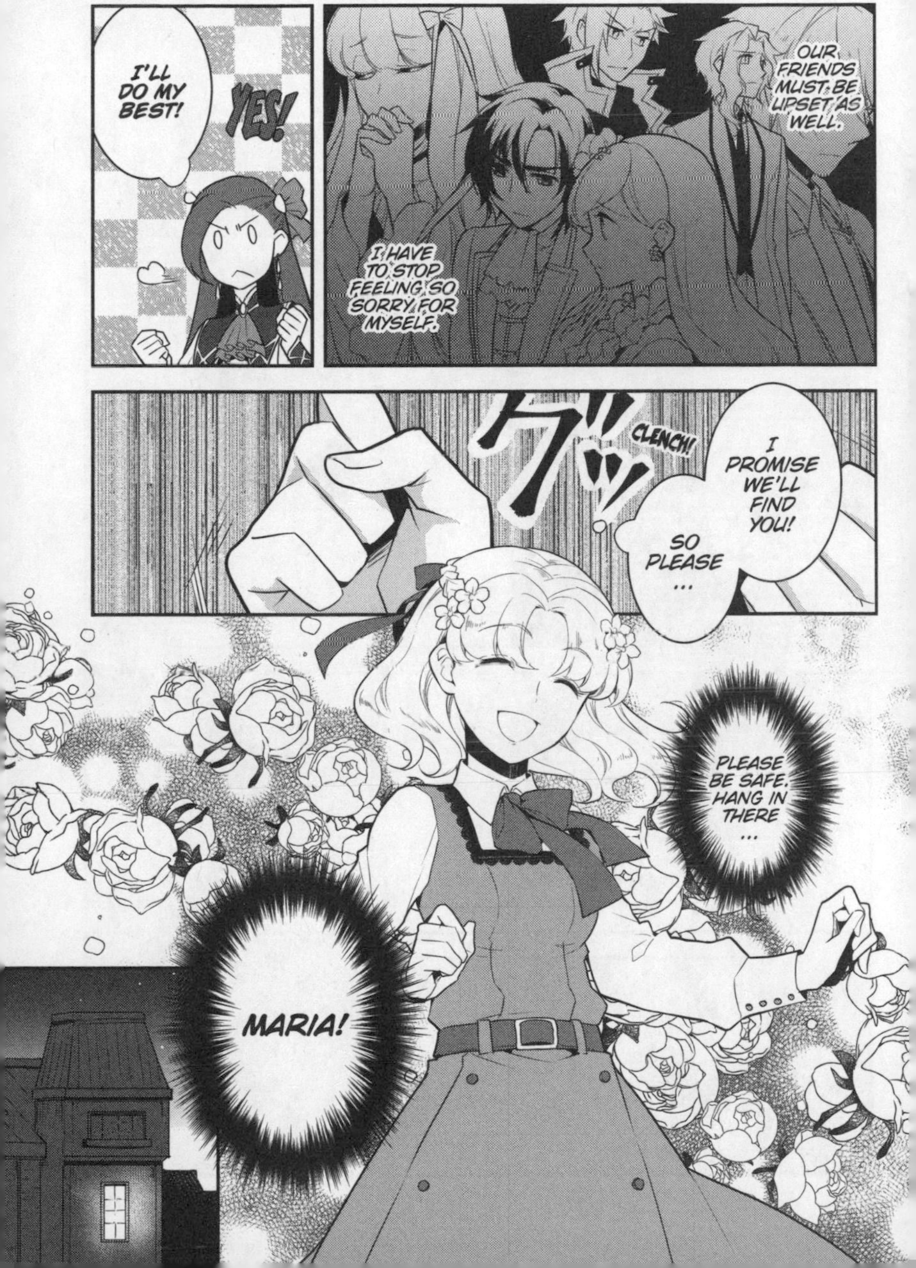
OUR FRIENDS MUST BE UPSET AS WELL.
I HAVE TO STOP FEELING SO SORRY FOR MYSELF.
I'LL DO MY BEST!
YES!
I PROMISE WE'LL FIND YOU!
SO PLEASE ...
CLENCH!
PLEASE BE SAFE. HANG IN THERE ...
MARIA!

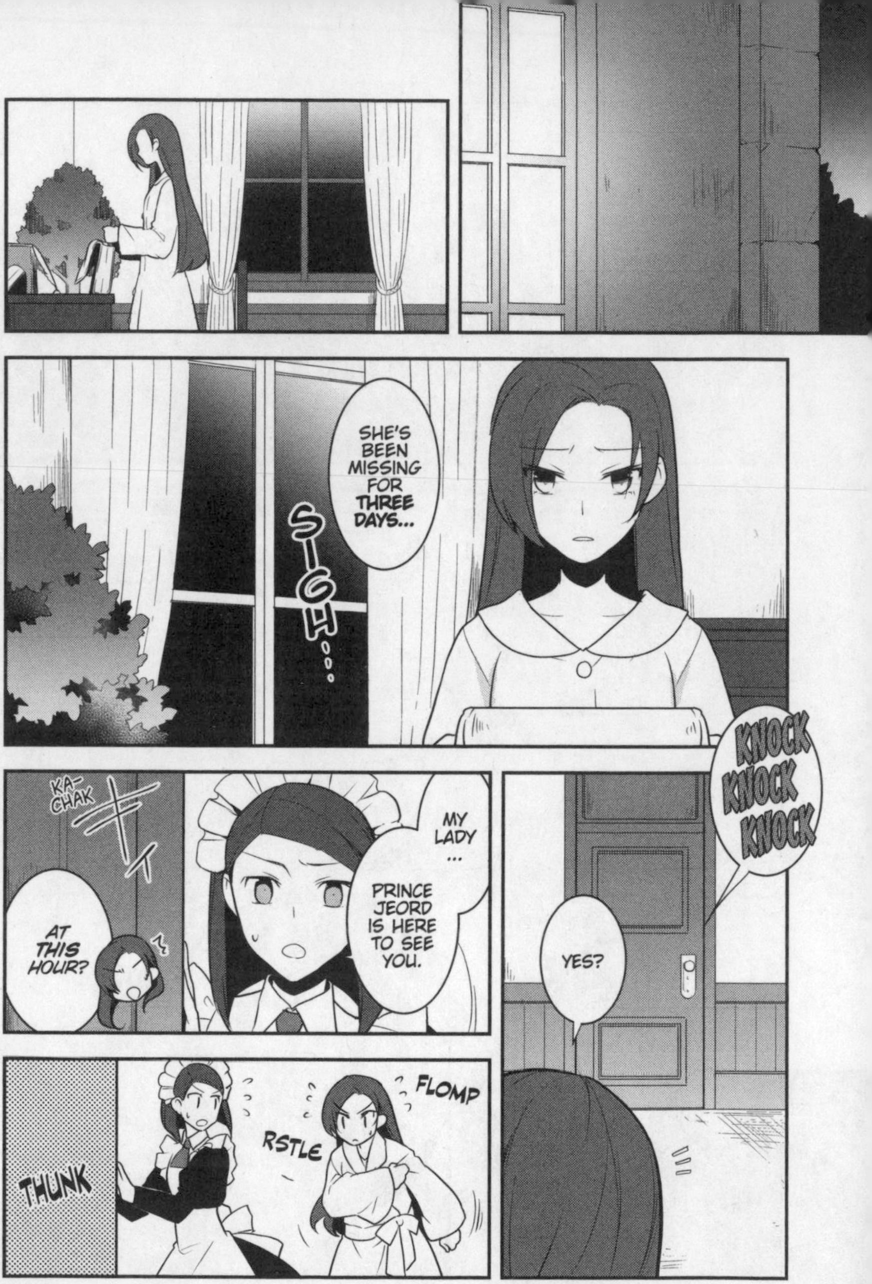
SHE'S BEEN MISSING FOR THREE DAYS...
SIGH...
KNOCK KNOCK KNOCK
YES?
MY LADY ... PRINCE JEORD IS HERE TO SEE YOU.
KA-CHAK
AT THIS HOUR?
FLOMP
RSTLE
THUNK

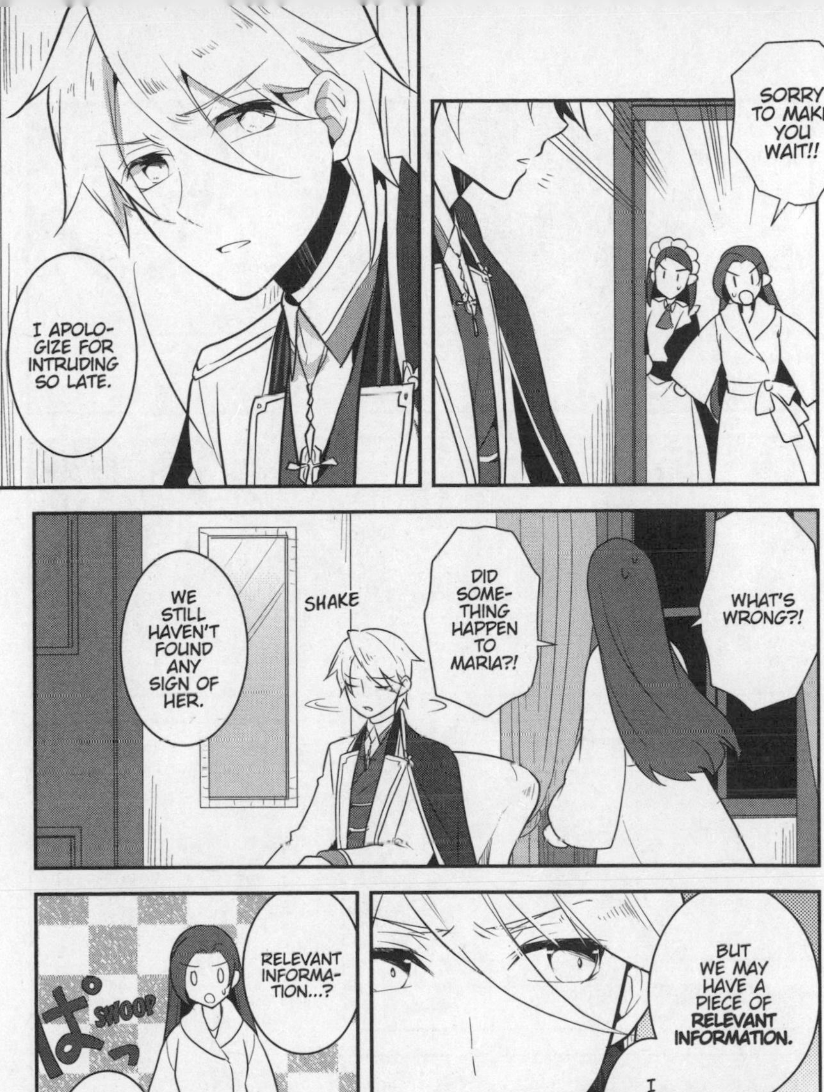
SORRY TO MAKE YOU WAIT!!
I APOLOGIZE FOR INTRUDING SO LATE.
WHAT'S WRONG?!
DID SOMETHING HAPPEN TO MARIA?!
SHAKE
WE STILL HAVEN'T FOUND ANY SIGN OF HER.
BUT WE MAY HAVE A PIECE OF RELEVANT INFORMATION.
I WANTED TO TELL YOU RIGHT AWAY.
RELEVANT INFORMATION...?
ぱっ
SWOOP
HAVE A LOOK AT THIS.

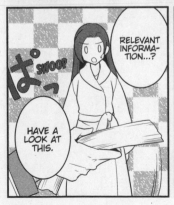

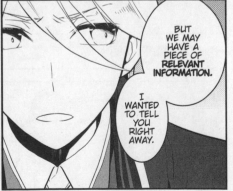

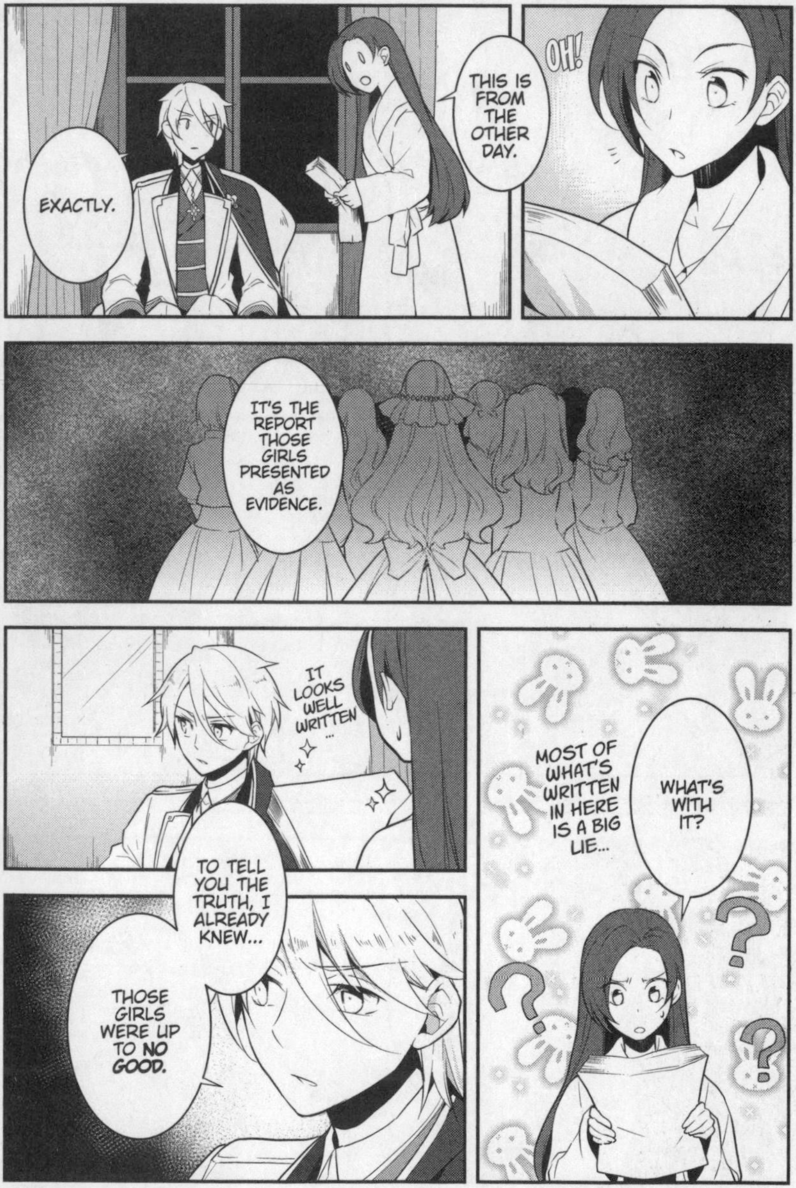
OH!
THIS IS FROM THE OTHER DAY.
EXACTLY.
IT'S THE REPORT THOSE GIRLS PRESENTED AS EVIDENCE.
WHAT'S WITH IT?
MOST OF WHAT'S WRITTEN IN HERE IS A BIG LIE...
IT LOOKS WELL WRITTEN ...
TO TELL YOU THE TRUTH, I ALREADY KNEW...
THOSE GIRLS WERE UP TO NO GOOD.

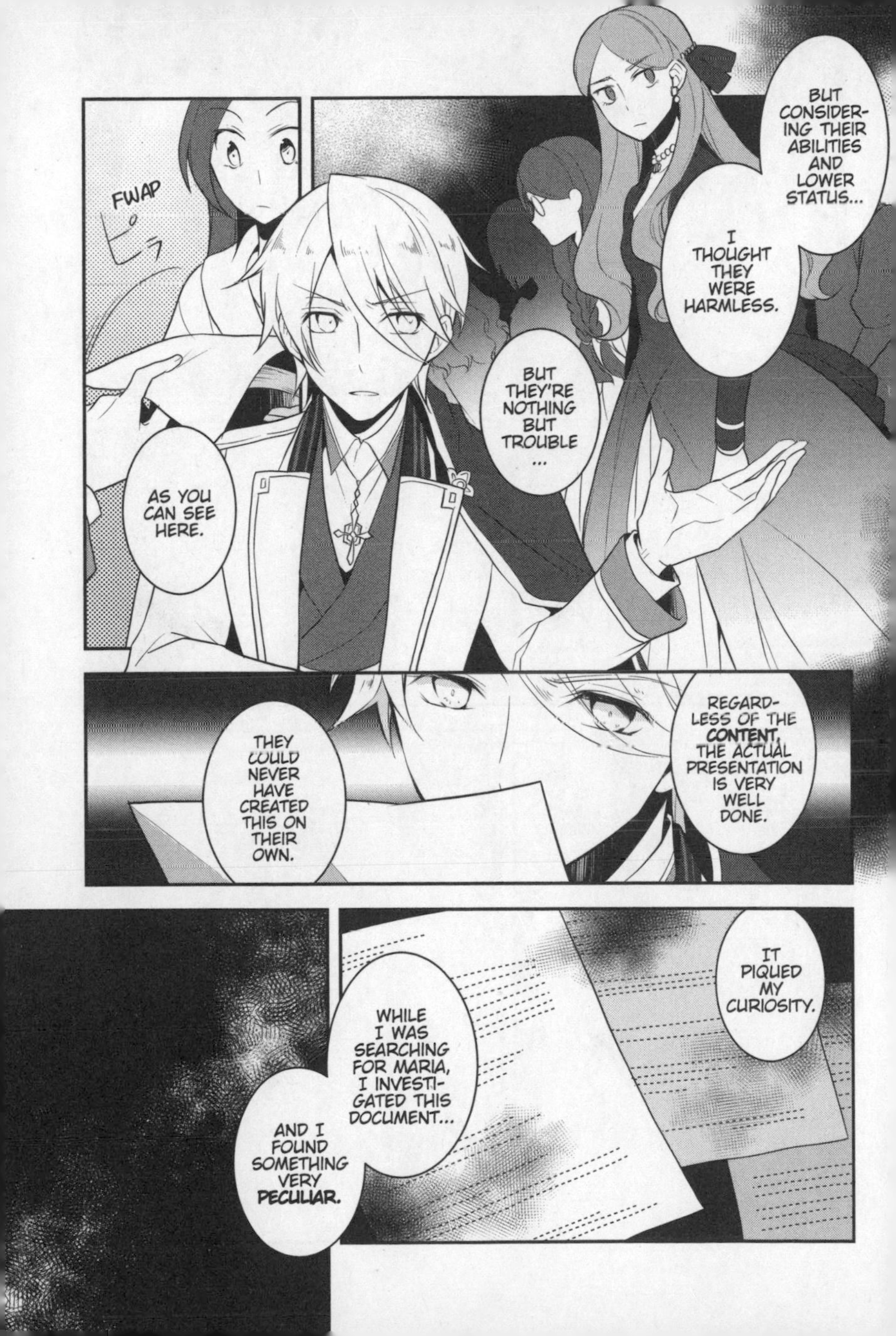
BUT CONSIDERING THEIR ABILITIES AND LOWER STATUS...
I THOUGHT THEY WERE HARMLESS.
BUT THEY'RE NOTHING BUT TROUBLE...
AS YOU CAN SEE HERE.
FWAP
ピラ
REGARDLESS OF THE CONTENT, THE ACTUAL PRESENTATION IS VERY WELL DONE.
THEY COULD NEVER HAVE CREATED THIS ON THEIR OWN.
IT PIQUED MY CURIOSITY.
WHILE I WAS SEARCHING FOR MARIA, I INVESTIGATED THIS DOCUMENT...
AND I FOUND SOMETHING VERY PECULIAR.

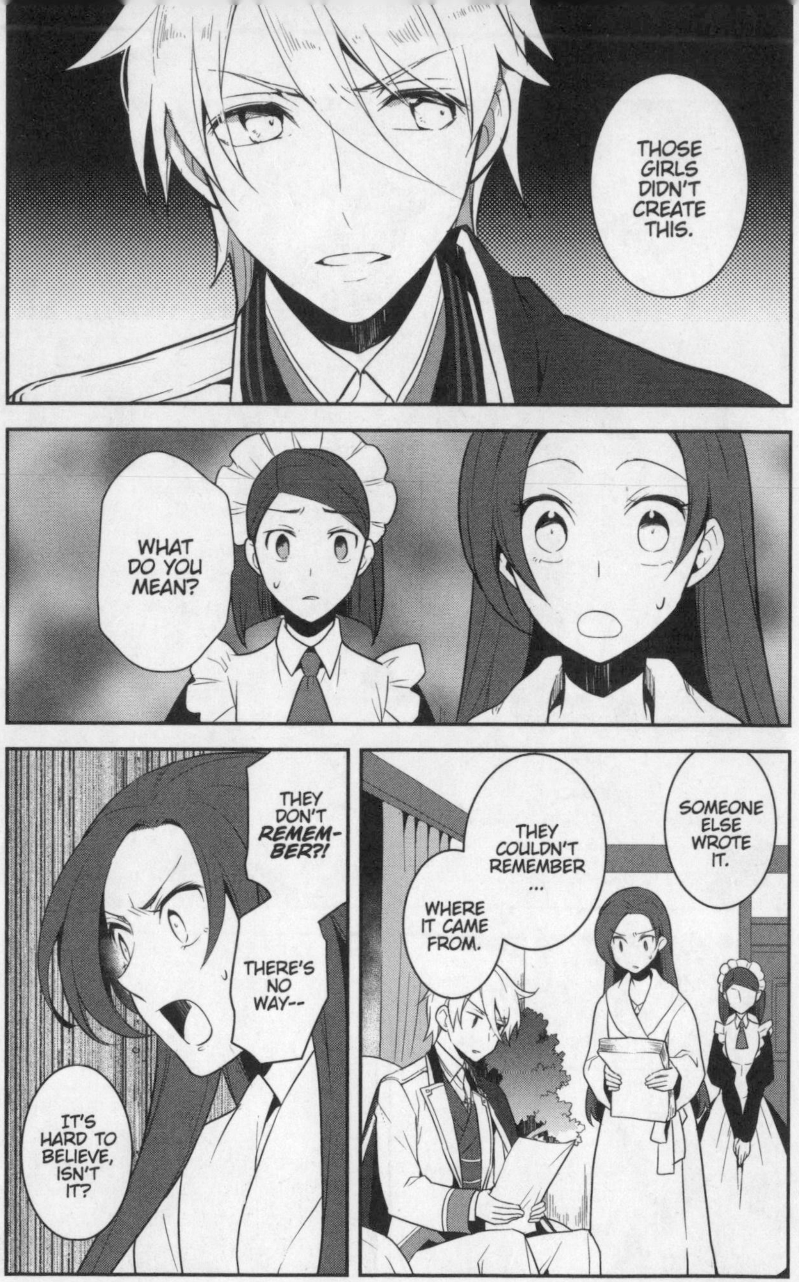
THOSE GIRLS DIDN'T CREATE THIS.
WHAT DO YOU MEAN?
SOMEONE ELSE WROTE IT.
THEY COULDN'T REMEMBER ...
WHERE IT CAME FROM.
THEY DON'T *REMEMBER?!*
THERE'S NO WAY--
IT'S HARD TO BELIEVE, ISN'T IT?

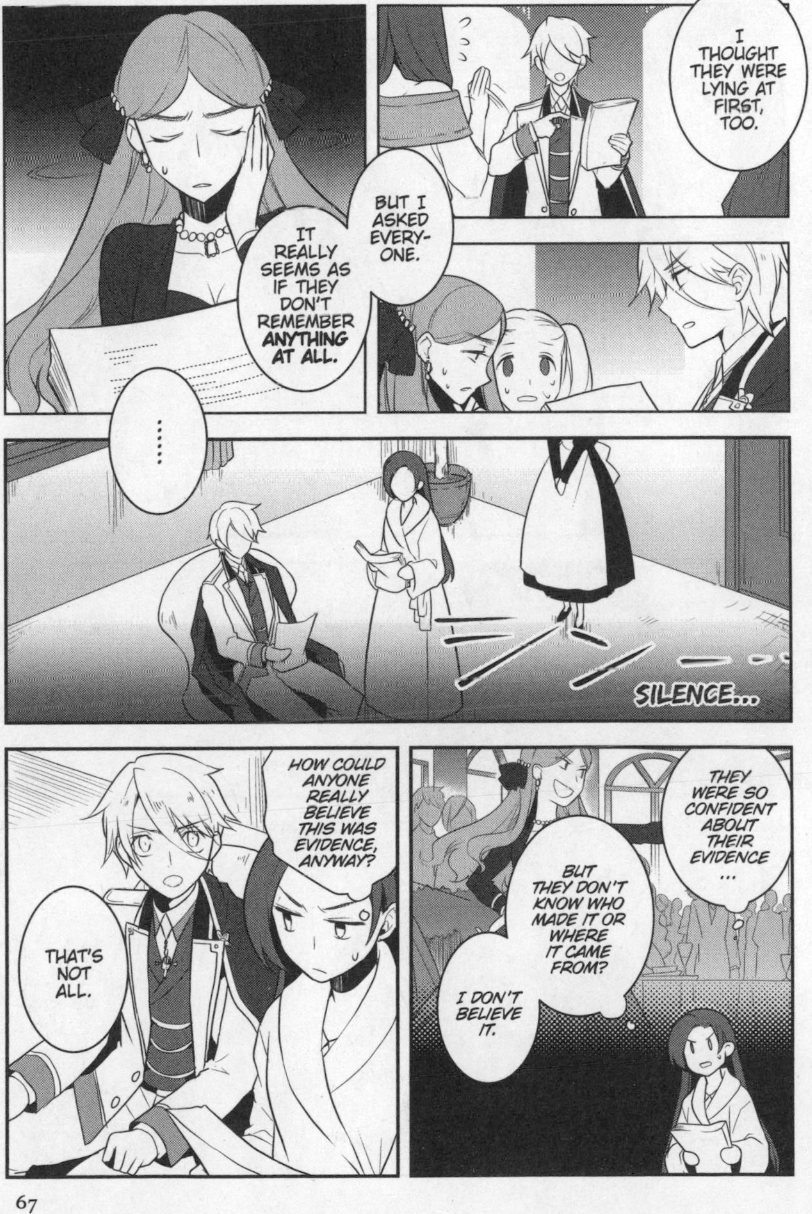
I THOUGHT THEY WERE LYING AT FIRST, TOO.
BUT I ASKED EVERY-ONE.
IT REALLY SEEMS AS IF THEY DON'T REMEMBER **ANYTHING AT ALL.**
......
SILENCE...
THEY WERE SO CONFIDENT ABOUT THEIR EVIDENCE ...
BUT THEY DON'T KNOW WHO MADE IT OR WHERE IT CAME FROM?
I DON'T BELIEVE IT.
HOW COULD ANYONE REALLY BELIEVE THIS WAS EVIDENCE, ANYWAY?
THAT'S NOT ALL.

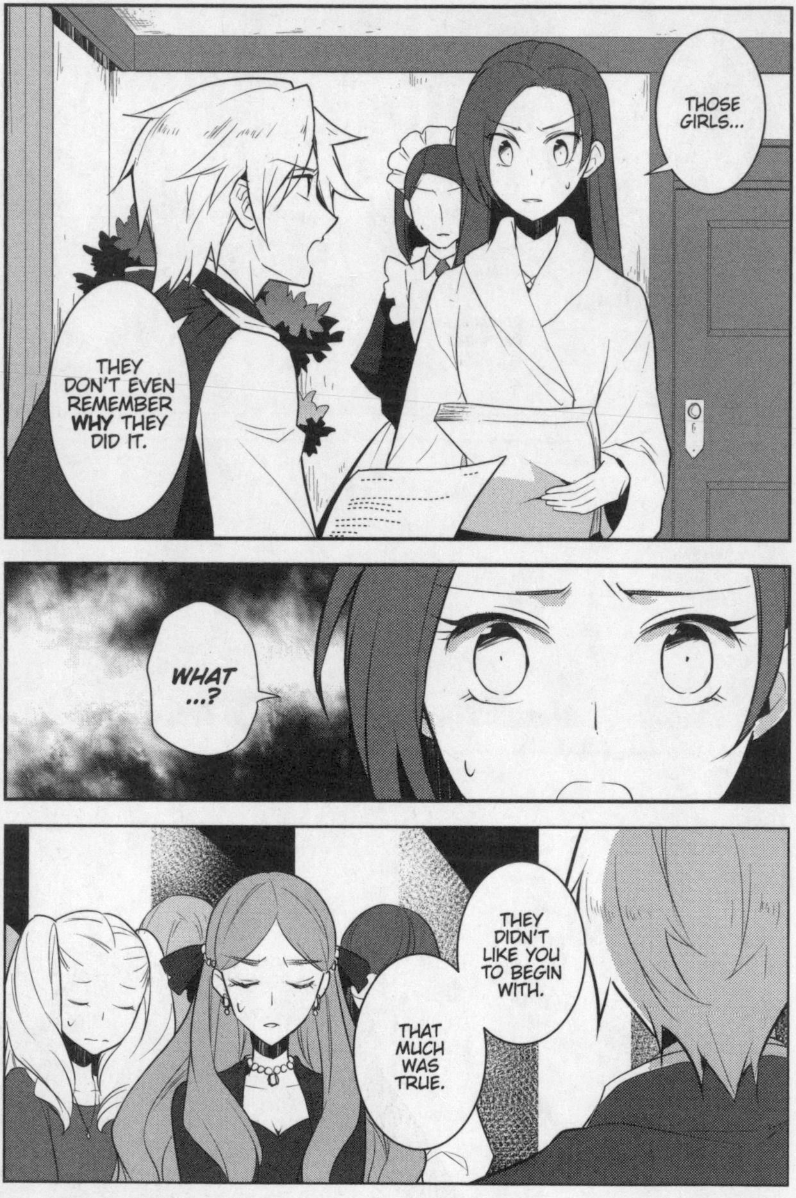
THOSE GIRLS...
THEY DON'T EVEN REMEMBER WHY THEY DID IT.
WHAT ...?
THEY DIDN'T LIKE YOU TO BEGIN WITH.
THAT MUCH WAS TRUE.

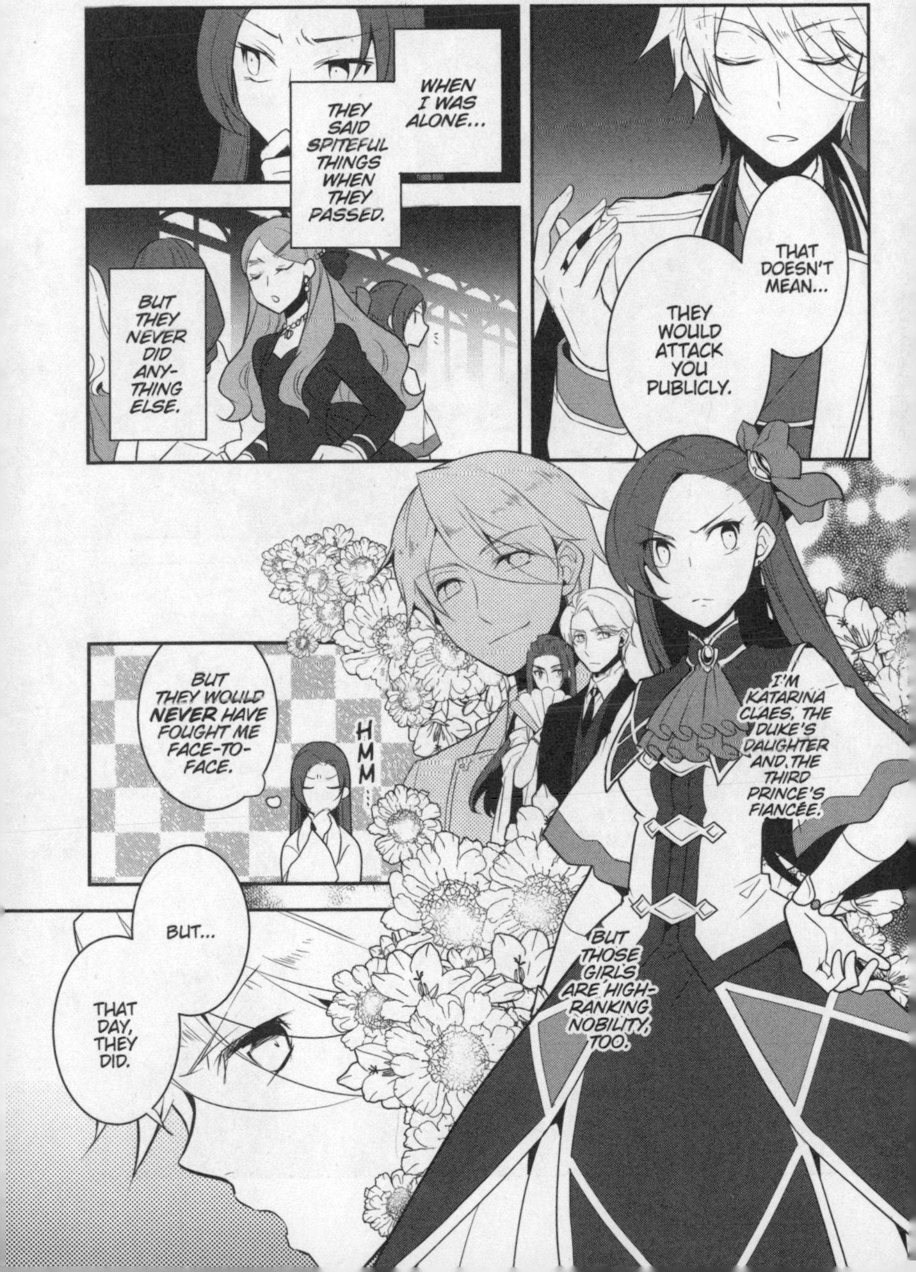
THAT DOESN'T MEAN...
THEY WOULD ATTACK YOU PUBLICLY.
WHEN I WAS ALONE...
THEY SAID SPITEFUL THINGS WHEN THEY PASSED.
BUT THEY NEVER DID ANY-THING ELSE.
I'M KATARINA CLAES, THE DUKE'S DAUGHTER AND THE THIRD PRINCE'S FIANCÉE.
BUT THOSE GIRLS ARE HIGH-RANKING NOBILITY, TOO.
BUT THEY WOULD NEVER HAVE FOUGHT ME FACE-TO-FACE.
HMM...
BUT...
THAT DAY, THEY DID.

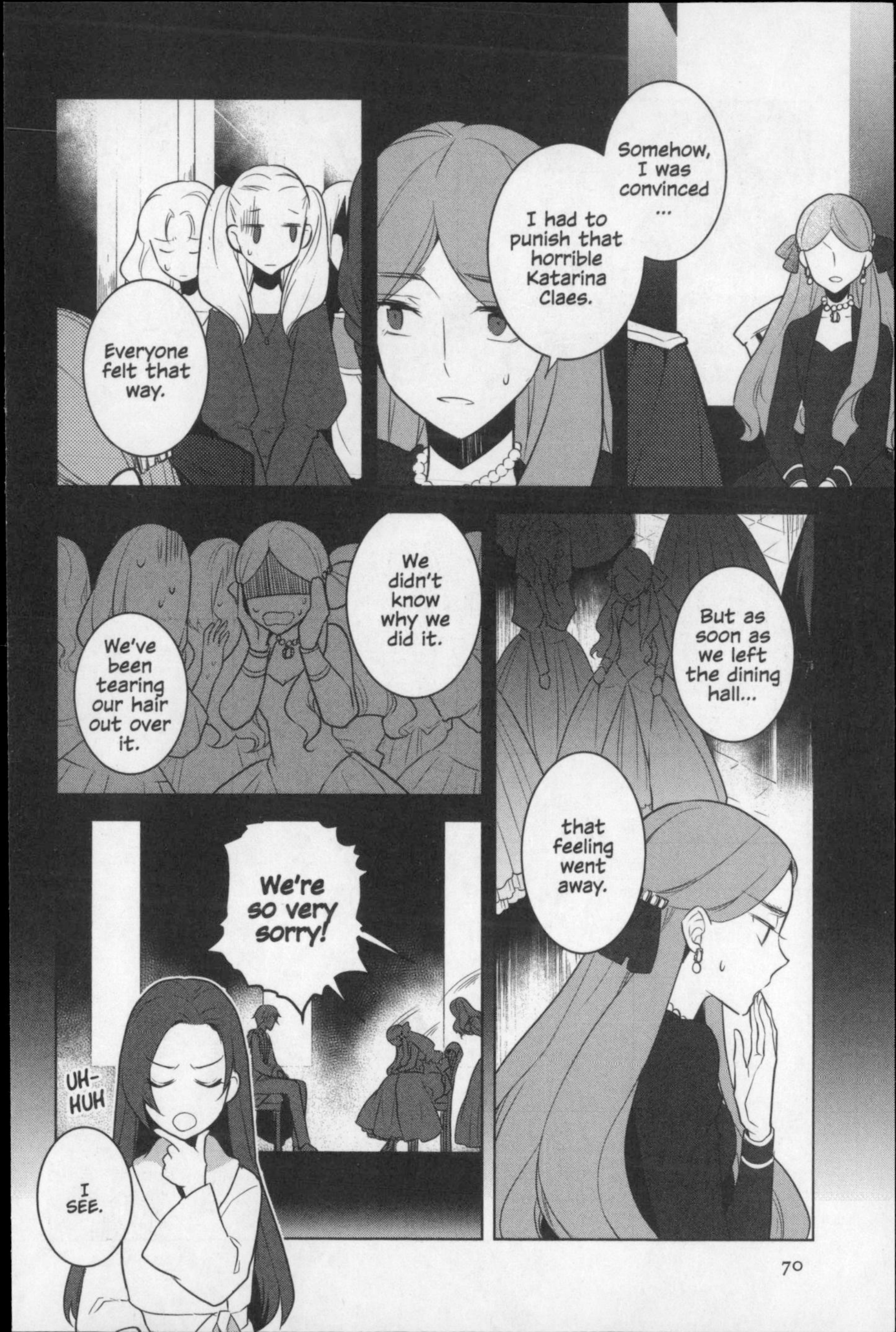
Somehow, I was convinced ...
I had to punish that horrible Katarina Claes.
Everyone felt that way.
But as soon as we left the dining hall...
that feeling went away.
We didn't know why we did it.
We've been tearing our hair out over it.
We're so very sorry!
UH-HUH
I SEE.

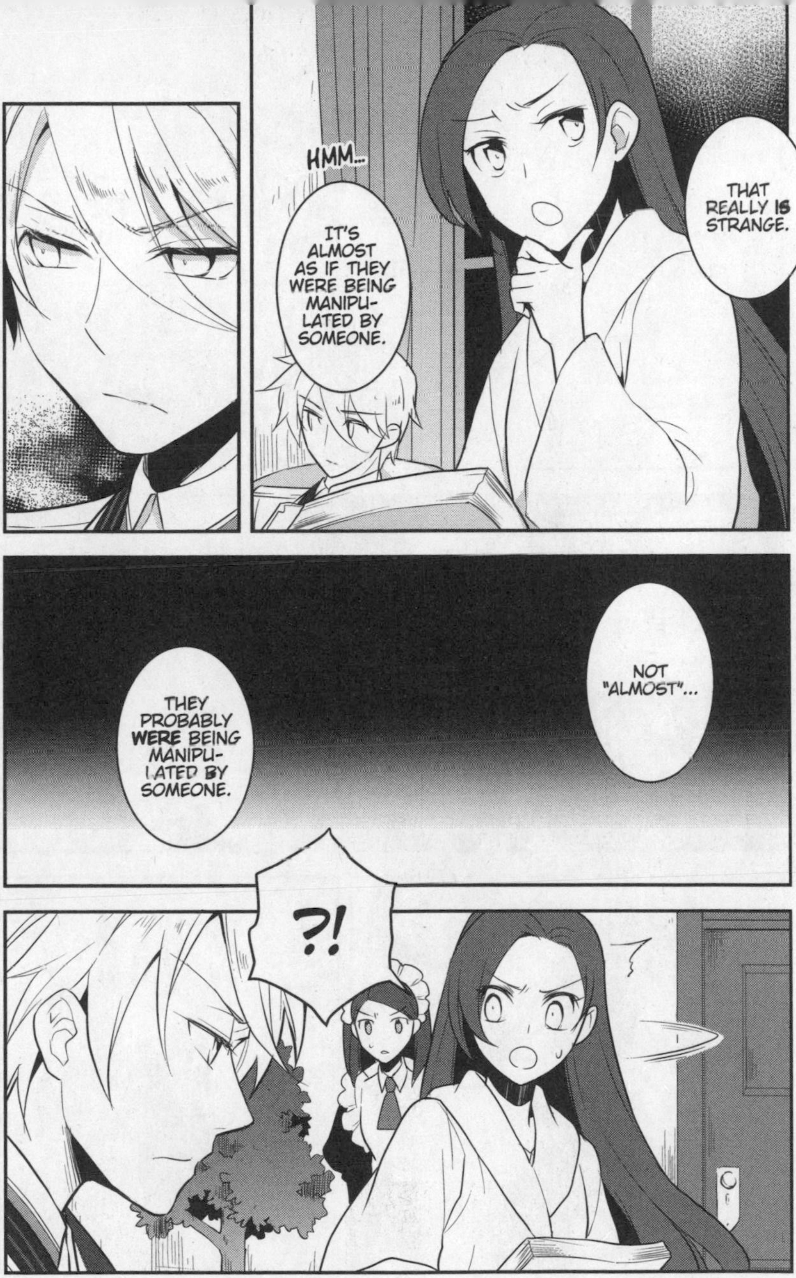
THAT REALLY IS STRANGE.
HMM...
IT'S ALMOST AS IF THEY WERE BEING MANIPULATED BY SOMEONE.
NOT "ALMOST"...
THEY PROBABLY WERE BEING MANIPULATED BY SOMEONE.
?!

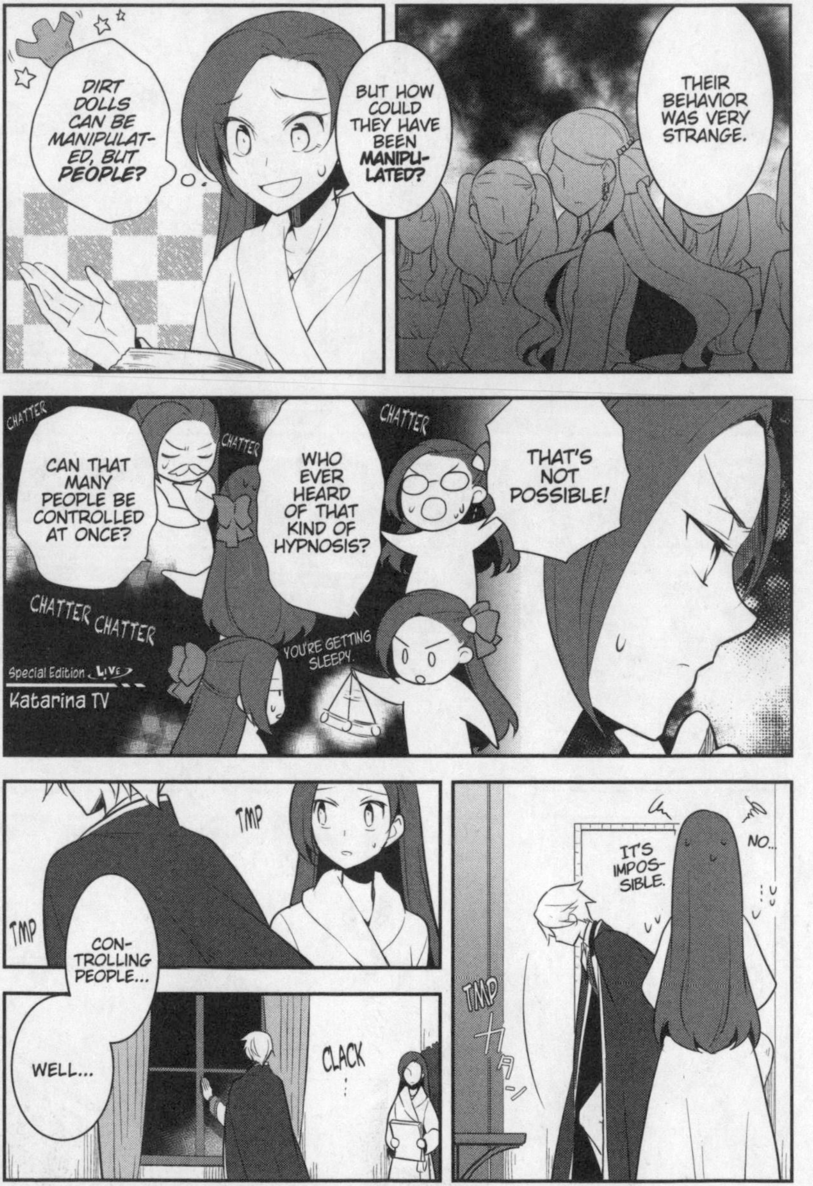
THEIR BEHAVIOR WAS VERY STRANGE.
BUT HOW COULD THEY HAVE BEEN MANIPULATED?
DIRT DOLLS CAN BE MANIPULATED, BUT PEOPLE?
THAT'S NOT POSSIBLE!
CHATTER
WHO EVER HEARD OF THAT KIND OF HYPNOSIS?
CHATTER
CHATTER
CAN THAT MANY PEOPLE BE CONTROLLED AT ONCE?
YOU'RE GETTING SLEEPY.
CHATTER CHATTER
Special Edition LIVE
Katarina TV
NO...
IT'S IMPOSSIBLE.
TMP
カタン
TMP
CONTROLLING PEOPLE...
TMP
CLACK
WELL...

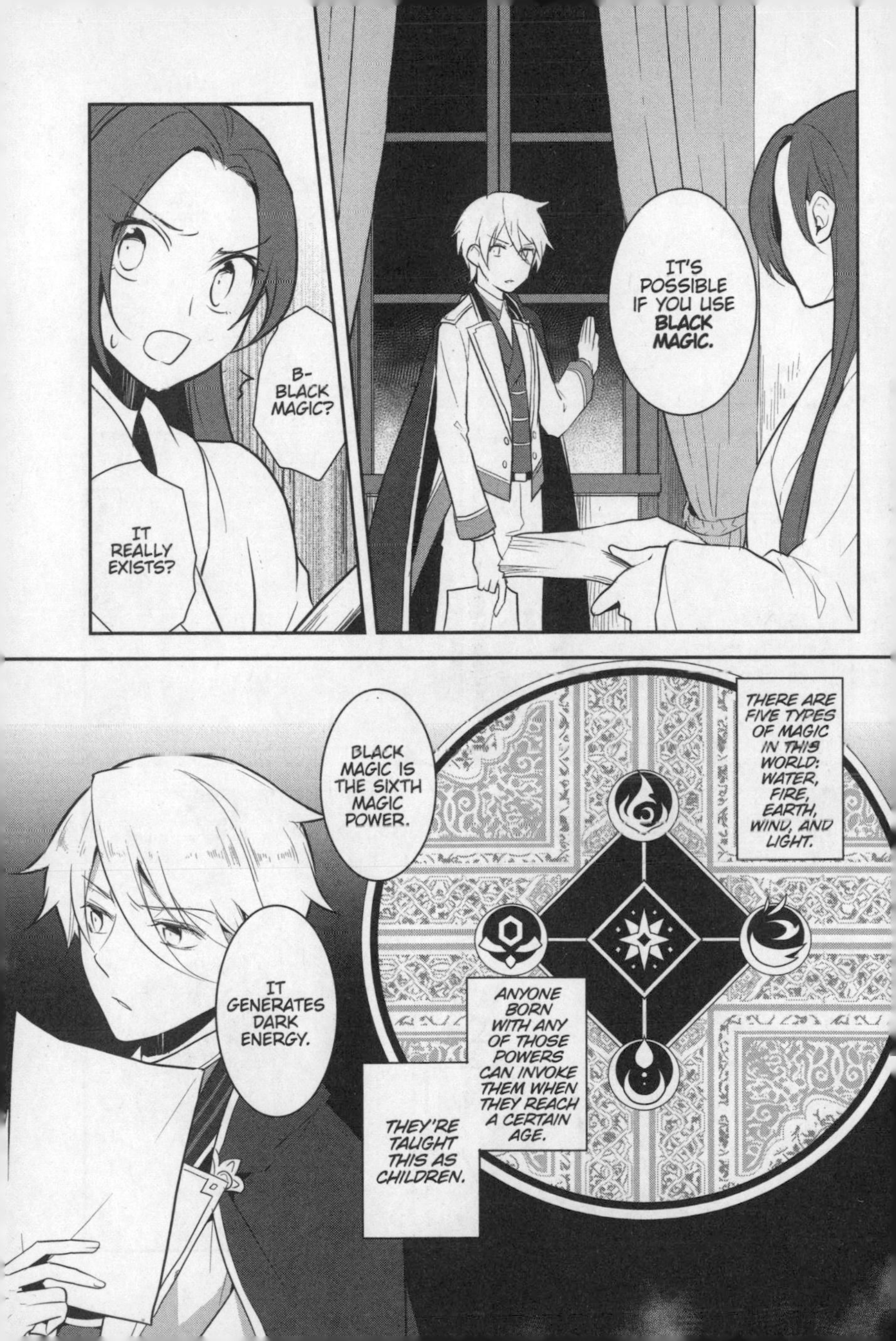
IT'S POSSIBLE IF YOU USE BLACK MAGIC.
B-BLACK MAGIC?
IT REALLY EXISTS?
THERE ARE FIVE TYPES OF MAGIC IN THIS WORLD: WATER, FIRE, EARTH, WIND, AND LIGHT.
BLACK MAGIC IS THE SIXTH MAGIC POWER.
ANYONE BORN WITH ANY OF THOSE POWERS CAN INVOKE THEM WHEN THEY REACH A CERTAIN AGE.
THEY'RE TAUGHT THIS AS CHILDREN.
IT GENERATES DARK ENERGY.

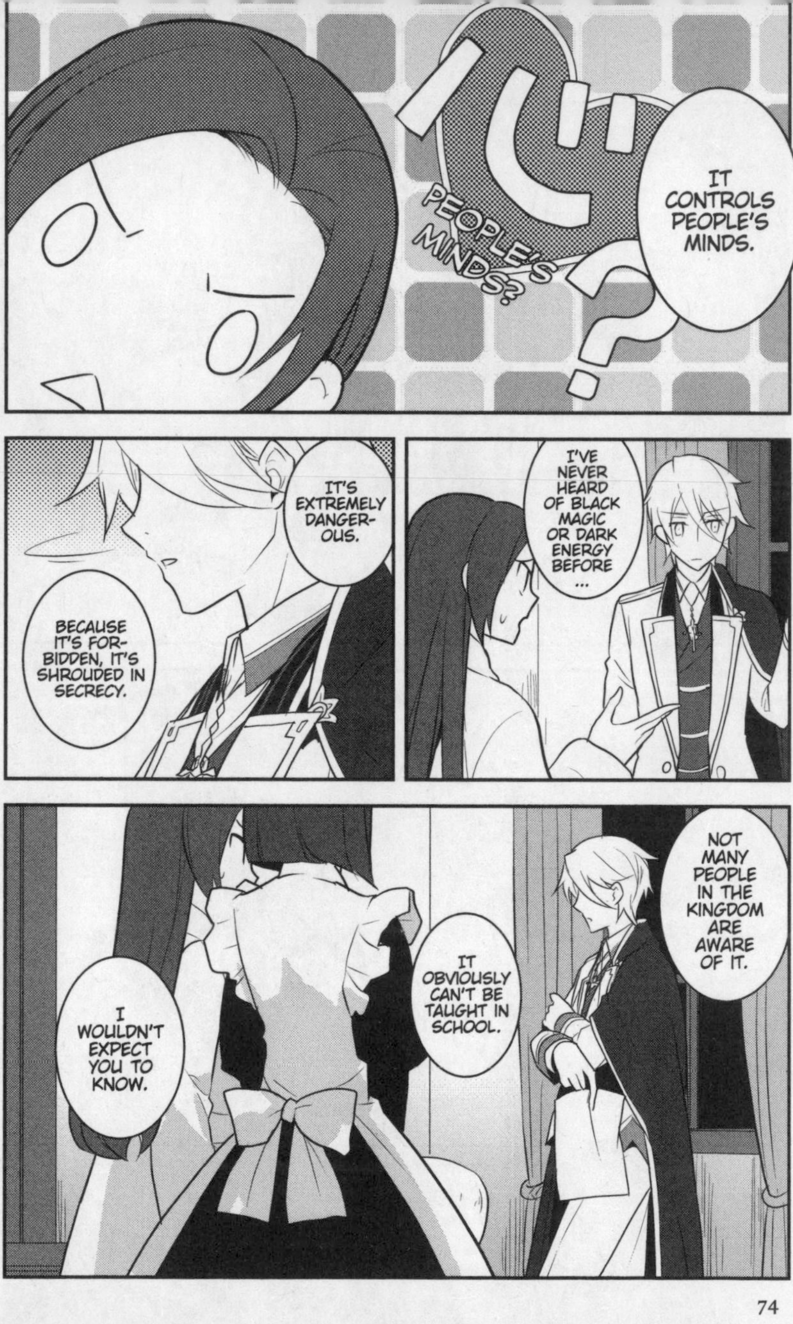
IT CONTROLS PEOPLE'S MINDS.
PEOPLE'S MINDS?!
I'VE NEVER HEARD OF BLACK MAGIC OR DARK ENERGY BEFORE ...
IT'S EXTREMELY DANGEROUS.
BECAUSE IT'S FORBIDDEN, IT'S SHROUDED IN SECRECY.
NOT MANY PEOPLE IN THE KINGDOM ARE AWARE OF IT.
IT OBVIOUSLY CAN'T BE TAUGHT IN SCHOOL.
I WOULDN'T EXPECT YOU TO KNOW.

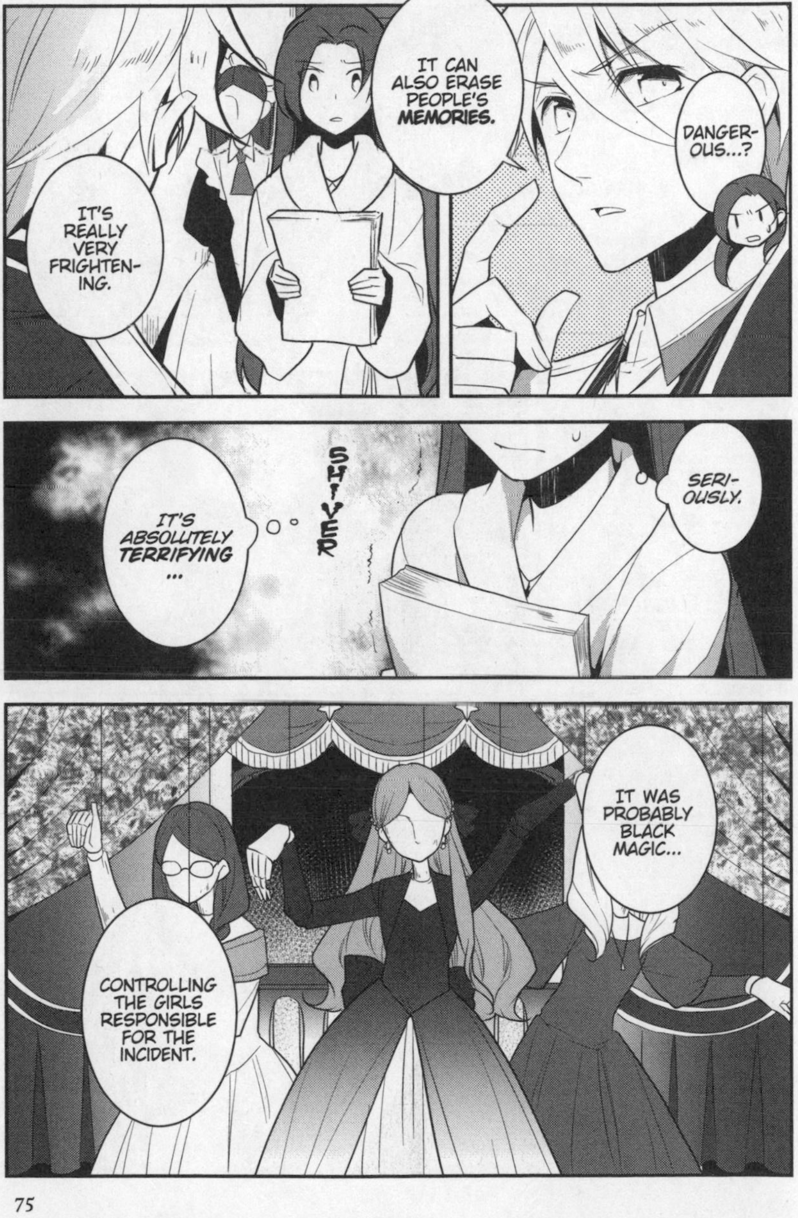
IT CAN ALSO ERASE PEOPLE'S MEMORIES.
DANGER-OUS...?
IT'S REALLY VERY FRIGHTEN-ING.
SERI-OUSLY.
SHIVER
IT'S ABSOLUTELY TERRIFYING ...
IT WAS PROBABLY BLACK MAGIC...
CONTROLLING THE GIRLS RESPONSIBLE FOR THE INCIDENT.

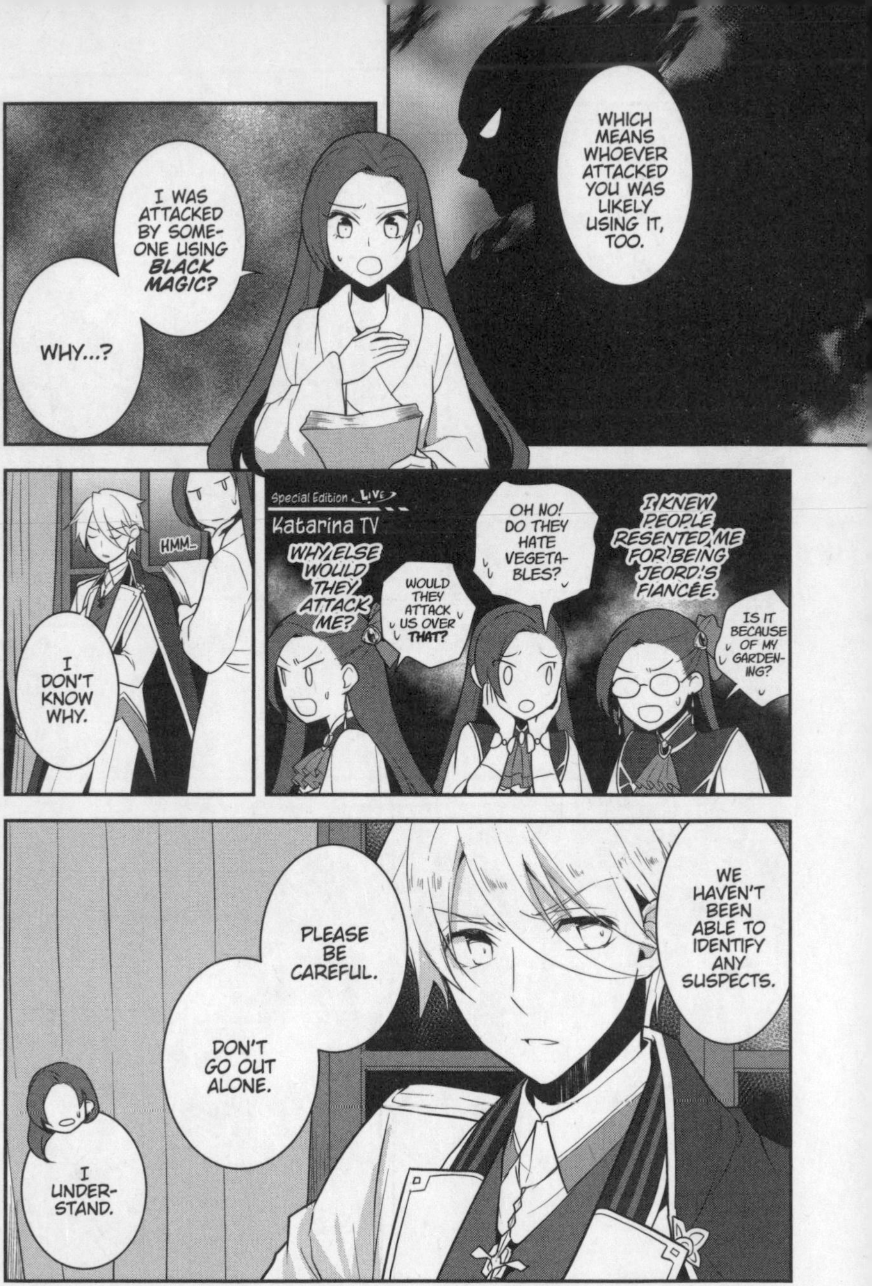
WHICH MEANS WHOEVER ATTACKED YOU WAS LIKELY USING IT, TOO.
I WAS ATTACKED BY SOME-ONE USING BLACK MAGIC?
WHY...?
Special Edition LIVE
Katarina TV
I KNEW PEOPLE RESENTED ME FOR BEING JEORD'S FIANCÉE.
IS IT BECAUSE OF MY GARDEN-ING?
OH NO! DO THEY HATE VEGETA-BLES?
WOULD THEY ATTACK US OVER THAT?
WHY ELSE WOULD THEY ATTACK ME?
HMM...
I DON'T KNOW WHY.
WE HAVEN'T BEEN ABLE TO IDENTIFY ANY SUSPECTS.
PLEASE BE CAREFUL.
DON'T GO OUT ALONE.
I UNDER-STAND.

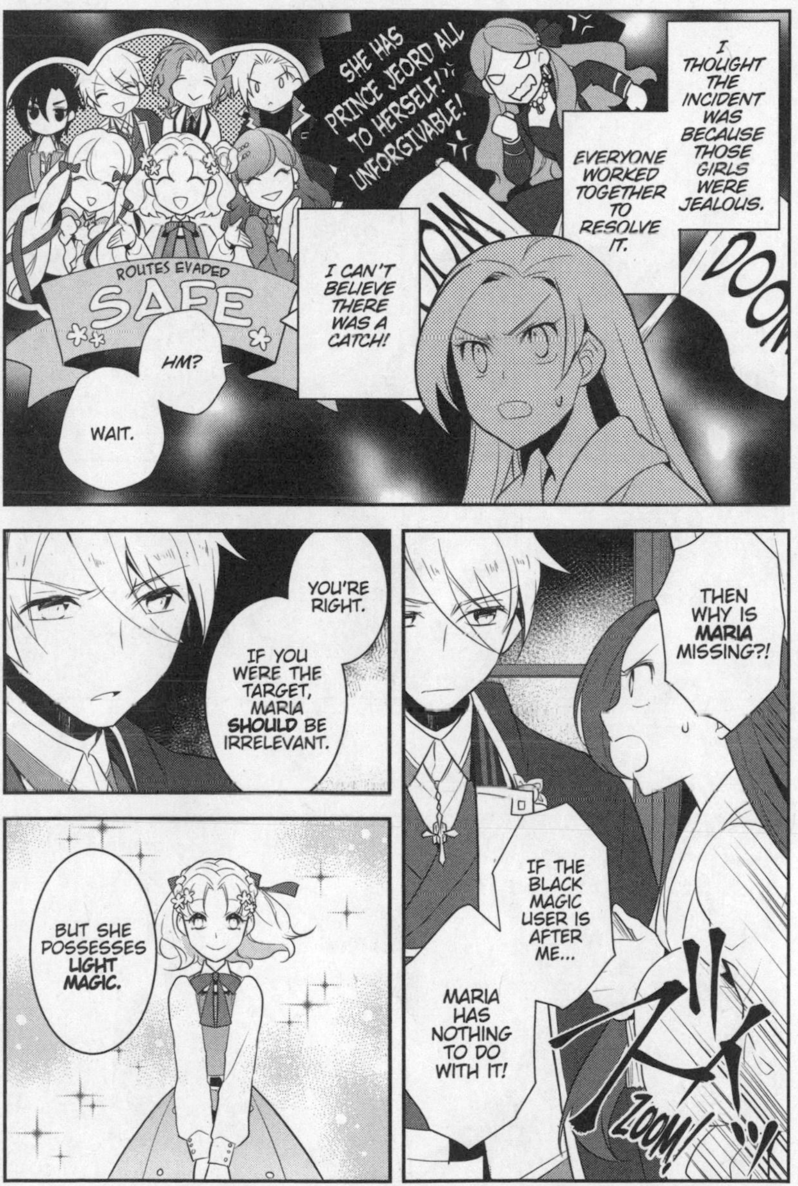
I THOUGHT THE INCIDENT WAS BECAUSE THOSE GIRLS WERE JEALOUS.
EVERYONE WORKED TOGETHER TO RESOLVE IT.
SHE HAS PRINCE JEORD ALL TO HERSELF! UNFORGIVABLE!
DOOM
ROUTES EVADED
SAFE
I CAN'T BELIEVE THERE WAS A CATCH!
HM?
WAIT.
THEN WHY IS MARIA MISSING?!
IF THE BLACK MAGIC USER IS AFTER ME...
MARIA HAS NOTHING TO DO WITH IT!
ZOOM!
YOU'RE RIGHT.
IF YOU WERE THE TARGET, MARIA SHOULD BE IRRELEVANT.
BUT SHE POSSESSES LIGHT MAGIC.

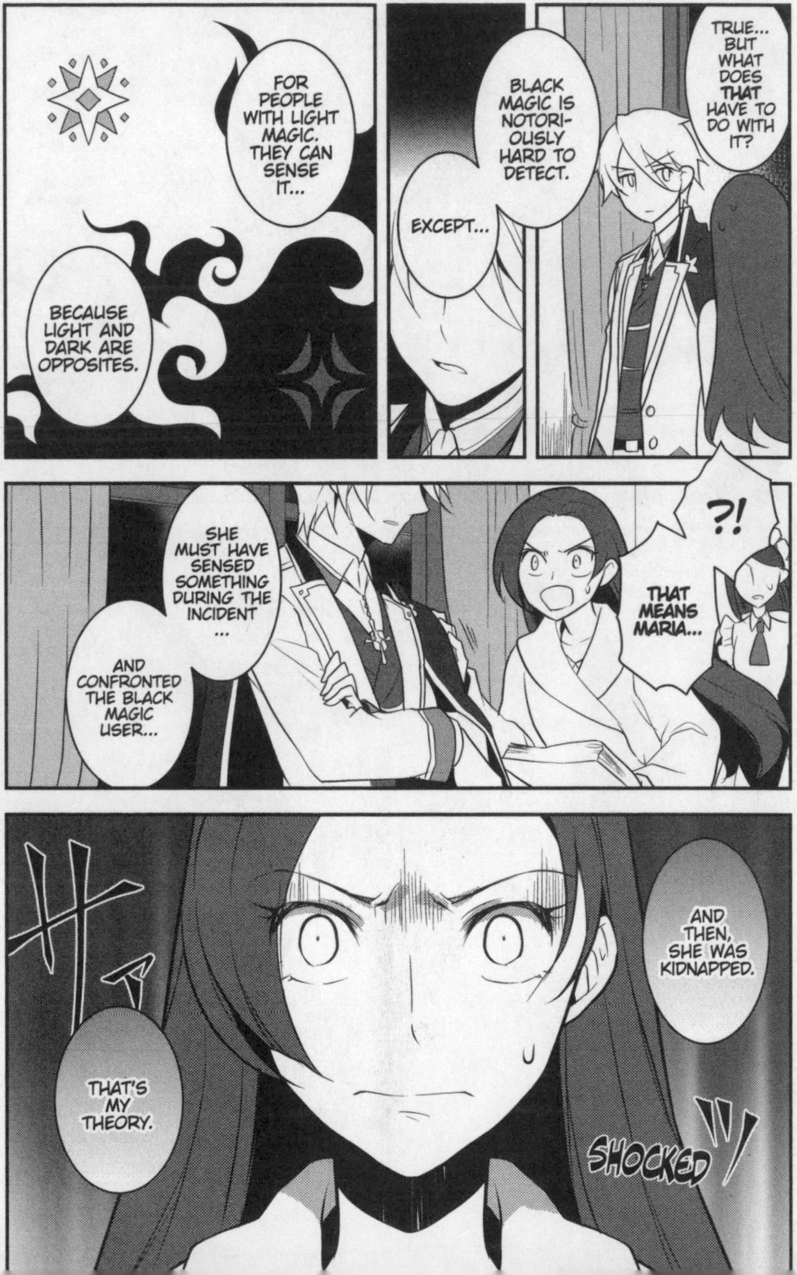
TRUE... BUT WHAT DOES THAT HAVE TO DO WITH IT?
BLACK MAGIC IS NOTORIOUSLY HARD TO DETECT.
EXCEPT...
FOR PEOPLE WITH LIGHT MAGIC. THEY CAN SENSE IT...
BECAUSE LIGHT AND DARK ARE OPPOSITES.
?!
THAT MEANS MARIA...
SHE MUST HAVE SENSED SOMETHING DURING THE INCIDENT ...
AND CONFRONTED THE BLACK MAGIC USER...
AND THEN, SHE WAS KIDNAPPED.
THAT'S MY THEORY.
SHOCKED

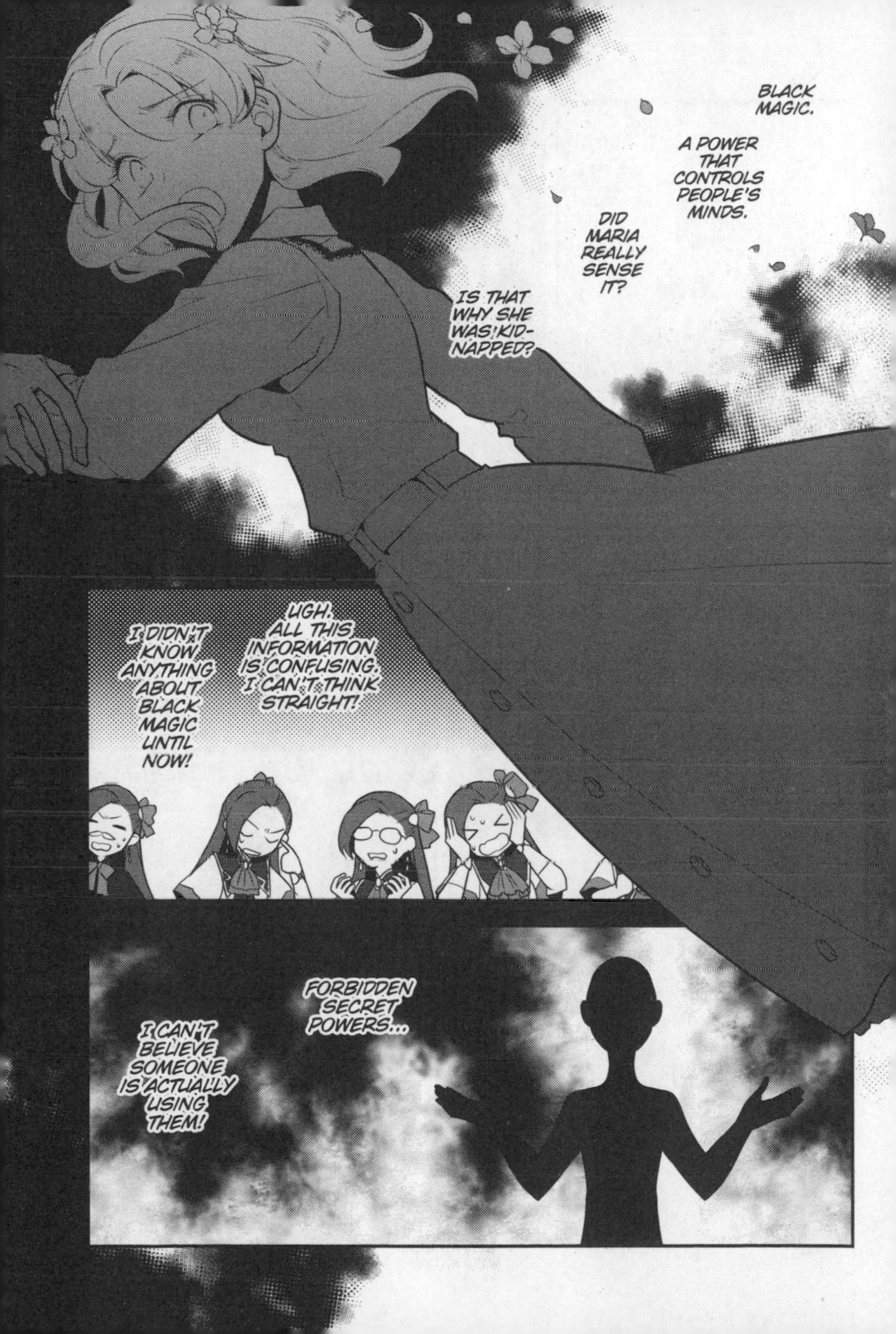
BLACK MAGIC.
A POWER THAT CONTROLS PEOPLE'S MINDS.
DID MARIA REALLY SENSE IT?
IS THAT WHY SHE WAS KID-NAPPED?
UGH. ALL THIS INFORMATION IS CONFUSING. I CAN'T THINK STRAIGHT!
I DIDN'T KNOW ANYTHING ABOUT BLACK MAGIC UNTIL NOW!
FORBIDDEN SECRET POWERS...
I CAN'T BELIEVE SOMEONE IS ACTUALLY USING THEM!

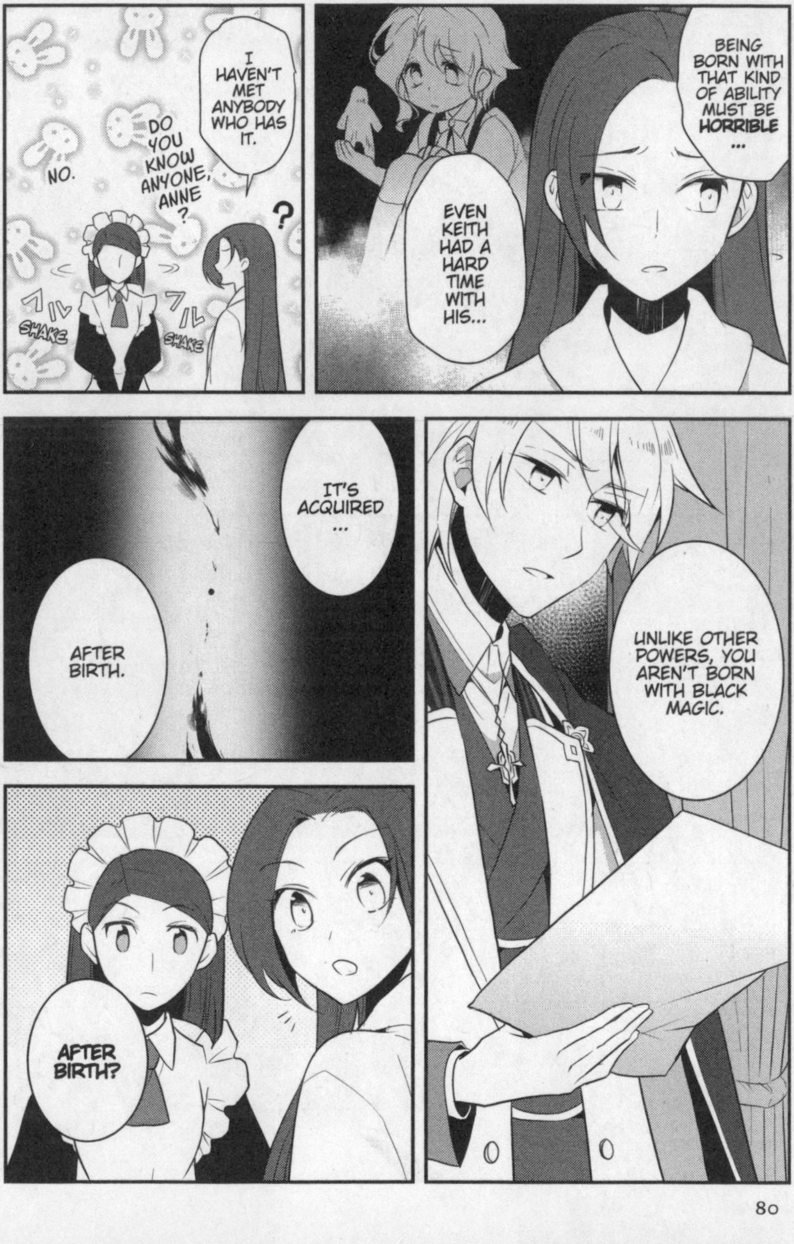
BEING BORN WITH THAT KIND OF ABILITY MUST BE **HORRIBLE** ...
EVEN KEITH HAD A HARD TIME WITH HIS...
I HAVEN'T MET ANYBODY WHO HAS IT.
DO YOU KNOW ANYONE, ANNE ?
?
NO.
SHAKE
SHAKE
UNLIKE OTHER POWERS, YOU AREN'T BORN WITH BLACK MAGIC.
IT'S ACQUIRED ...
AFTER BIRTH.
AFTER BIRTH?

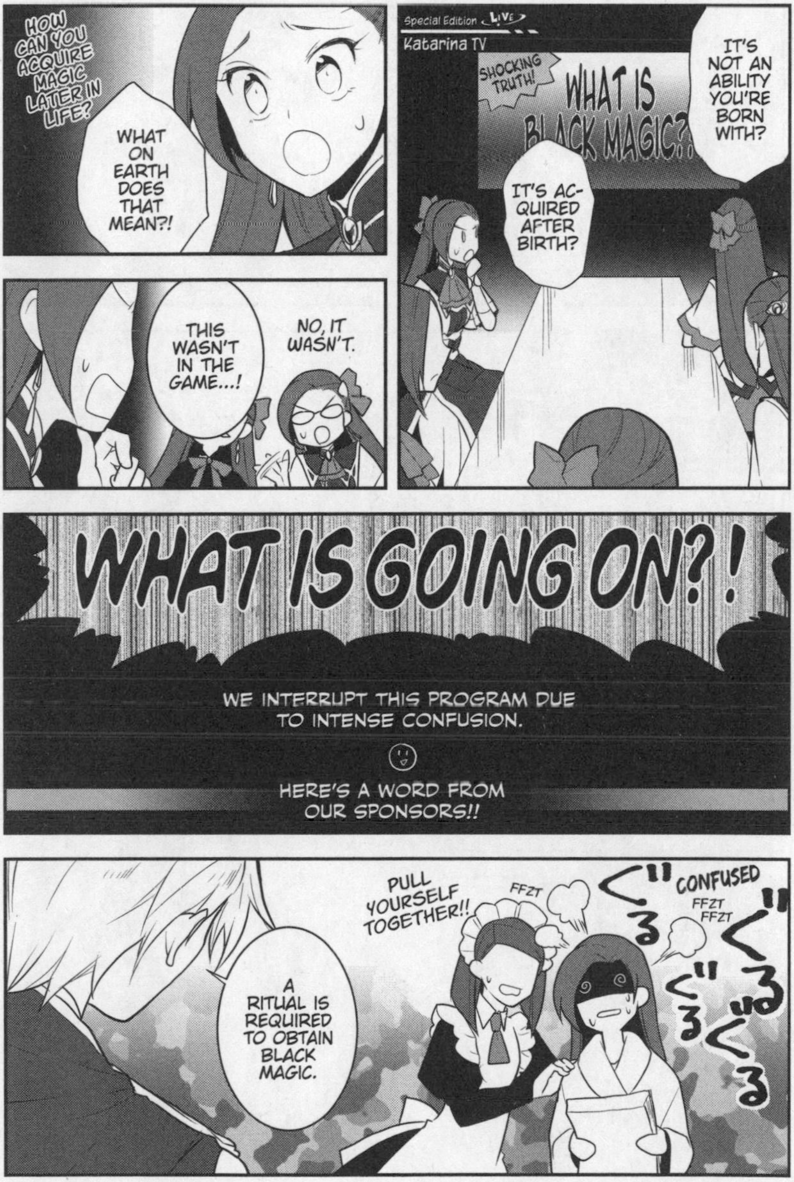
Special Edition LIVE
Katarina TV
IT'S NOT AN ABILITY YOU'RE BORN WITH?
SHOCKING TRUTH!
WHAT IS BLACK MAGIC?!
IT'S ACQUIRED AFTER BIRTH?
HOW CAN YOU ACQUIRE MAGIC LATER IN LIFE?
WHAT ON EARTH DOES THAT MEAN?!
THIS WASN'T IN THE GAME...!
NO, IT WASN'T.
WHAT IS GOING ON?!
WE INTERRUPT THIS PROGRAM DUE TO INTENSE CONFUSION.
HERE'S A WORD FROM OUR SPONSORS!!
ぐるぐる
ぐるぐる
ぐるぐる
CONFUSED
FFZT FFZT
PULL YOURSELF TOGETHER!!
FFZT
A RITUAL IS REQUIRED TO OBTAIN BLACK MAGIC.

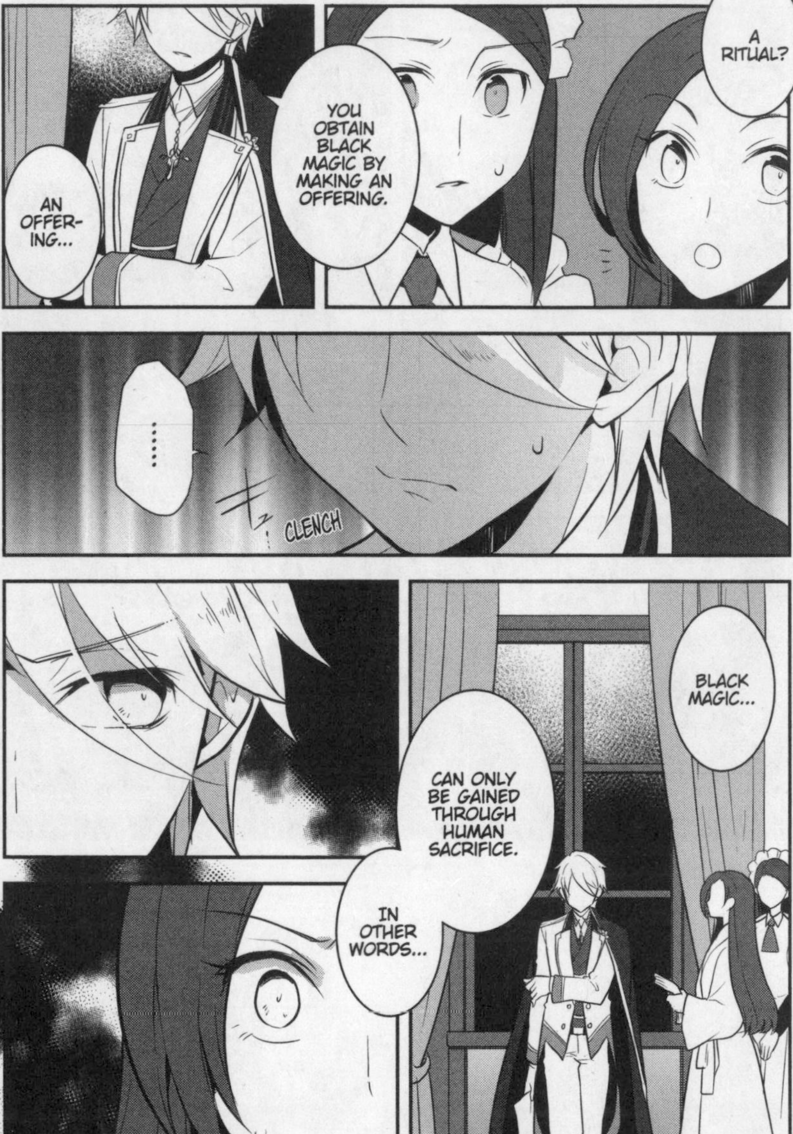
A RITUAL?
YOU OBTAIN BLACK MAGIC BY MAKING AN OFFERING.
AN OFFERING...
......
CLENCH
BLACK MAGIC...
CAN ONLY BE GAINED THROUGH HUMAN SACRIFICE.
IN OTHER WORDS...

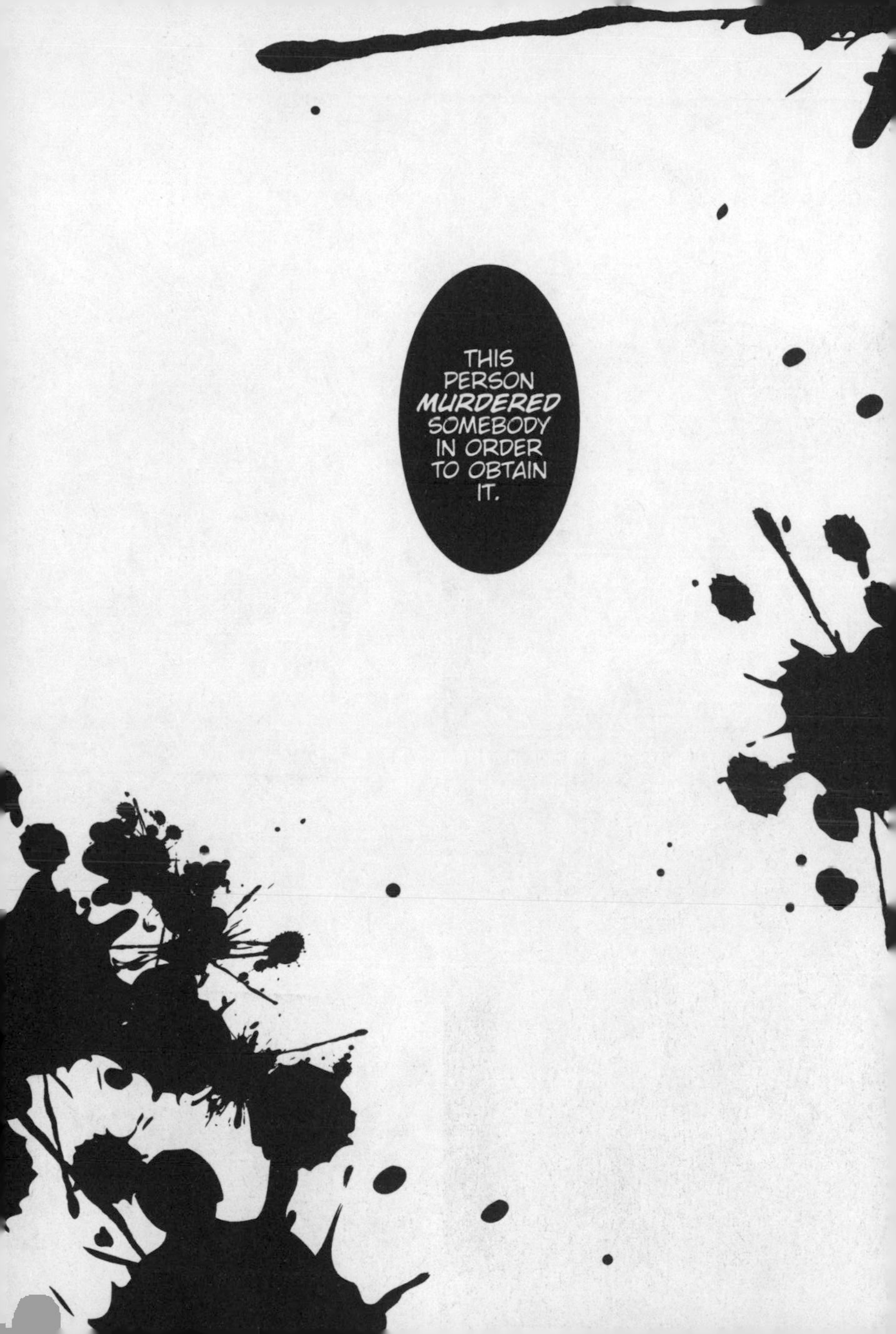
THIS PERSON MURDERED SOMEBODY IN ORDER TO OBTAIN IT.

My Next Life
as a VILLAINESS:
ALL ROUTES
LEAD TO DOOM!

Chapter 16: The Approaching Footsteps of Doom (Part 4)

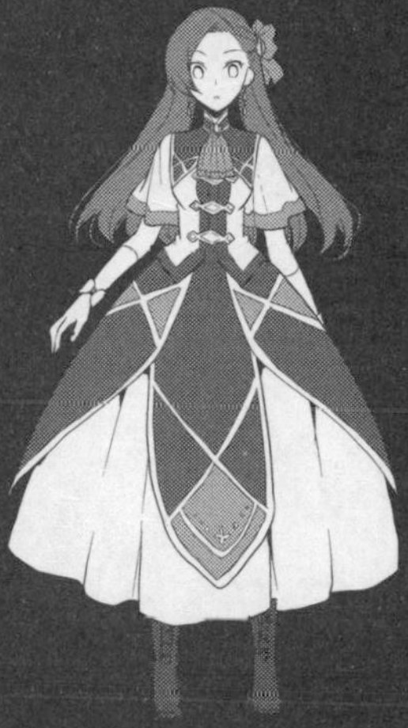

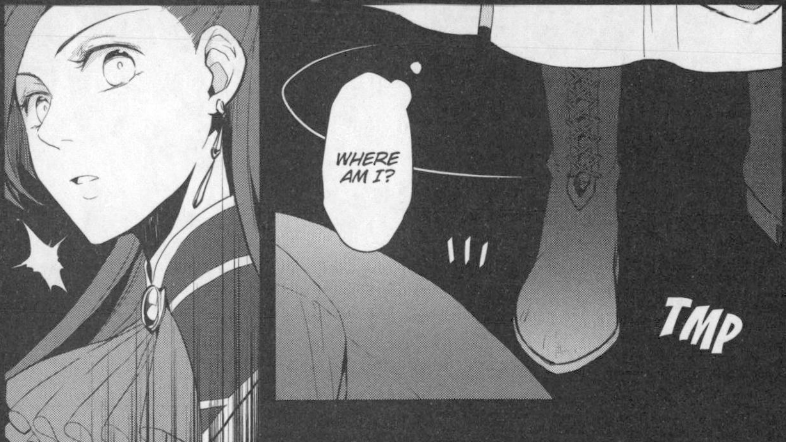
WHERE AM I?
TMP

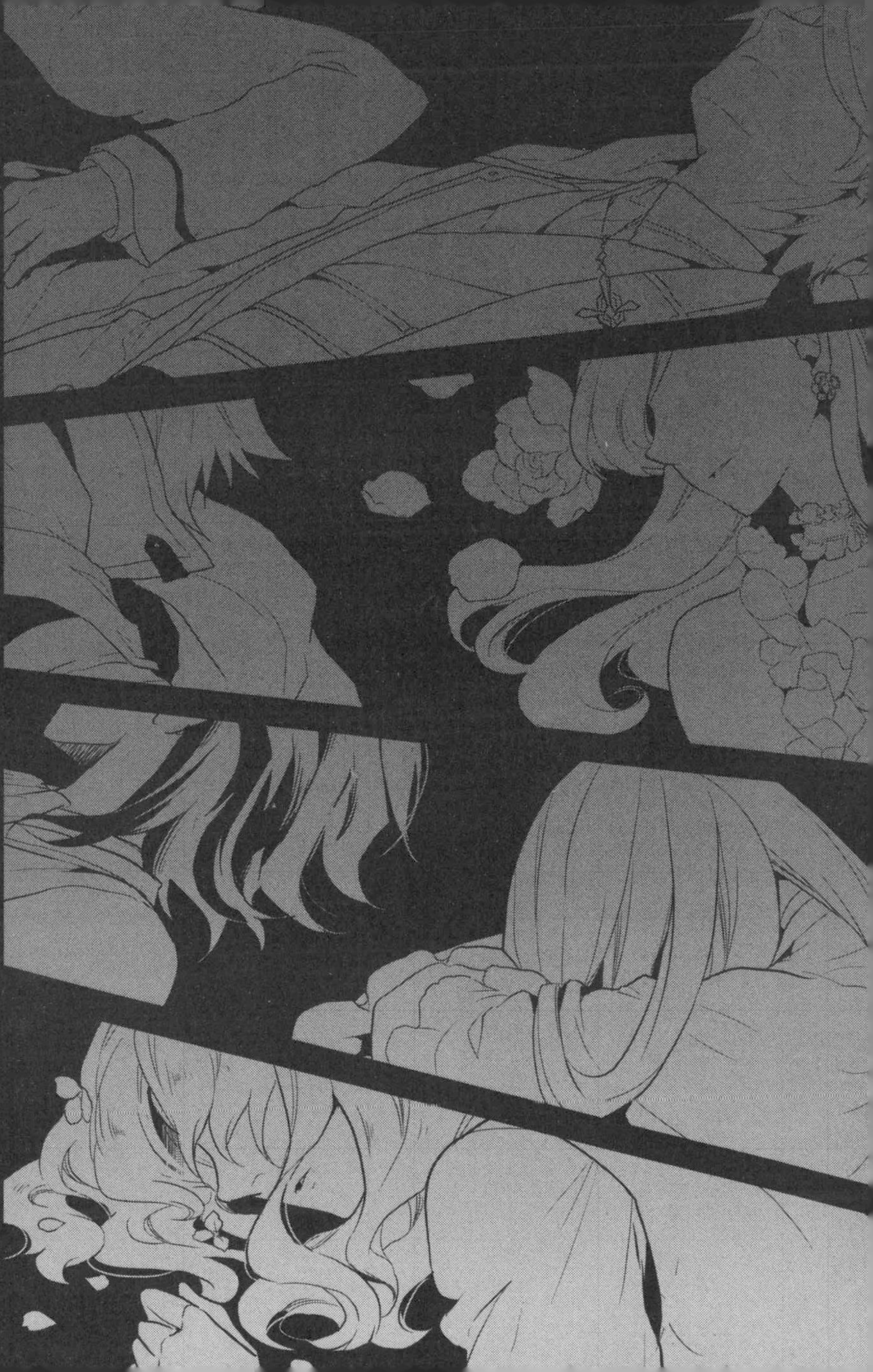

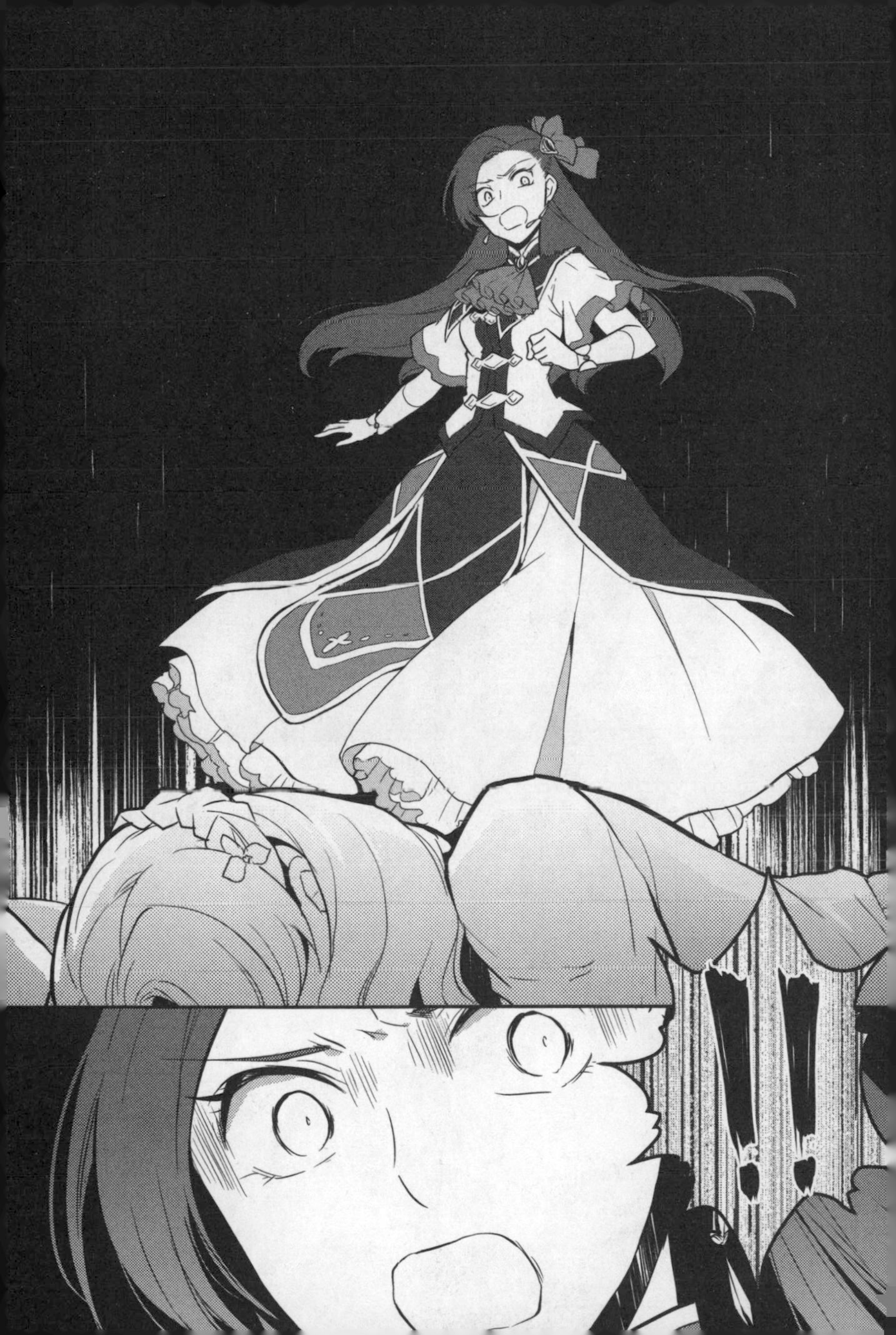
!!

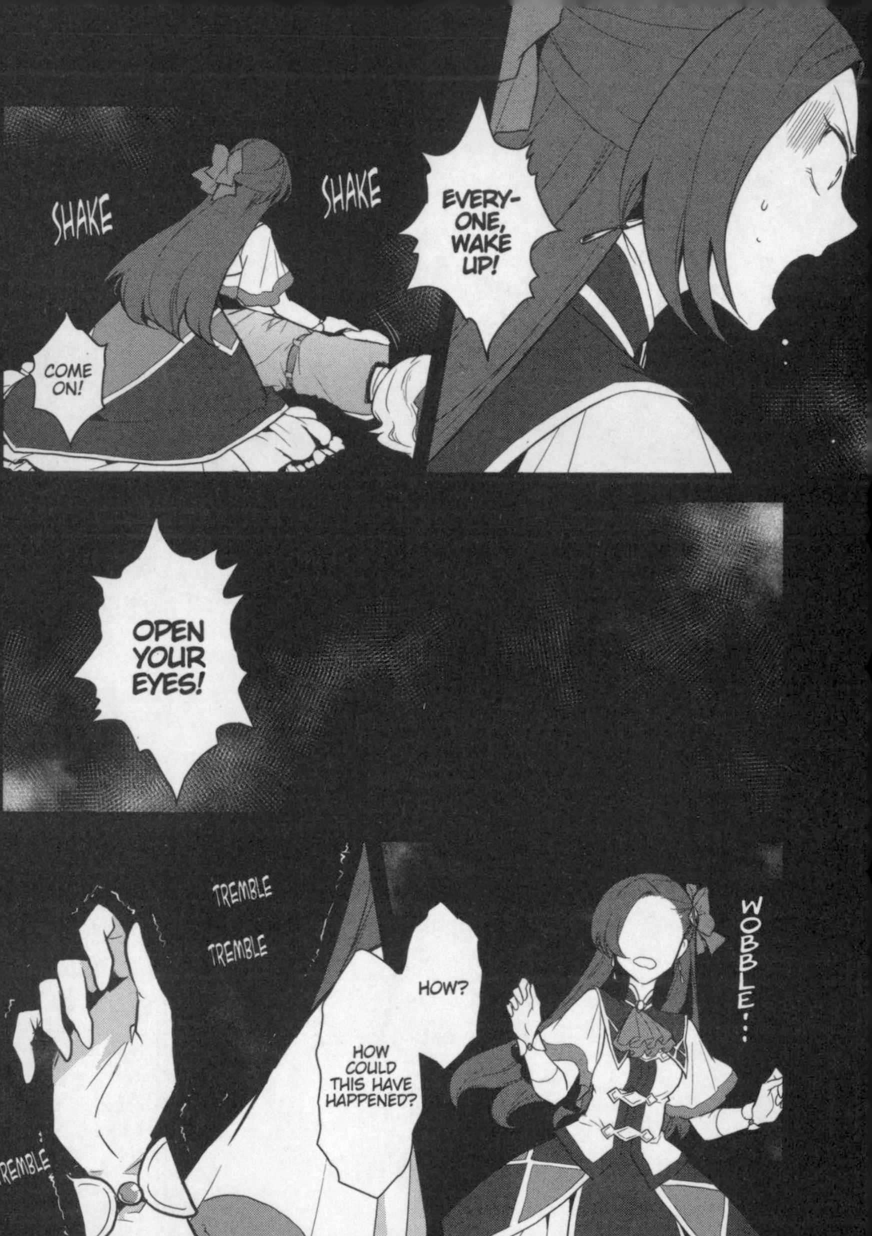
EVERY-ONE, WAKE UP!
SHAKE
SHAKE
COME ON!
OPEN YOUR EYES!
WOBBLE...
HOW?
HOW COULD THIS HAVE HAPPENED?
TREMBLE
TREMBLE
TREMBLE

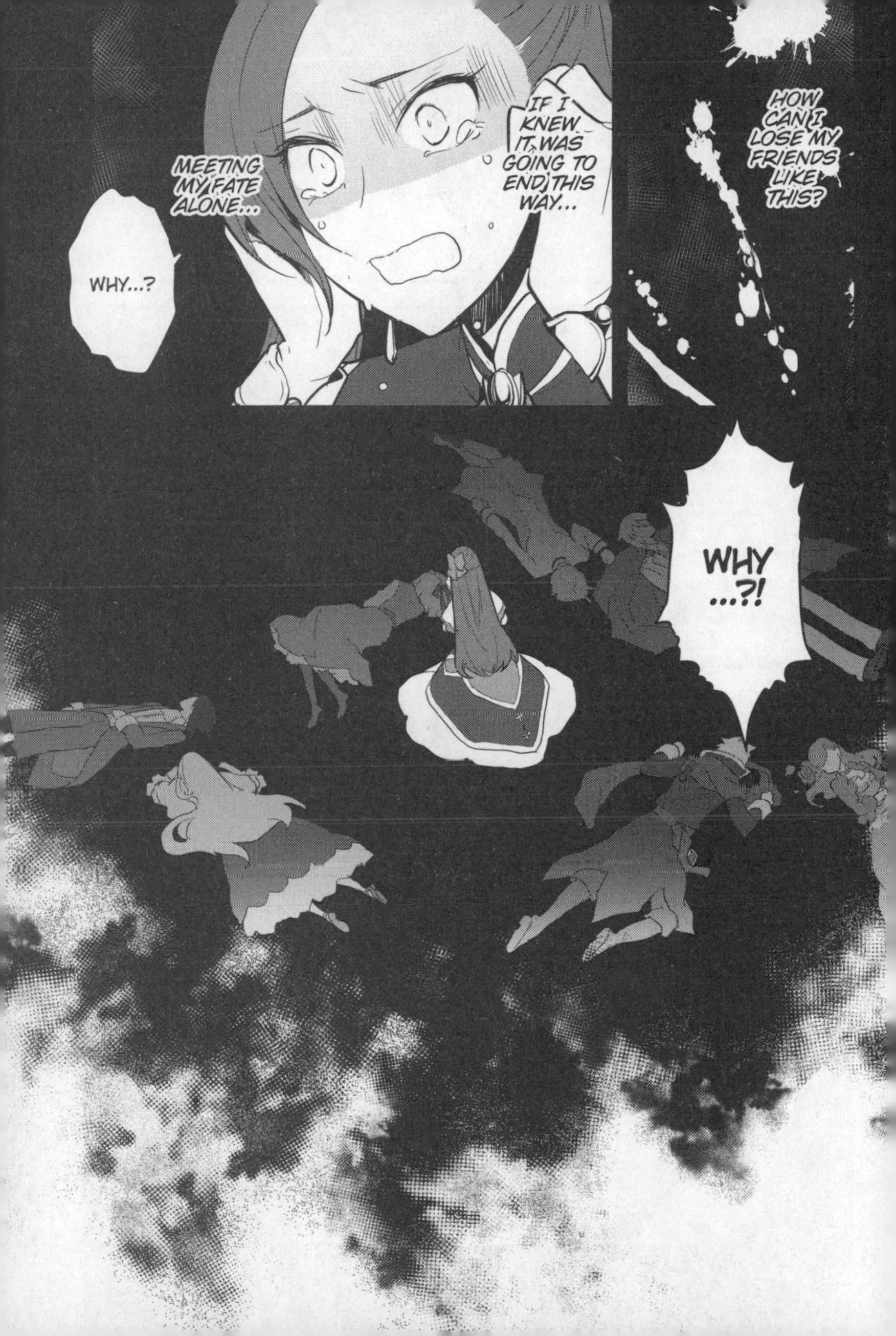

HOW CAN I LOSE MY FRIENDS LIKE THIS?
IF I KNEW IT WAS GOING TO END THIS WAY...
MEETING MY FATE ALONE...
WHY...?
WHY ...?!

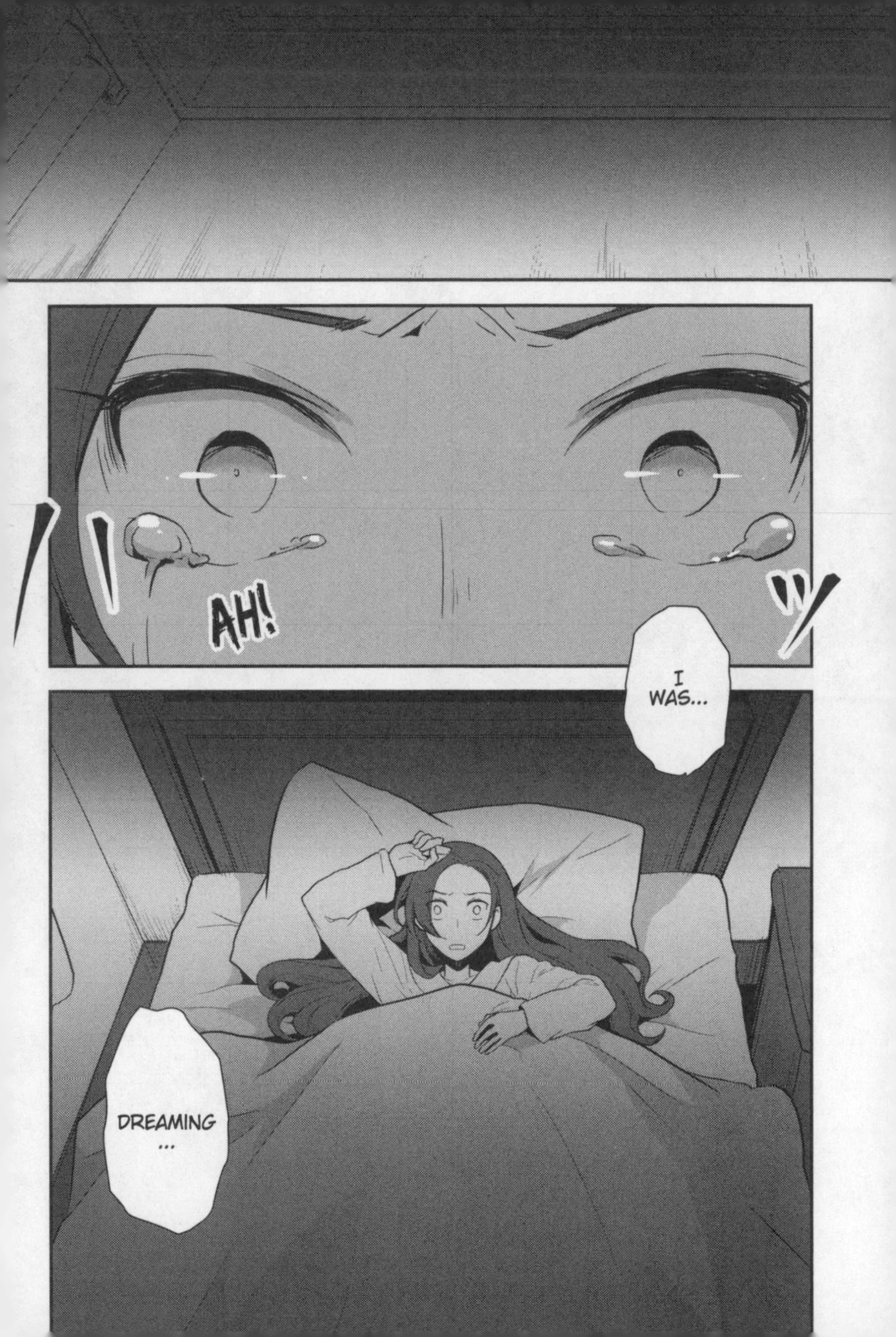
AH!
I WAS...
DREAMING ...

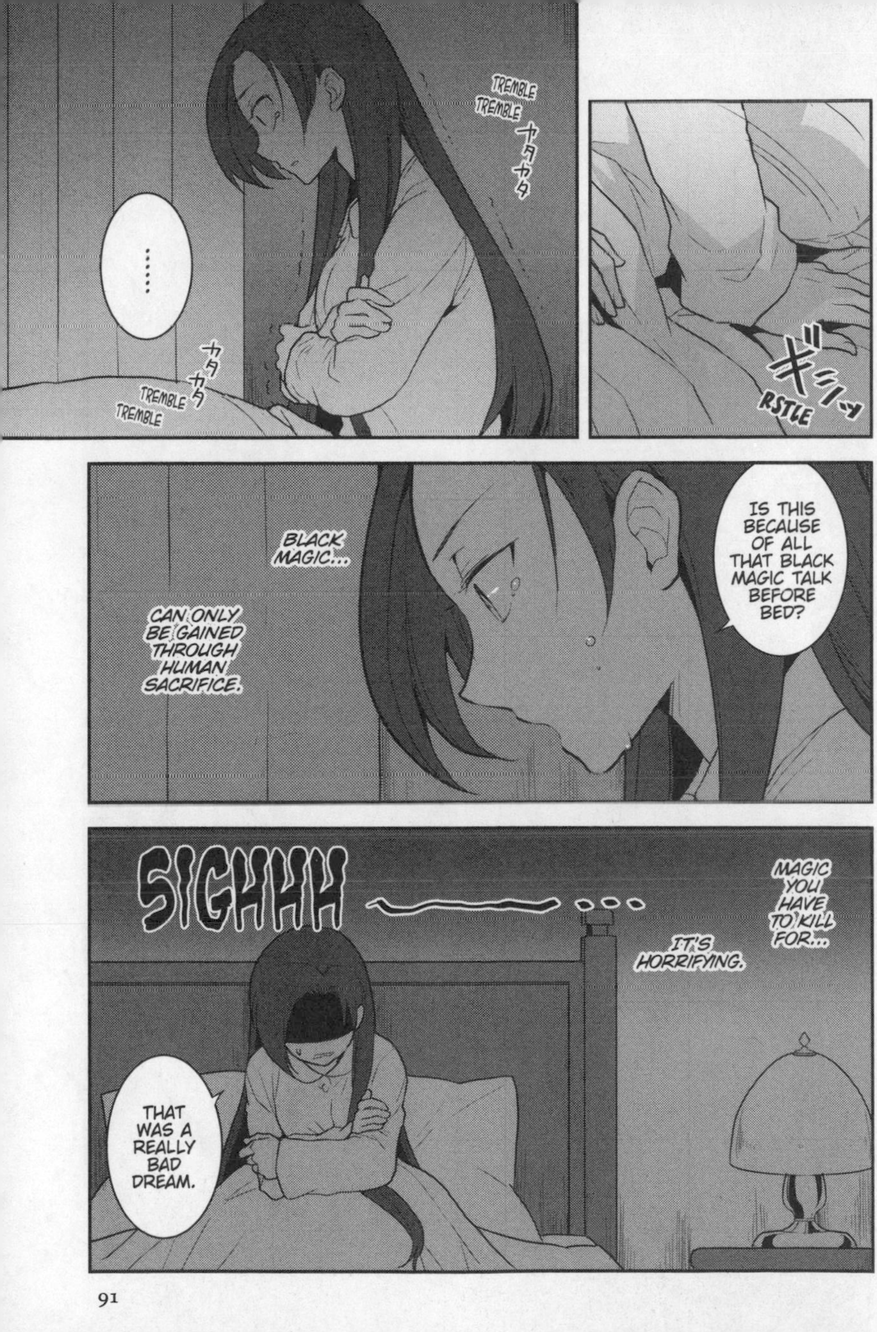

ギシッ
RSTLE
TREMBLE TREMBLE
カタカタ
......
カタカタ
TREMBLE TREMBLE
IS THIS BECAUSE OF ALL THAT BLACK MAGIC TALK BEFORE BED?
BLACK MAGIC...
CAN ONLY BE GAINED THROUGH HUMAN SACRIFICE.
MAGIC YOU HAVE TO KILL FOR...
IT'S HORRIFYING.
SIGHHH~...
THAT WAS A REALLY BAD DREAM.

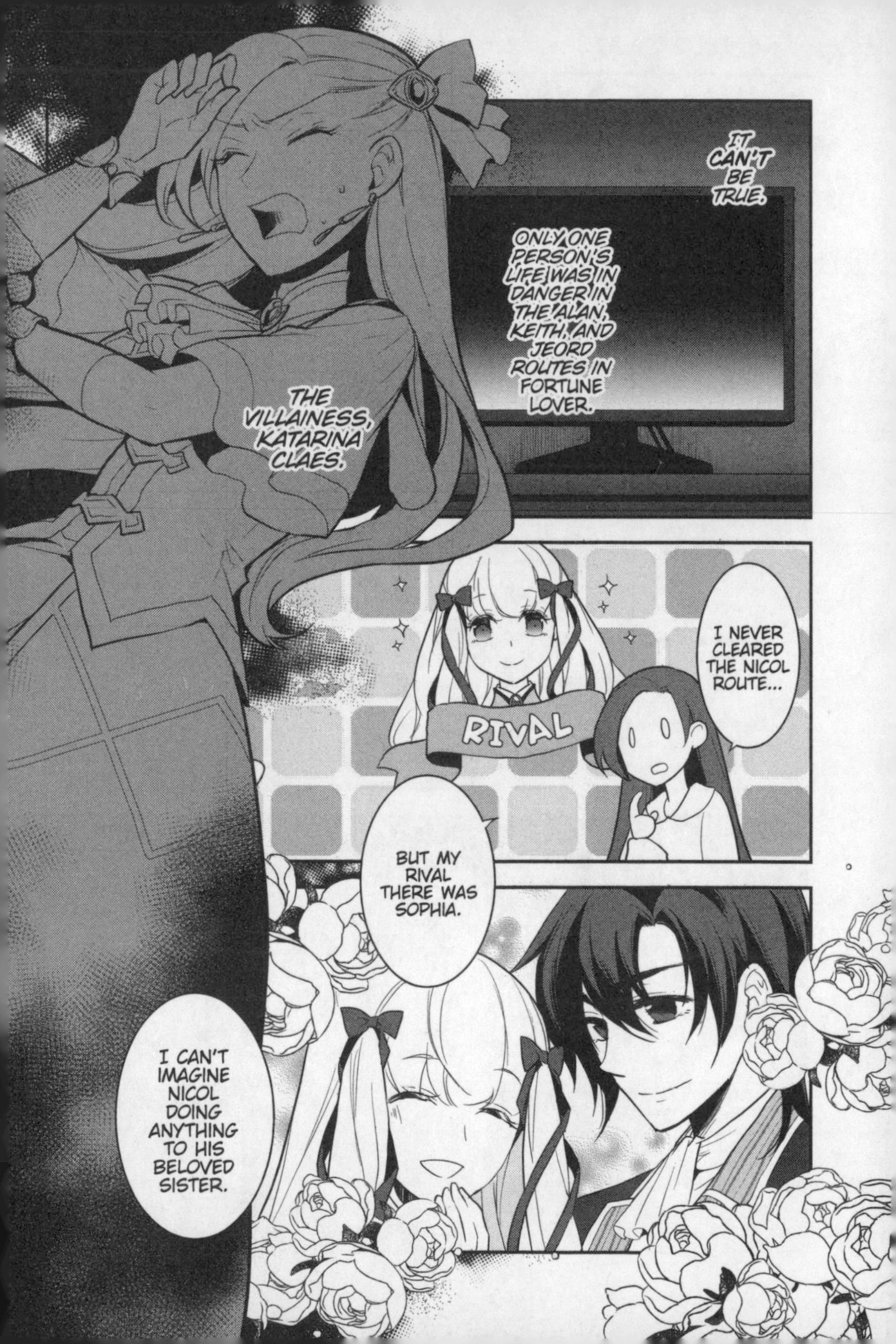
IT CAN'T BE TRUE.
ONLY ONE PERSON'S LIFE WAS IN DANGER IN THE ALAN, KEITH, AND JEORD ROUTES IN FORTUNE LOVER.
THE VILLAINESS, KATARINA CLAES.
I NEVER CLEARED THE NICOL ROUTE...
RIVAL
BUT MY RIVAL THERE WAS SOPHIA.
I CAN'T IMAGINE NICOL DOING ANYTHING TO HIS BELOVED SISTER.

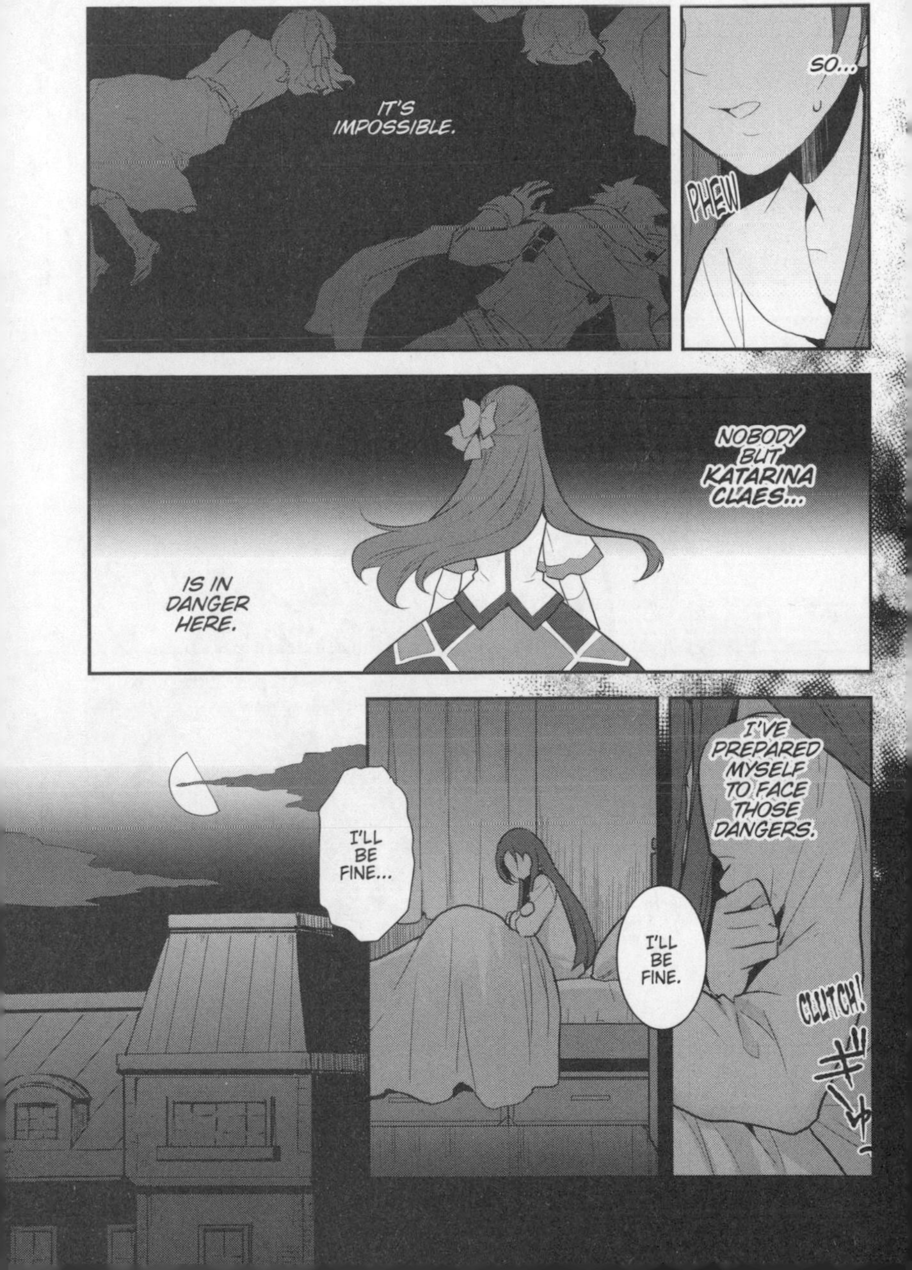
SO...
PHEW
IT'S IMPOSSIBLE.
NOBODY BUT KATARINA CLAES...
IS IN DANGER HERE.
I'VE PREPARED MYSELF TO FACE THOSE DANGERS.
CLUTCH!
I'LL BE FINE.
I'LL BE FINE...

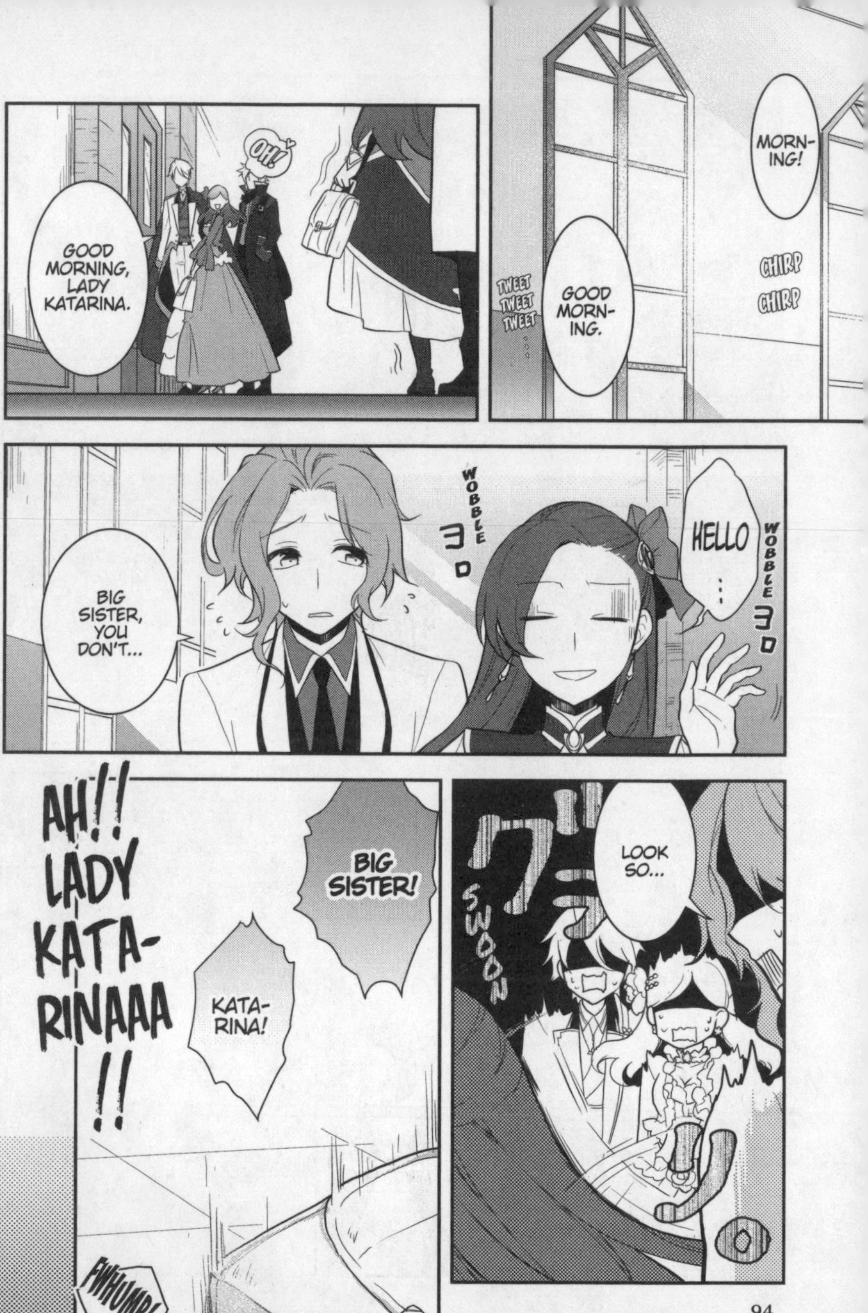
MORN-ING!
GOOD MORN-ING.
TWEET TWEET TWEET
CHIRP CHIRP
OH!
GOOD MORNING, LADY KATARINA.
HELLO...
WOBBLE
WOBBLE
BIG SISTER, YOU DON'T...
LOOK SO...
SWOON
BIG SISTER!
KATA-RINA!
AH!! LADY KATA-RINAAA!!
FWHUMP!

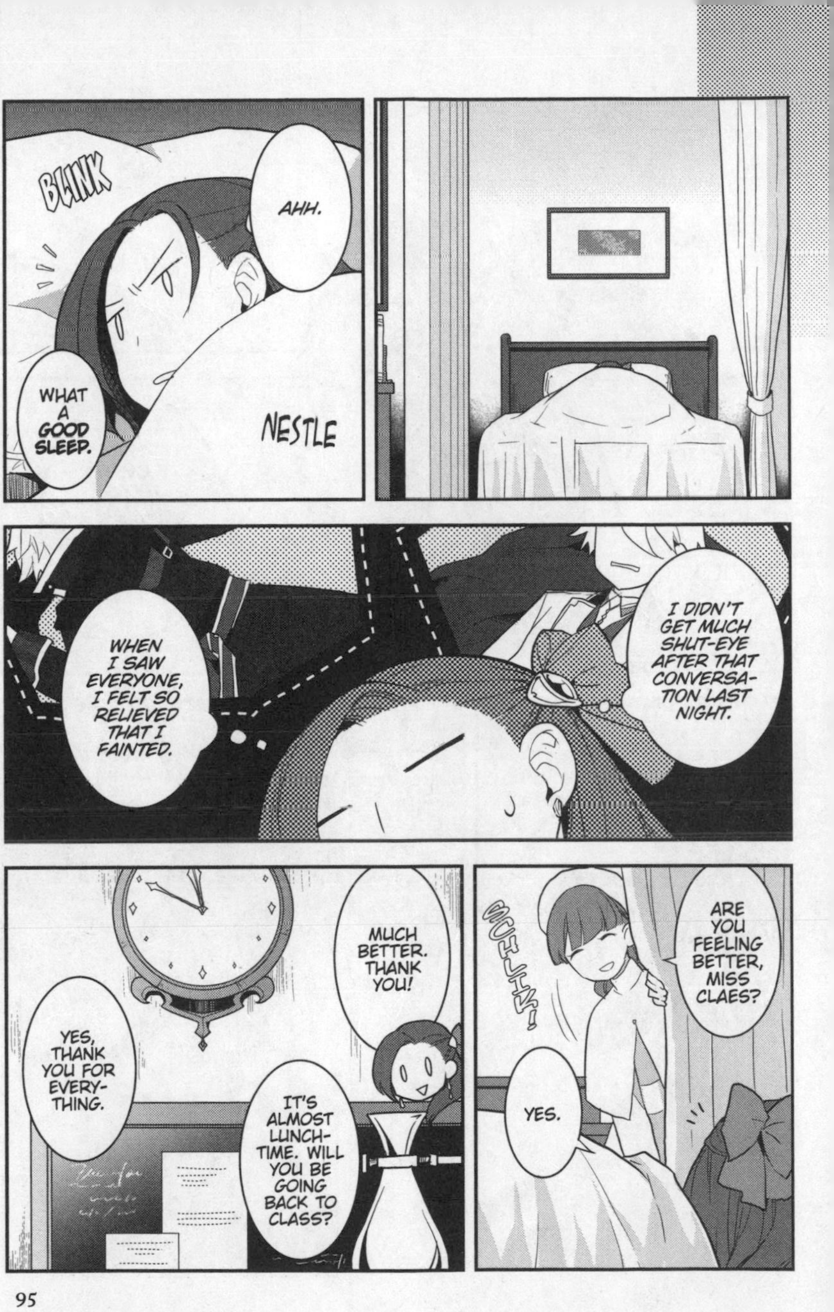
AHH.
BLINK
WHAT A GOOD SLEEP.
NESTLE
I DIDN'T GET MUCH SHUT-EYE AFTER THAT CONVERSATION LAST NIGHT.
WHEN I SAW EVERYONE, I FELT SO RELIEVED THAT I FAINTED.
ARE YOU FEELING BETTER, MISS CLAES?
SCHLIK!
YES.
MUCH BETTER. THANK YOU!
IT'S ALMOST LUNCHTIME. WILL YOU BE GOING BACK TO CLASS?
YES, THANK YOU FOR EVERYTHING.

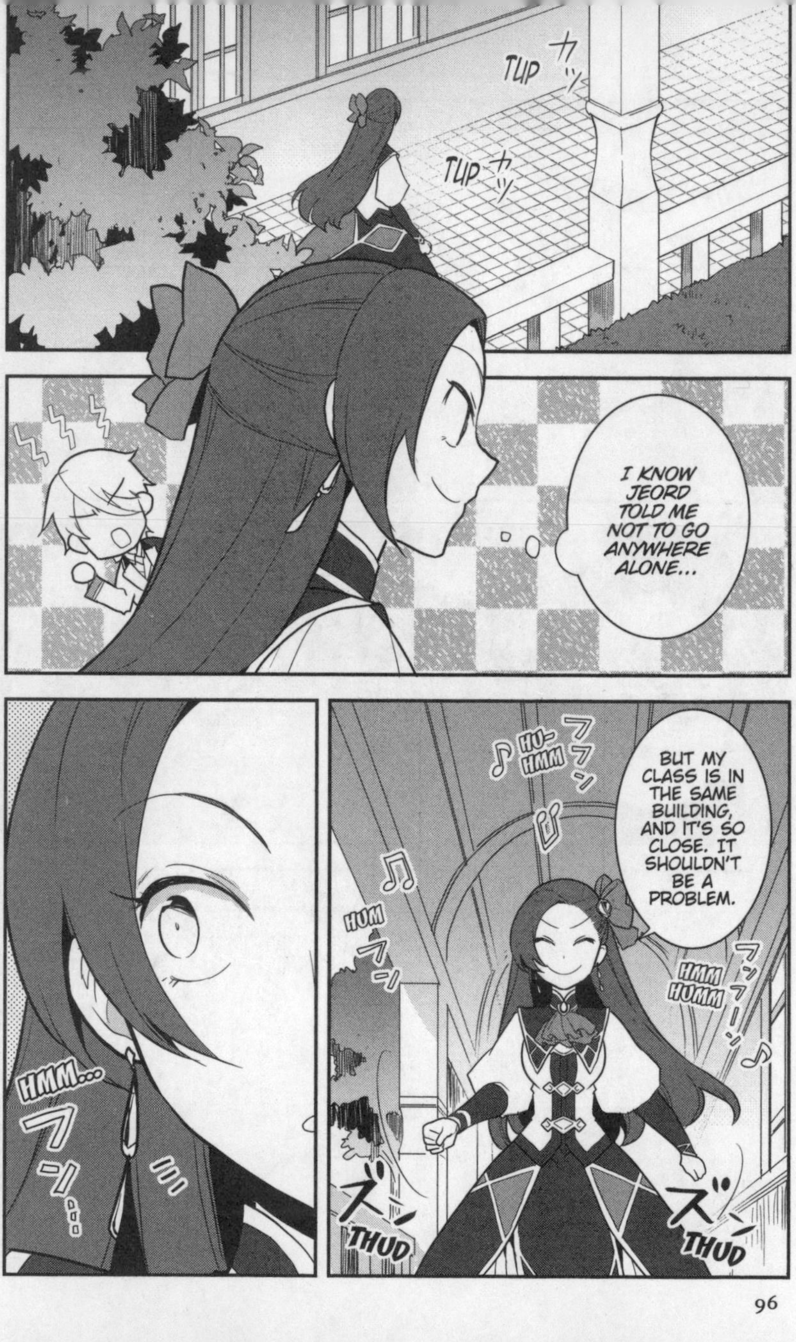
TUP
カッ
TUP
カッ
I KNOW JEORD TOLD ME NOT TO GO ANYWHERE ALONE...
HO-HMM
フフーッ
BUT MY CLASS IS IN THE SAME BUILDING, AND IT'S SO CLOSE. IT SHOULDN'T BE A PROBLEM.
HUM
フフーン
HMM HUMM
フンフーン
THUD
THUD
HMM...
フフーン...

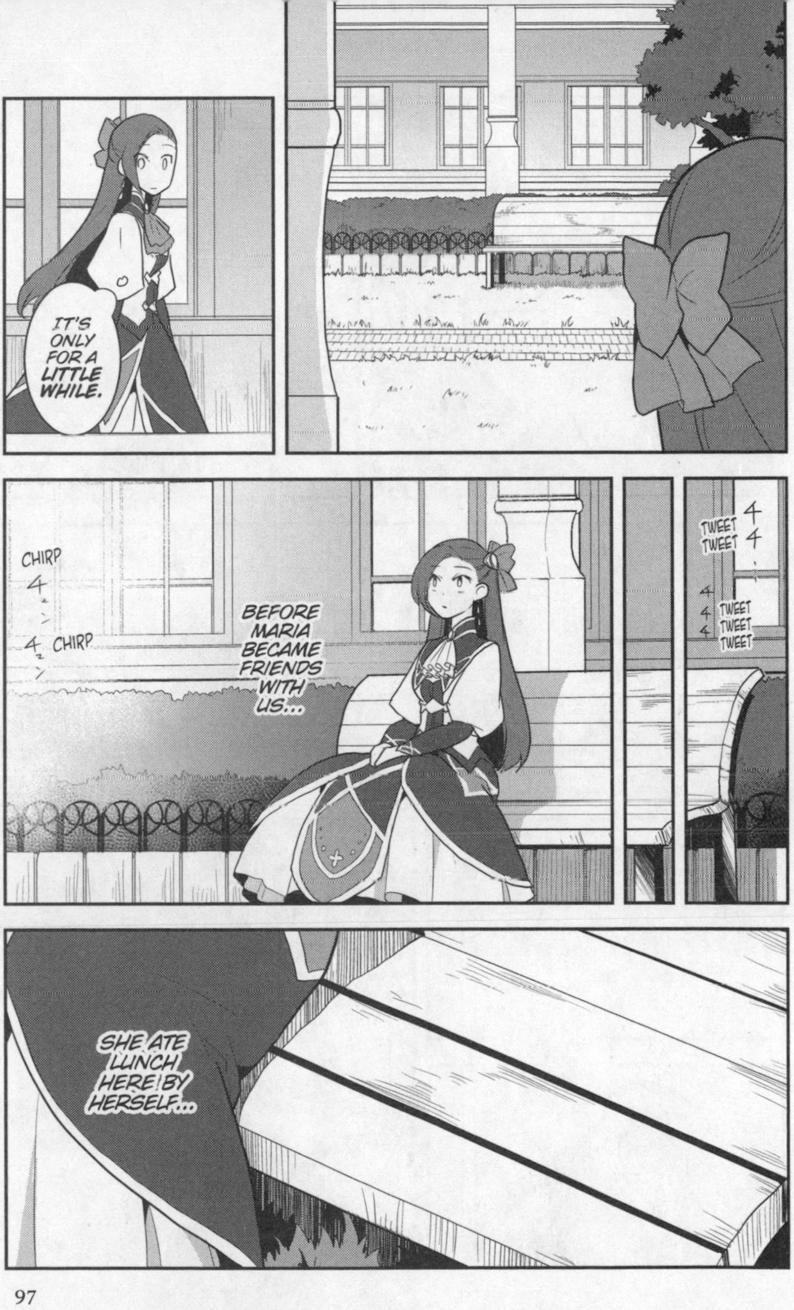
IT'S ONLY FOR A LITTLE WHILE.
TWEET TWEET
TWEET TWEET TWEET
BEFORE MARIA BECAME FRIENDS WITH US...
CHIRP
CHIRP
SHE ATE LUNCH HERE BY HERSELF...

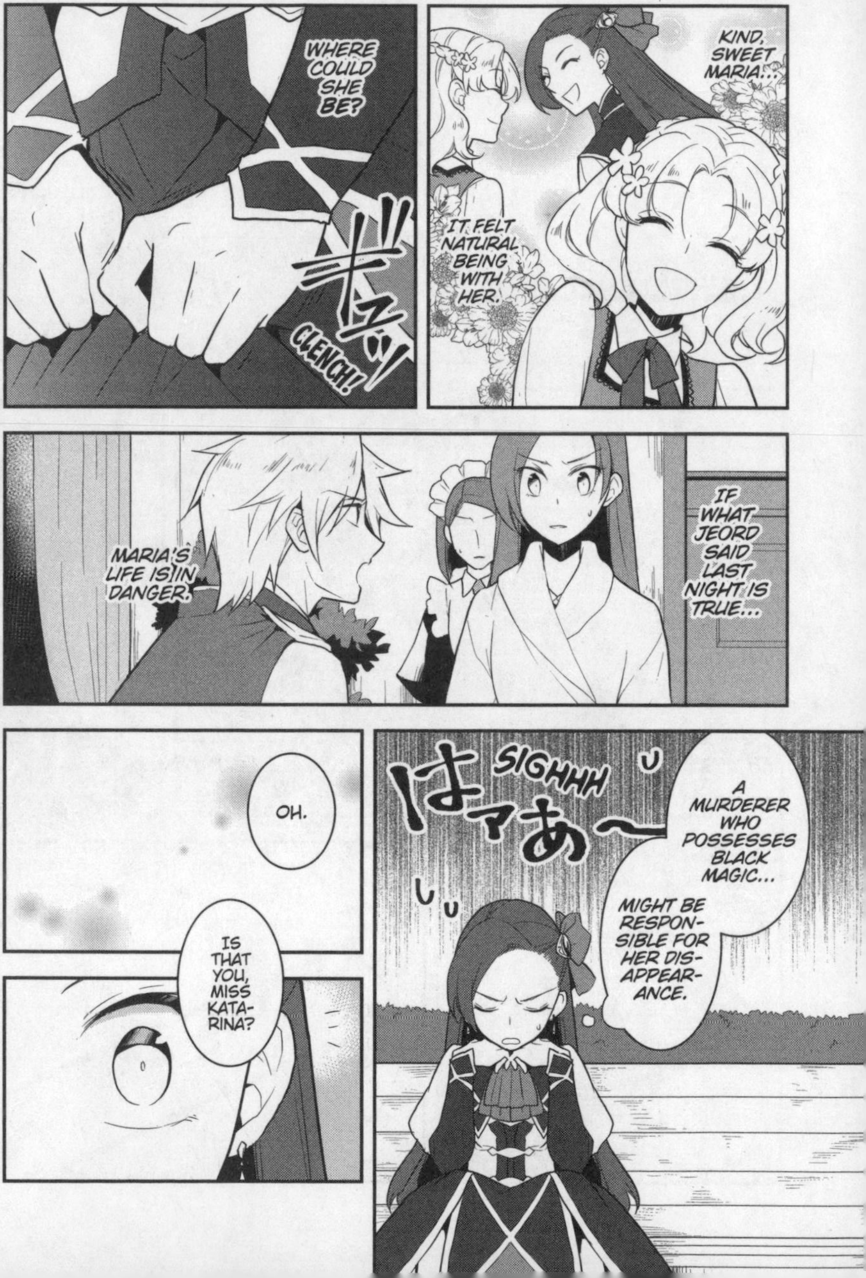
KIND, SWEET MARIA...
IT FELT NATURAL BEING WITH HER.
WHERE COULD SHE BE?
ギュッ
CLENCH!
IF WHAT JEORD SAID LAST NIGHT IS TRUE...
MARIA'S LIFE IS IN DANGER.
はァあ～
SIGHHH
A MURDERER WHO POSSESSES BLACK MAGIC...
MIGHT BE RESPONSIBLE FOR HER DISAPPEARANCE.
OH.
IS THAT YOU, MISS KATARINA?

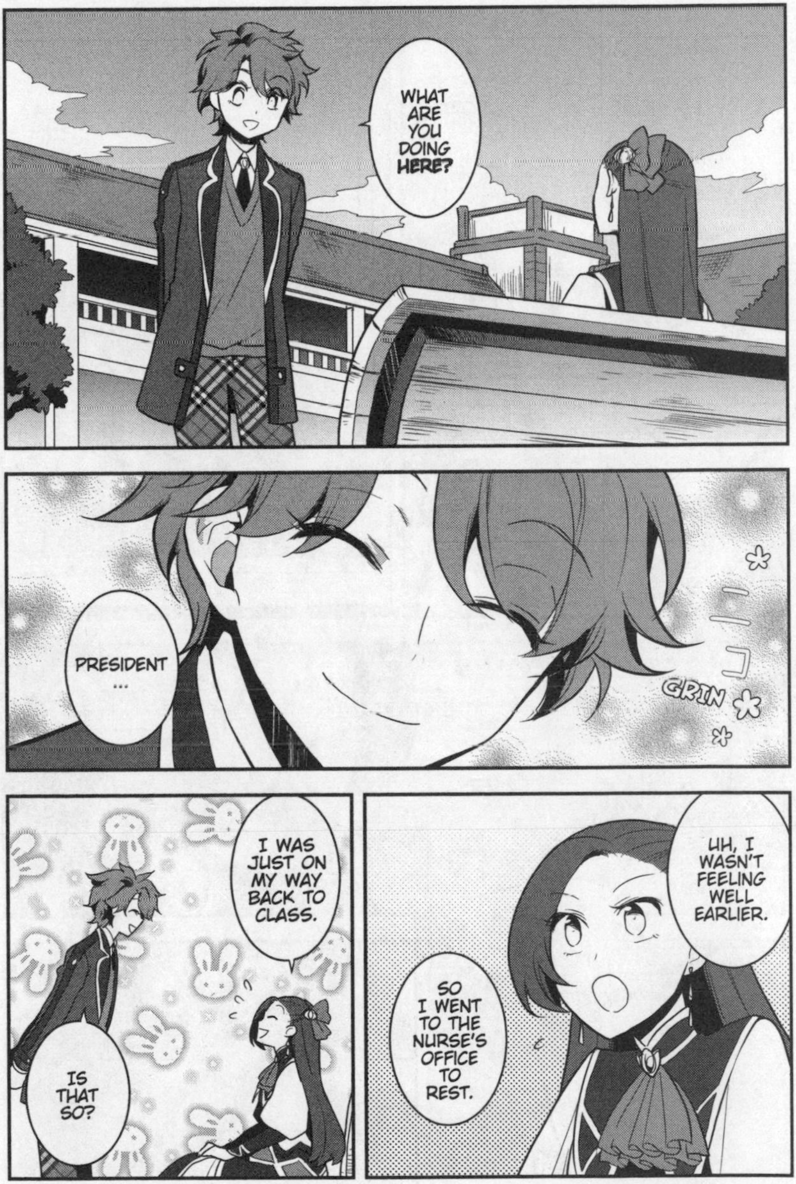

WHAT ARE YOU DOING HERE?
ニコ
GRIN
PRESIDENT ...
UH, I WASN'T FEELING WELL EARLIER.
SO I WENT TO THE NURSE'S OFFICE TO REST.
I WAS JUST ON MY WAY BACK TO CLASS.
IS THAT SO?

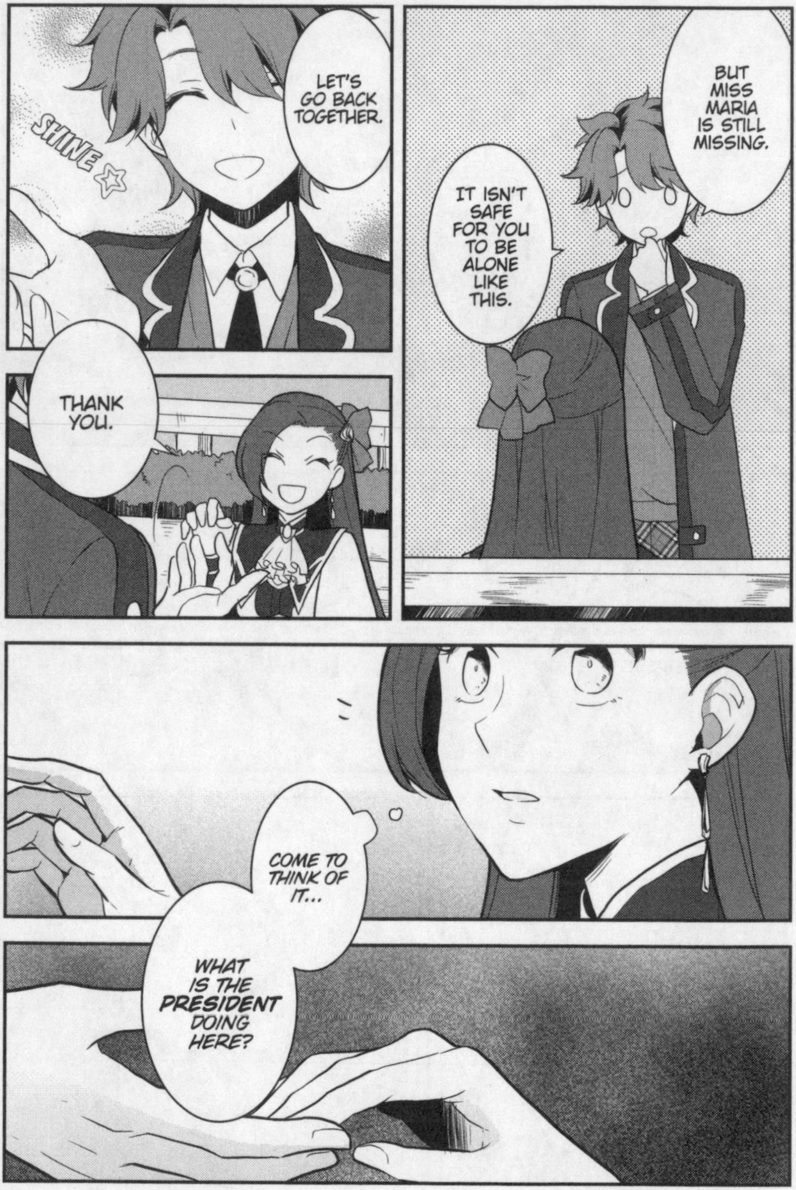
BUT MISS MARIA IS STILL MISSING.
IT ISN'T SAFE FOR YOU TO BE ALONE LIKE THIS.
LET'S GO BACK TOGETHER.
SHINE
THANK YOU.
COME TO THINK OF IT...
WHAT IS THE PRESIDENT DOING HERE?

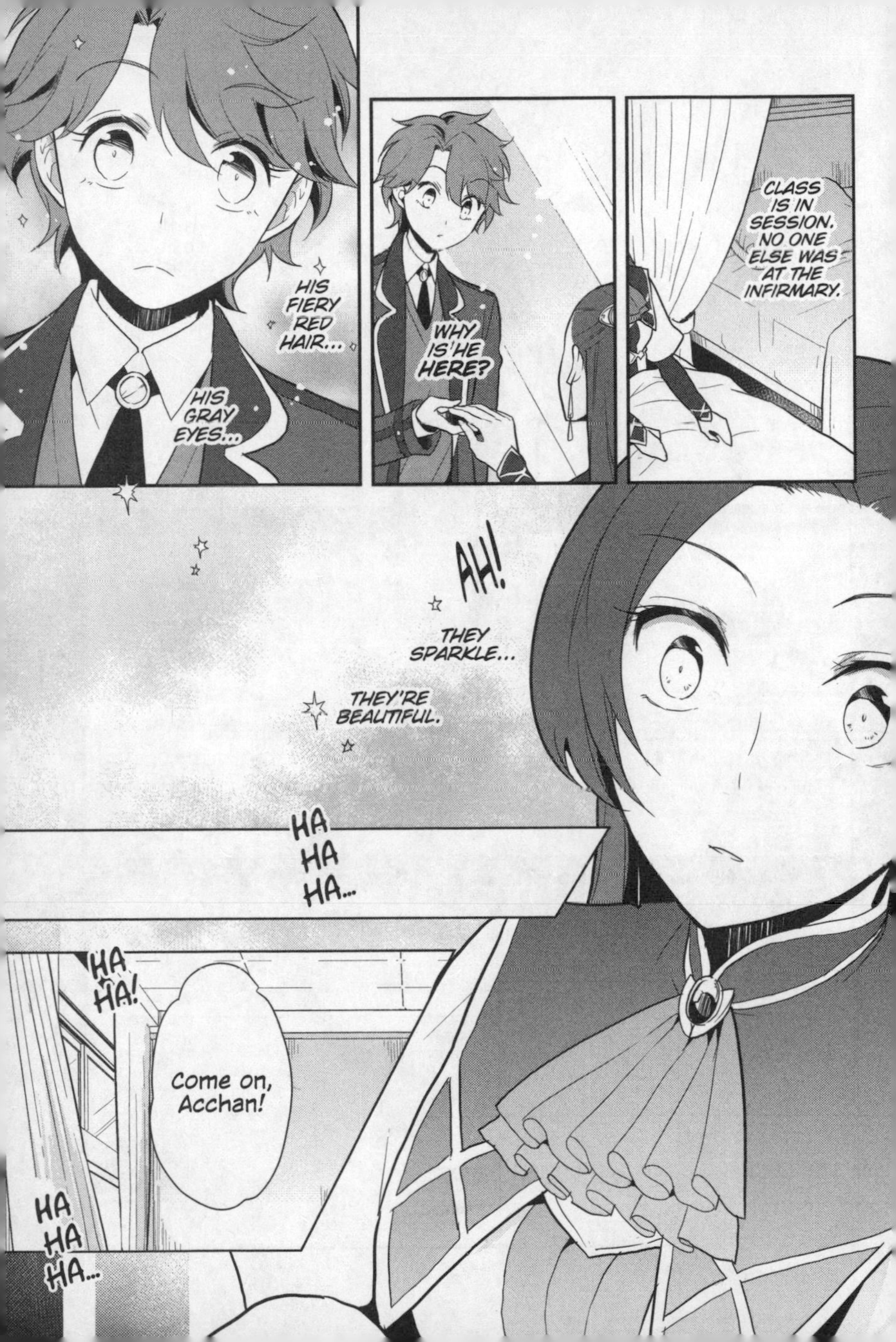
CLASS IS IN SESSION. NO ONE ELSE WAS AT THE INFIRMARY.
WHY IS HE HERE?
HIS FIERY RED HAIR...
HIS GRAY EYES...
AH!
THEY SPARKLE...
THEY'RE BEAUTIFUL.
HA HA HA...
HA HA!
Come on, Acchan!
HA HA HA...

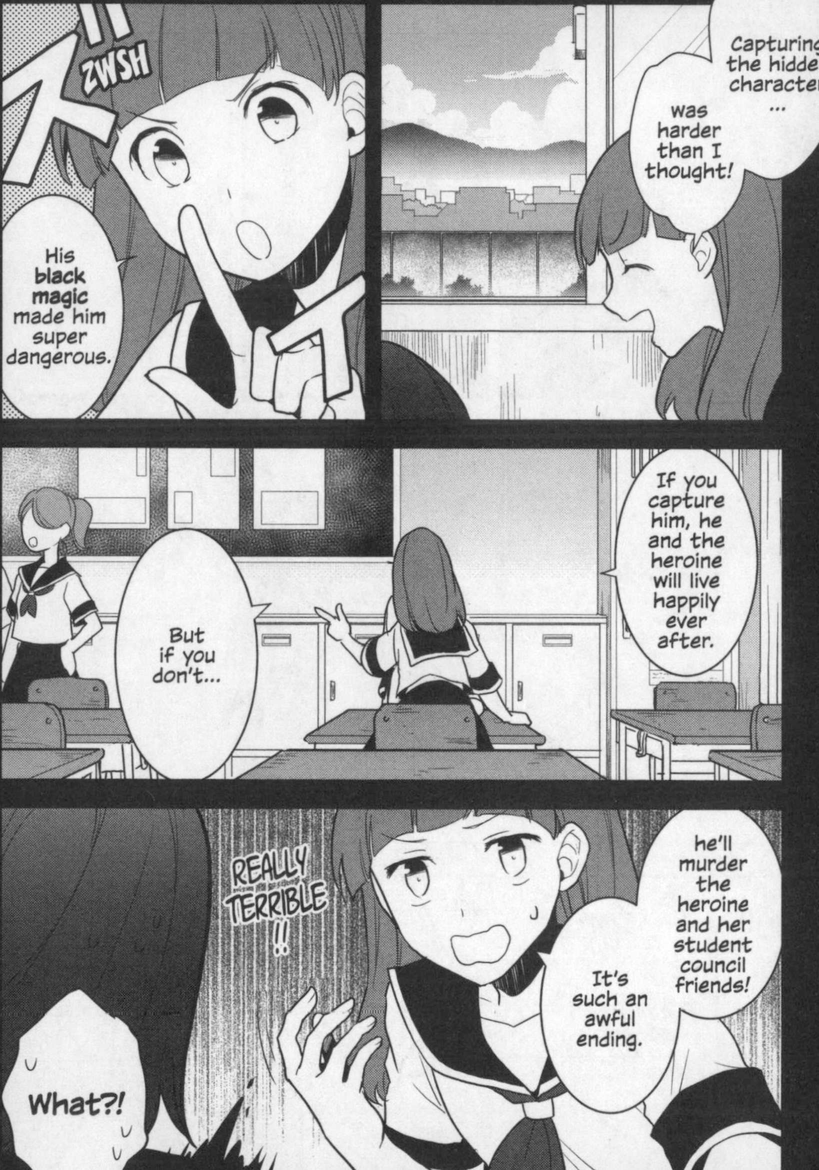

Capturing the hidden character ...
was harder than I thought!
ZWSH
His black magic made him super dangerous.
If you capture him, he and the heroine will live happily ever after.
But if you don't...
he'll murder the heroine and her student council friends!
It's such an awful ending.
REALLY TERRIBLE !!
What?!

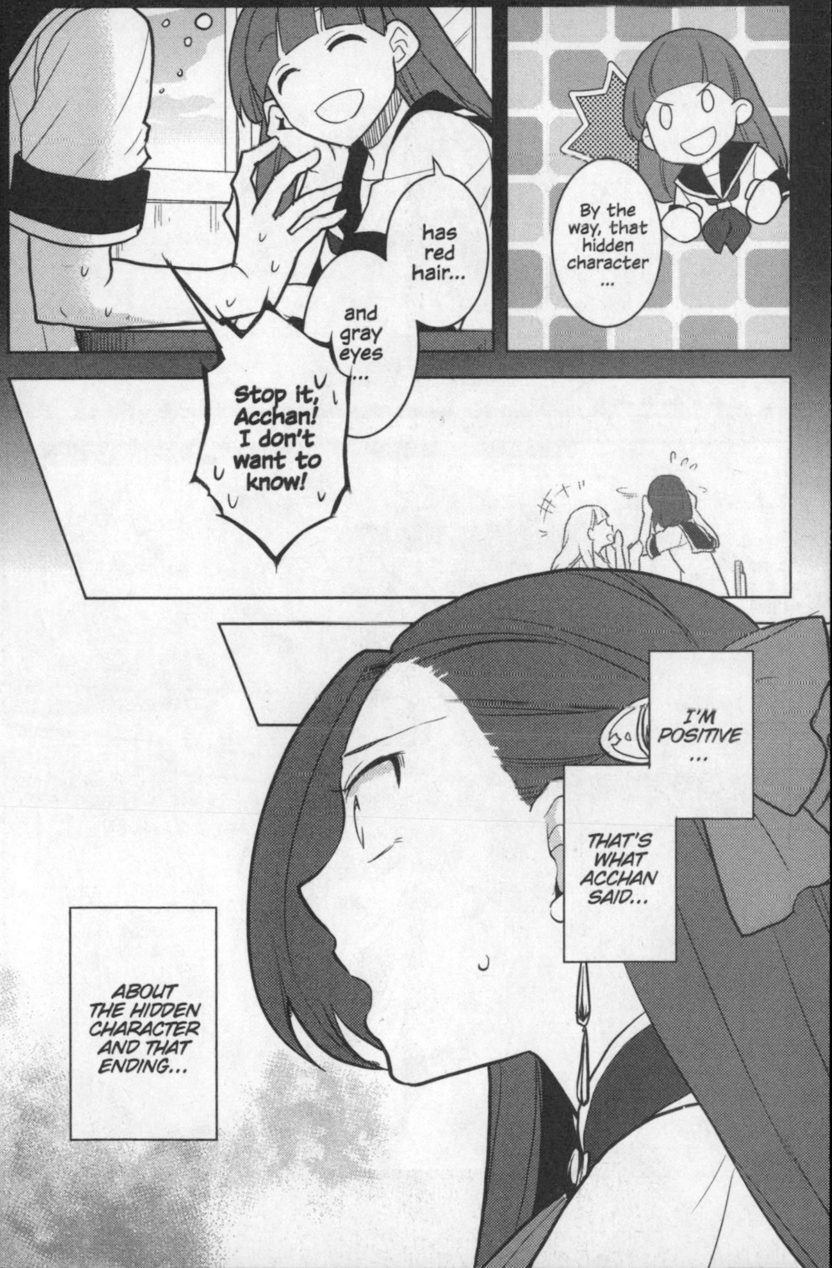
By the way, that hidden character...
has red hair...
and gray eyes...
Stop it, Acchan! I don't want to know!
I'M POSITIVE...
THAT'S WHAT ACCHAN SAID...
ABOUT THE HIDDEN CHARACTER AND THAT ENDING...

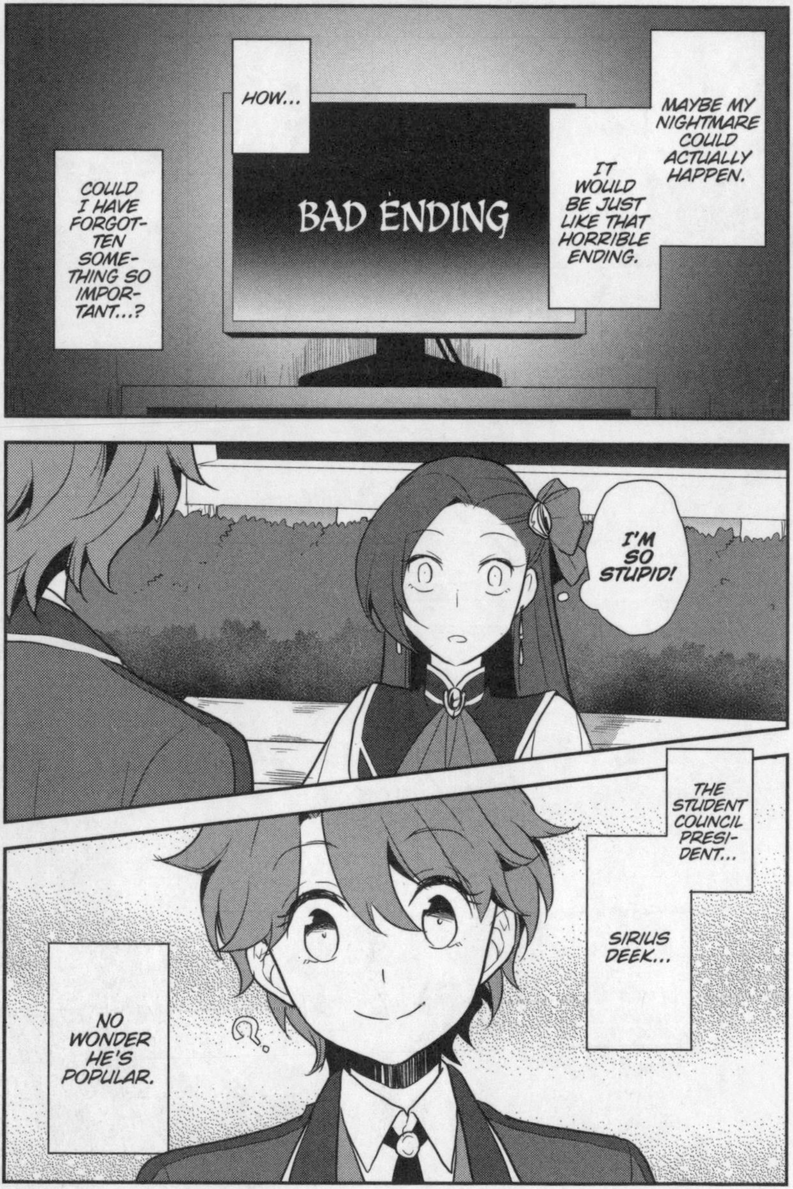
MAYBE MY NIGHTMARE COULD ACTUALLY HAPPEN.
HOW...
IT WOULD BE JUST LIKE THAT HORRIBLE ENDING.
BAD ENDING
COULD I HAVE FORGOTTEN SOMETHING SO IMPORTANT...?
I'M SO STUPID!
THE STUDENT COUNCIL PRESIDENT...
SIRIUS DEEK...
NO WONDER HE'S POPULAR.

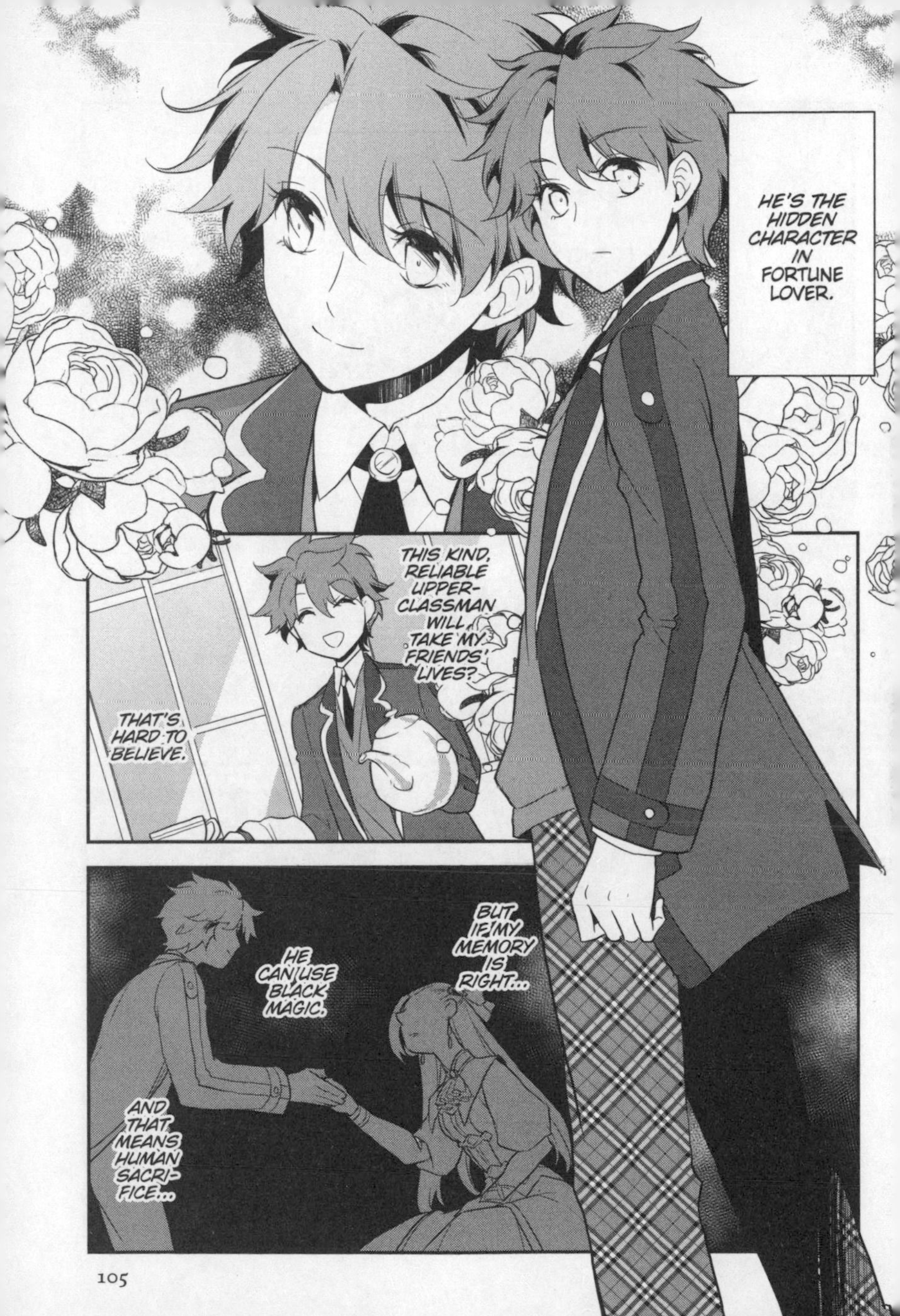
HE'S THE HIDDEN CHARACTER IN FORTUNE LOVER.
THIS KIND, RELIABLE UPPER-CLASSMAN WILL TAKE MY FRIENDS' LIVES?
THAT'S HARD TO BELIEVE.
BUT IF MY MEMORY IS RIGHT...
HE CAN USE BLACK MAGIC.
AND THAT MEANS HUMAN SACRI-FICE...

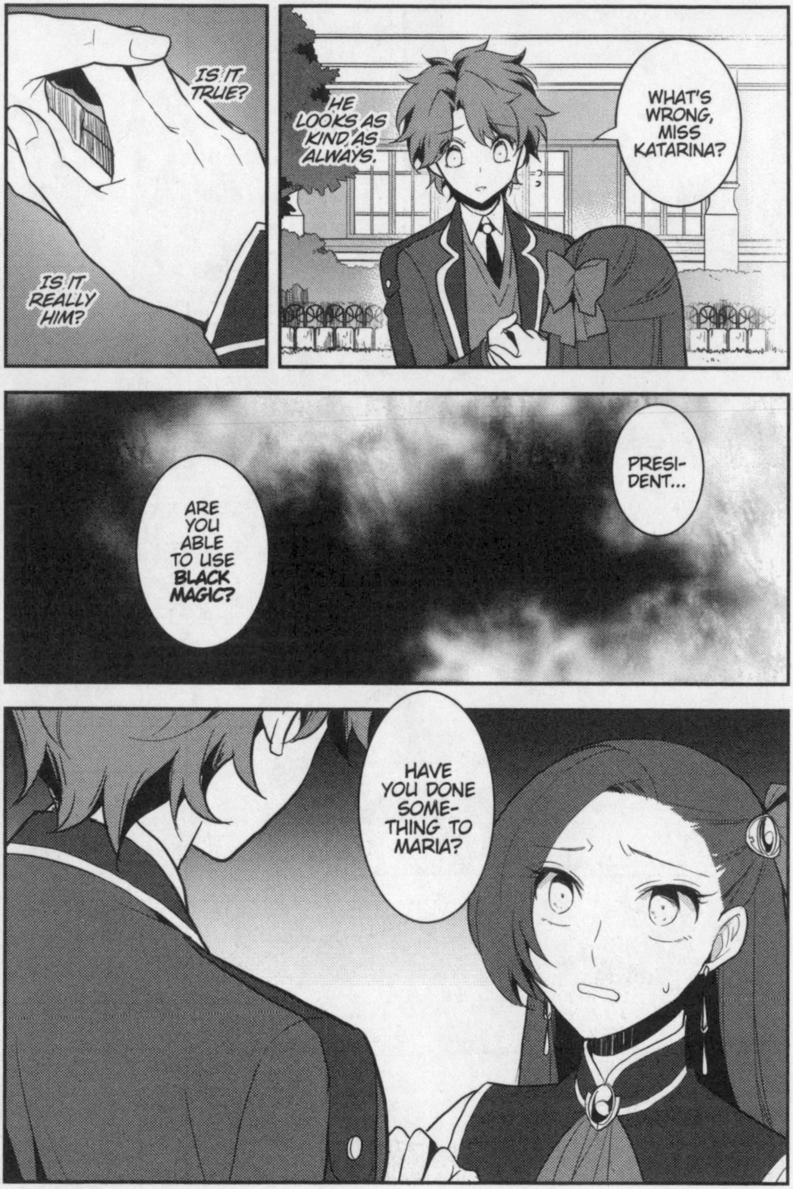
WHAT'S WRONG, MISS KATARINA?
HE LOOKS AS KIND AS ALWAYS.
IS IT TRUE?
IS IT REALLY HIM?
PRESIDENT...
ARE YOU ABLE TO USE BLACK MAGIC?
HAVE YOU DONE SOMETHING TO MARIA?

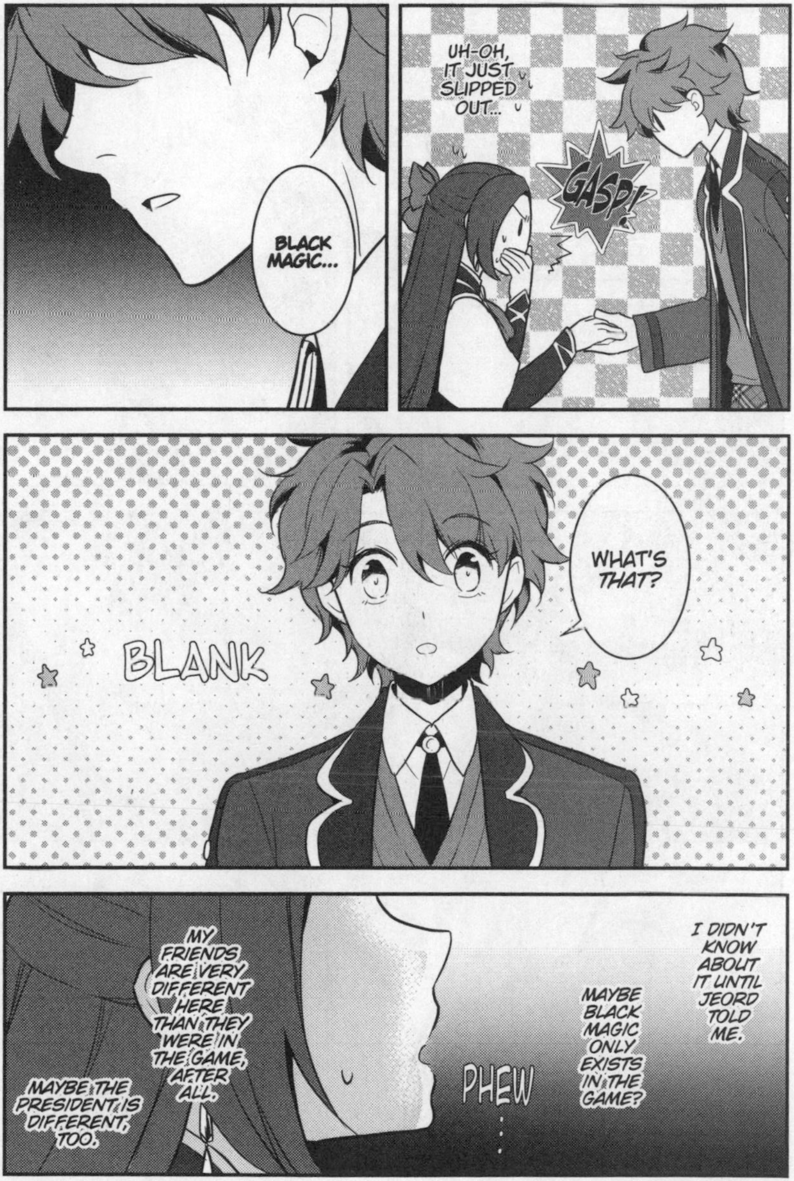
UH-OH, IT JUST SLIPPED OUT...
GASP!
BLACK MAGIC...
WHAT'S THAT?
BLANK
I DIDN'T KNOW ABOUT IT UNTIL JEORD TOLD ME.
MAYBE BLACK MAGIC ONLY EXISTS IN THE GAME?
PHEW
...
MY FRIENDS ARE VERY DIFFERENT HERE THAN THEY WERE IN THE GAME, AFTER ALL.
MAYBE THE PRESIDENT IS DIFFERENT, TOO.

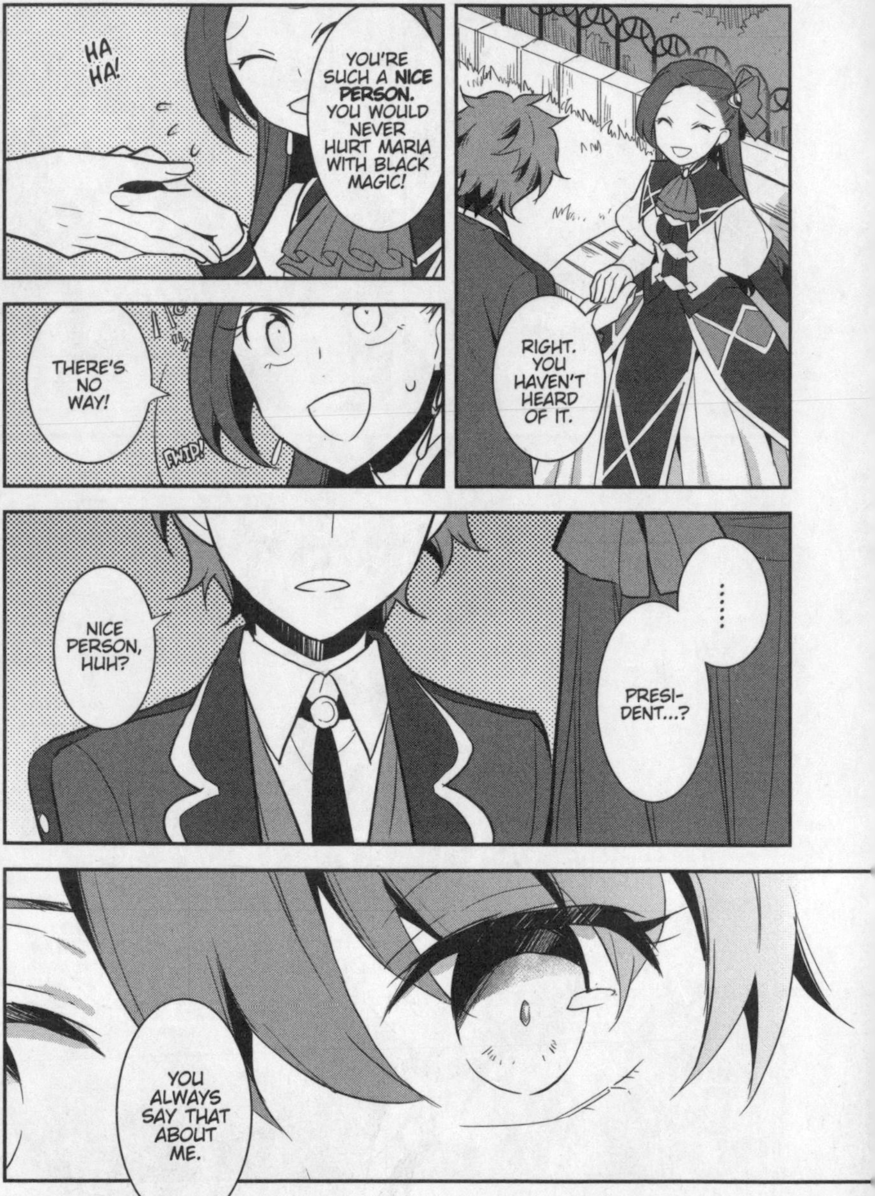
RIGHT. YOU HAVEN'T HEARD OF IT.
YOU'RE SUCH A **NICE PERSON.** YOU WOULD NEVER HURT MARIA WITH BLACK MAGIC!
HA HA!
THERE'S NO WAY!
FWIP!
...... PRESIDENT...?
NICE PERSON, HUH?
YOU ALWAYS SAY THAT ABOUT ME.

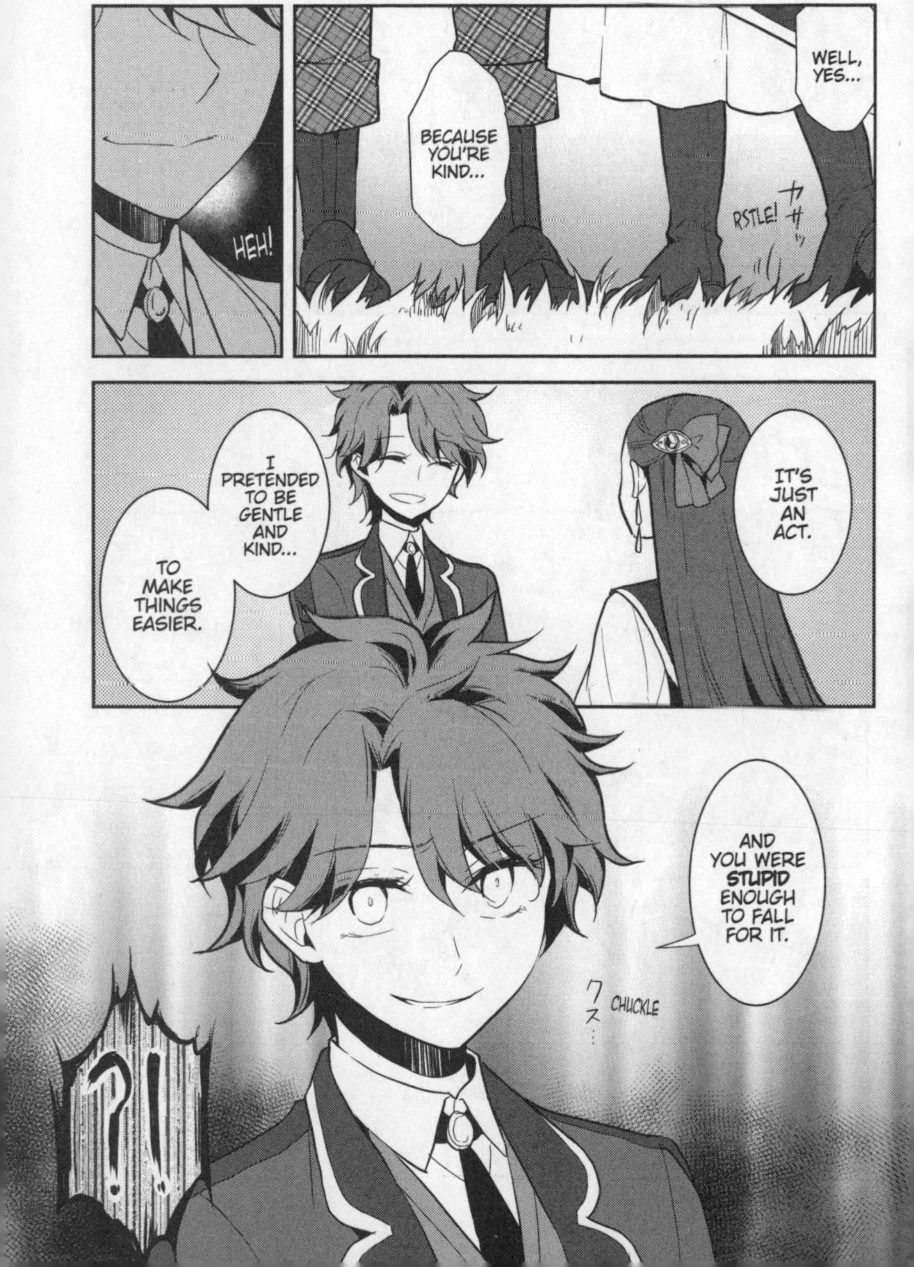
WELL, YES...
BECAUSE YOU'RE KIND...
RSTLE! カサッ
HEH!
IT'S JUST AN ACT.
I PRETENDED TO BE GENTLE AND KIND...
TO MAKE THINGS EASIER.
AND YOU WERE **STUPID** ENOUGH TO FALL FOR IT.
クス…
CHUCKLE
?!

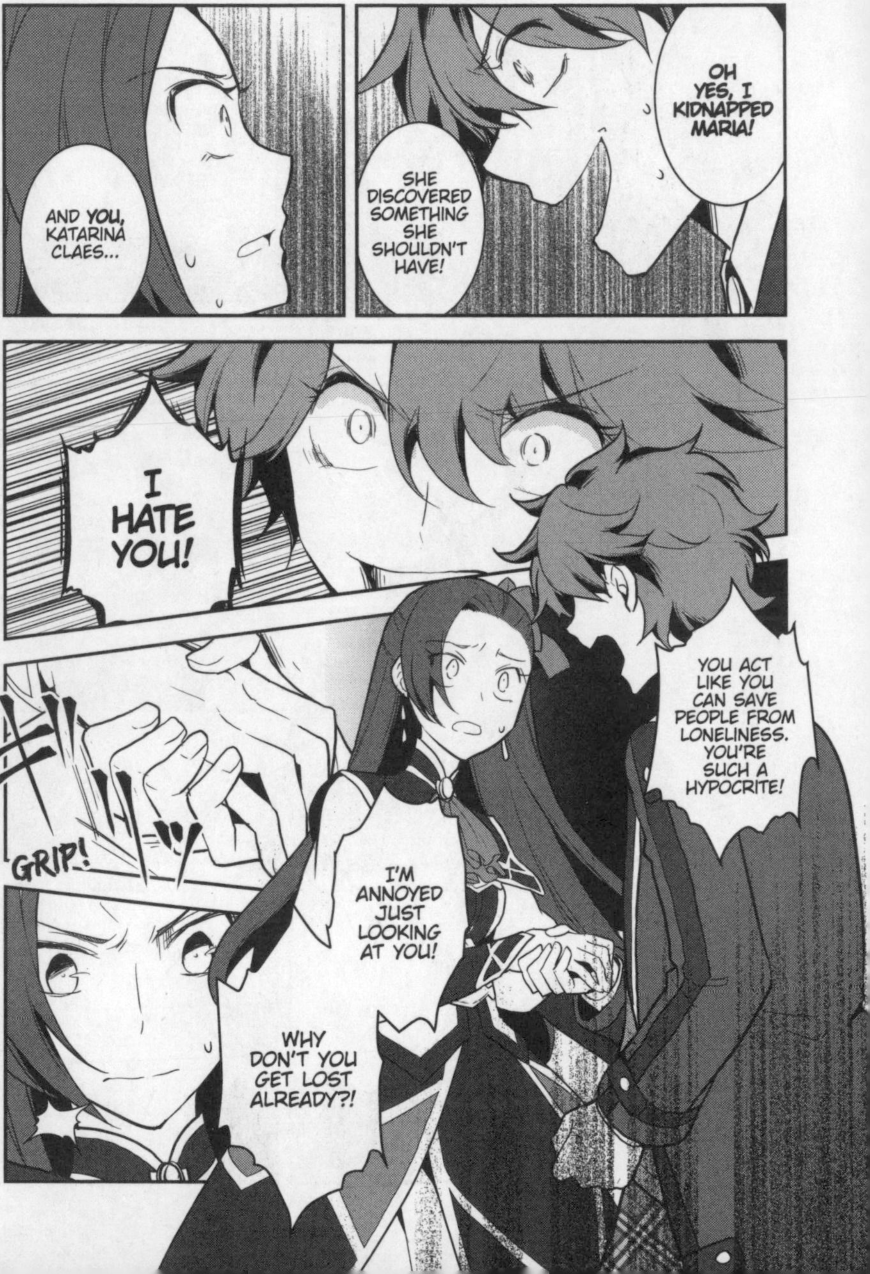

OH YES, I KIDNAPPED MARIA!
SHE DISCOVERED SOMETHING SHE SHOULDN'T HAVE!
AND YOU, KATARINA CLAES...
I HATE YOU!
YOU ACT LIKE YOU CAN SAVE PEOPLE FROM LONELINESS. YOU'RE SUCH A HYPOCRITE!
GRIP!
I'M ANNOYED JUST LOOKING AT YOU!
WHY DON'T YOU GET LOST ALREADY?!

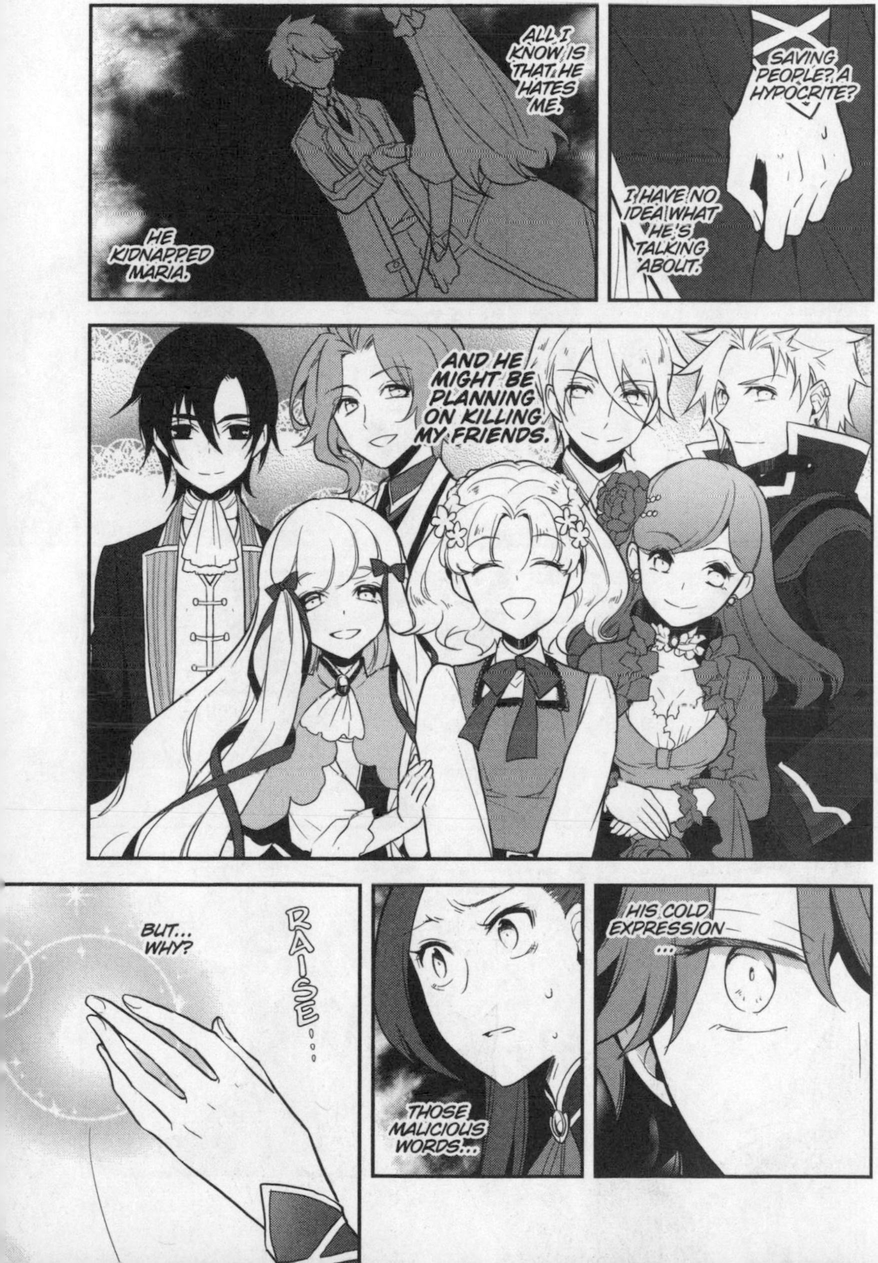
SAVING PEOPLE? A HYPOCRITE?
I HAVE NO IDEA WHAT HE'S TALKING ABOUT.
ALL I KNOW IS THAT HE HATES ME.
HE KIDNAPPED MARIA.
AND HE MIGHT BE PLANNING ON KILLING MY FRIENDS.
HIS COLD EXPRESSION...
THOSE MALICIOUS WORDS...
RAISE...
BUT... WHY?

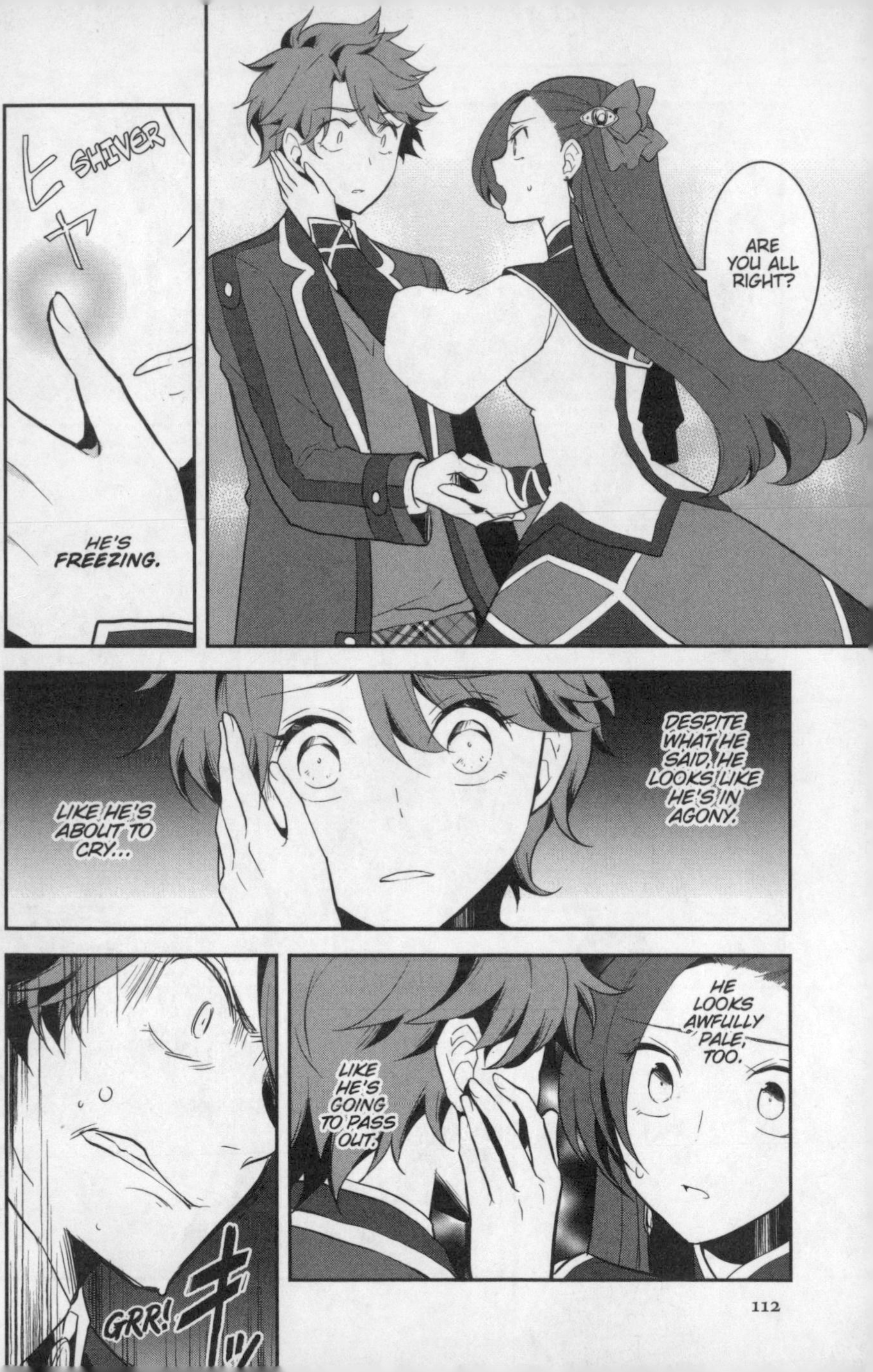
ARE YOU ALL RIGHT?
SHIVER
HE'S FREEZING.
DESPITE WHAT HE SAID, HE LOOKS LIKE HE'S IN AGONY.
LIKE HE'S ABOUT TO CRY...
HE LOOKS AWFULLY PALE, TOO.
LIKE HE'S GOING TO PASS OUT.
GRR!

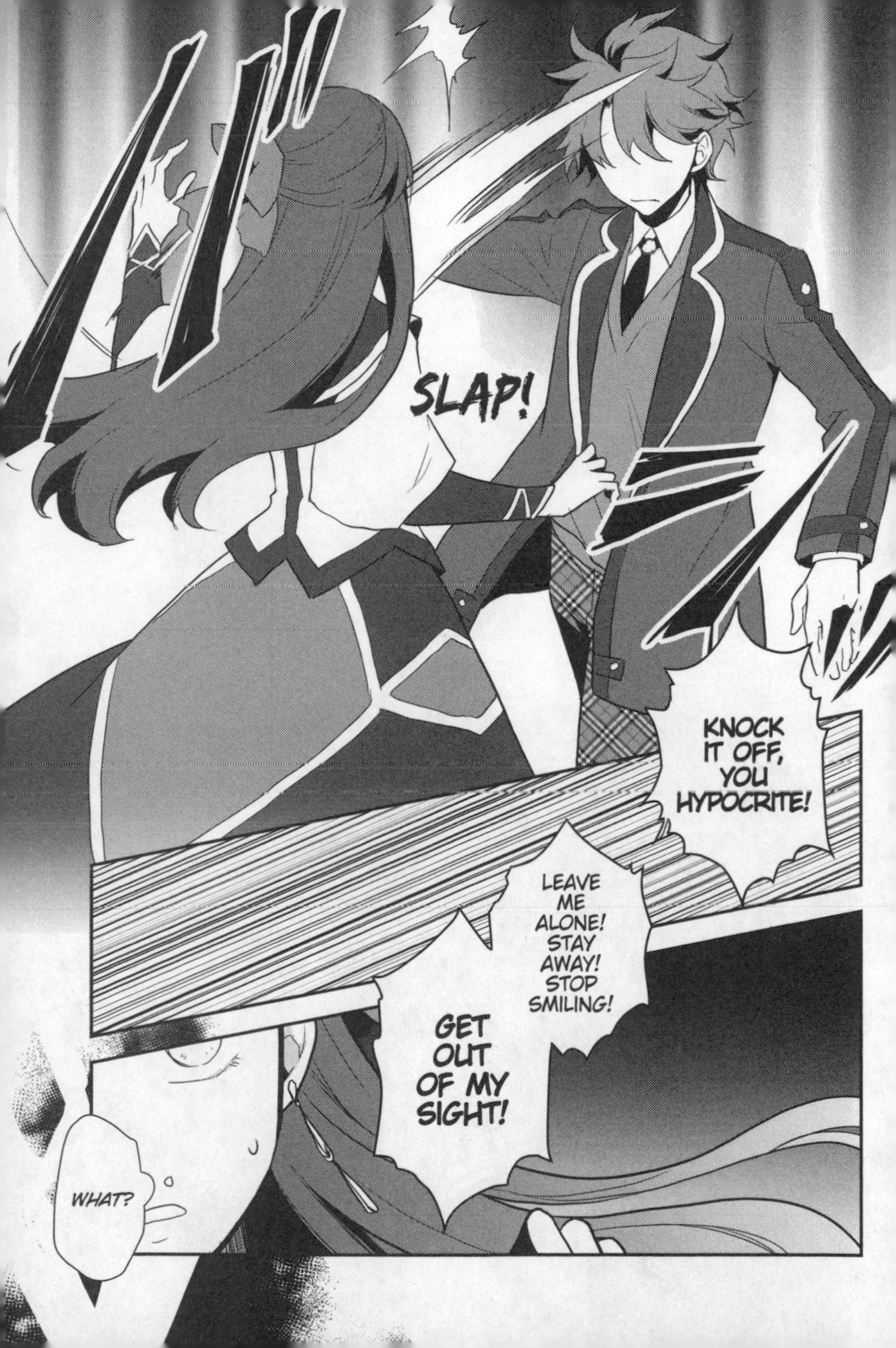
SLAP!
KNOCK IT OFF, YOU HYPOCRITE!
LEAVE ME ALONE! STAY AWAY! STOP SMILING!
GET OUT OF MY SIGHT!
WHAT?

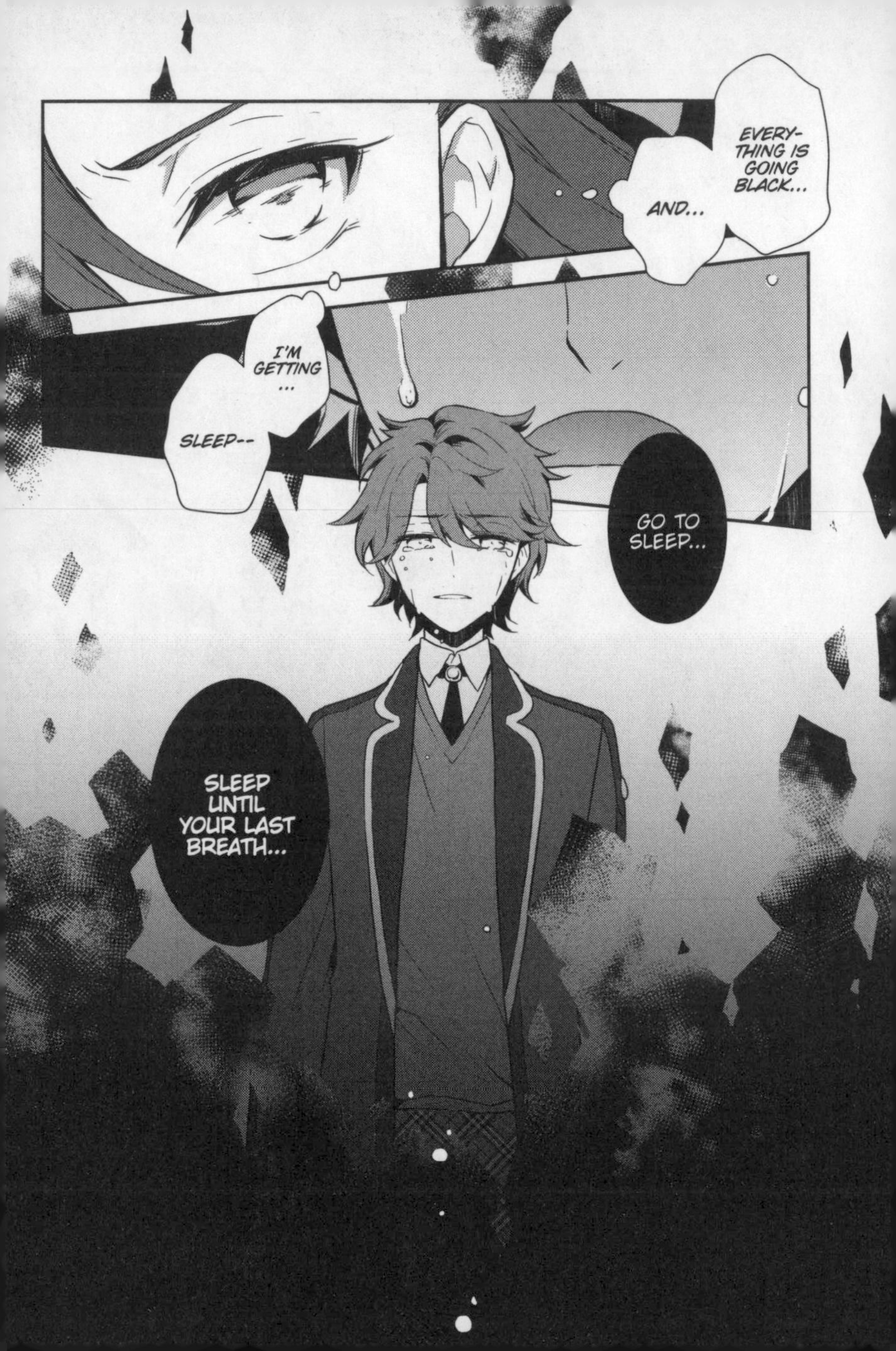
EVERY-THING IS GOING BLACK...
AND...
I'M GETTING ...
SLEEP--
GO TO SLEEP...
SLEEP UNTIL YOUR LAST BREATH...

Chapter 17

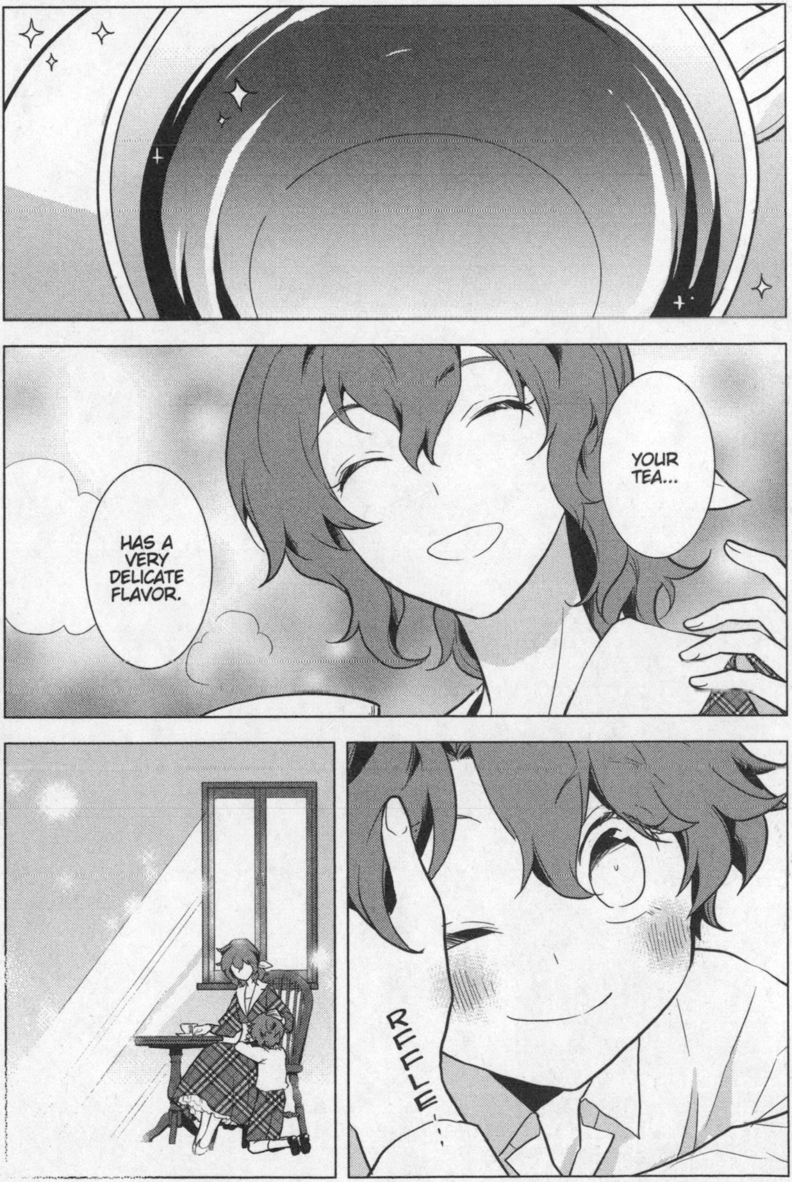
YOUR TEA...
HAS A VERY DELICATE FLAVOR.
RFFLE...

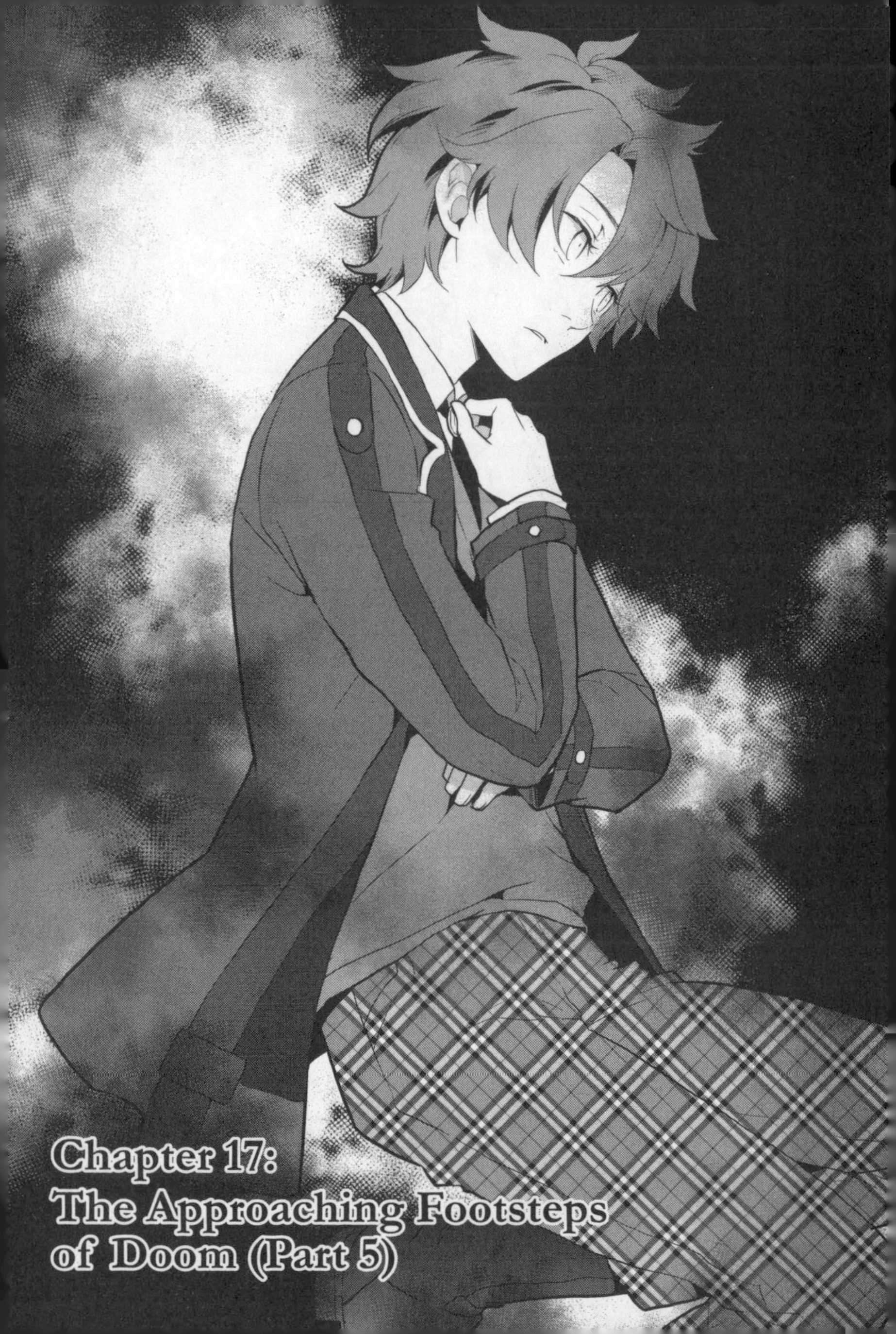

Chapter 17: The Approaching Footsteps of Doom (Part 5)

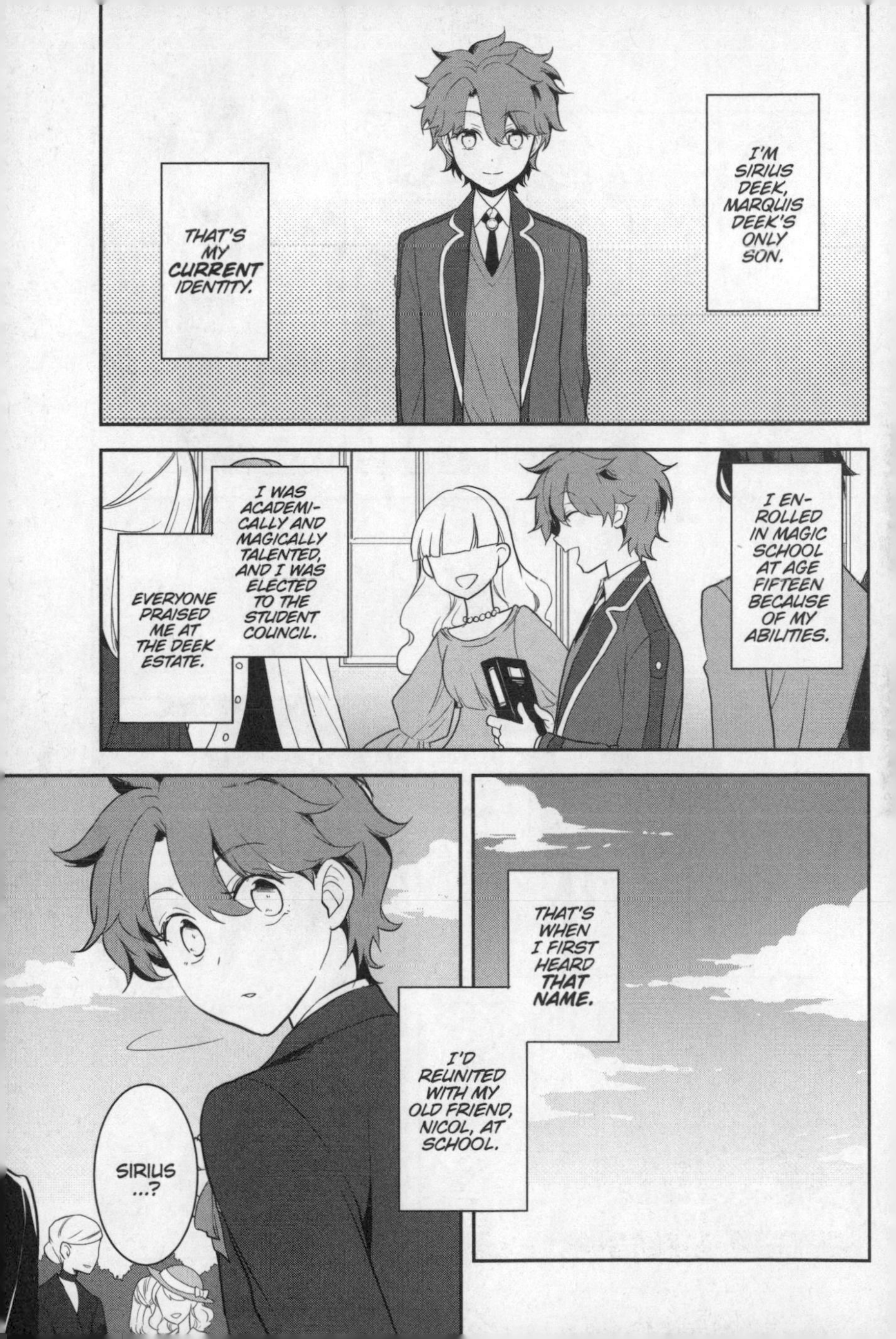
I'M SIRIUS DEEK, MARQUIS DEEK'S ONLY SON.
THAT'S MY **CURRENT** IDENTITY.
I EN-ROLLED IN MAGIC SCHOOL AT AGE FIFTEEN BECAUSE OF MY ABILITIES.
I WAS ACADEMI-CALLY AND MAGICALLY TALENTED, AND I WAS ELECTED TO THE STUDENT COUNCIL.
EVERYONE PRAISED ME AT THE DEEK ESTATE.
THAT'S WHEN I FIRST HEARD **THAT** NAME.
I'D REUNITED WITH MY OLD FRIEND, NICOL, AT SCHOOL.
SIRIUS ...?

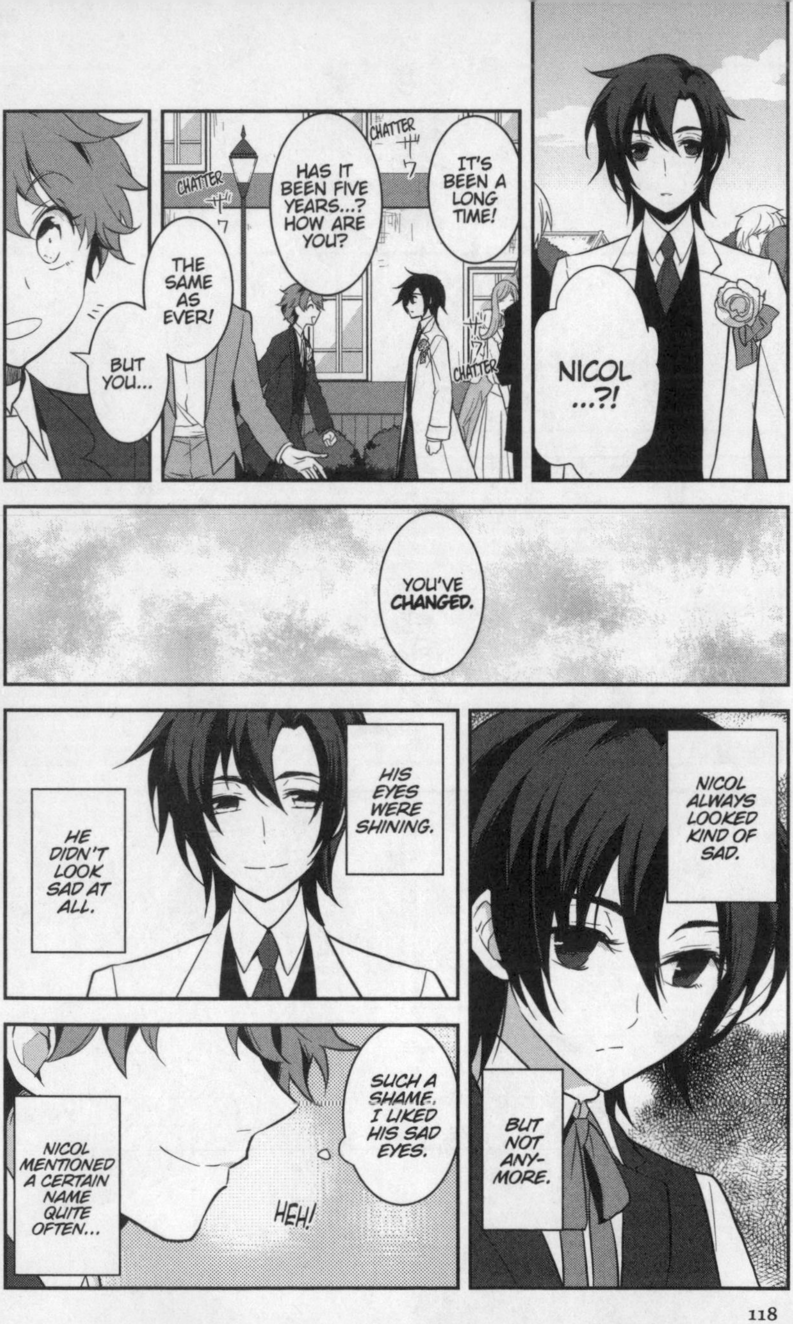
NICOL ...?!
IT'S BEEN A LONG TIME!
CHATTER
HAS IT BEEN FIVE YEARS...? HOW ARE YOU?
CHATTER
THE SAME AS EVER!
CHATTER
BUT YOU...
YOU'VE CHANGED.
NICOL ALWAYS LOOKED KIND OF SAD.
BUT NOT ANYMORE.
HIS EYES WERE SHINING.
HE DIDN'T LOOK SAD AT ALL.
SUCH A SHAME. I LIKED HIS SAD EYES.
HEH!
NICOL MENTIONED A CERTAIN NAME QUITE OFTEN...

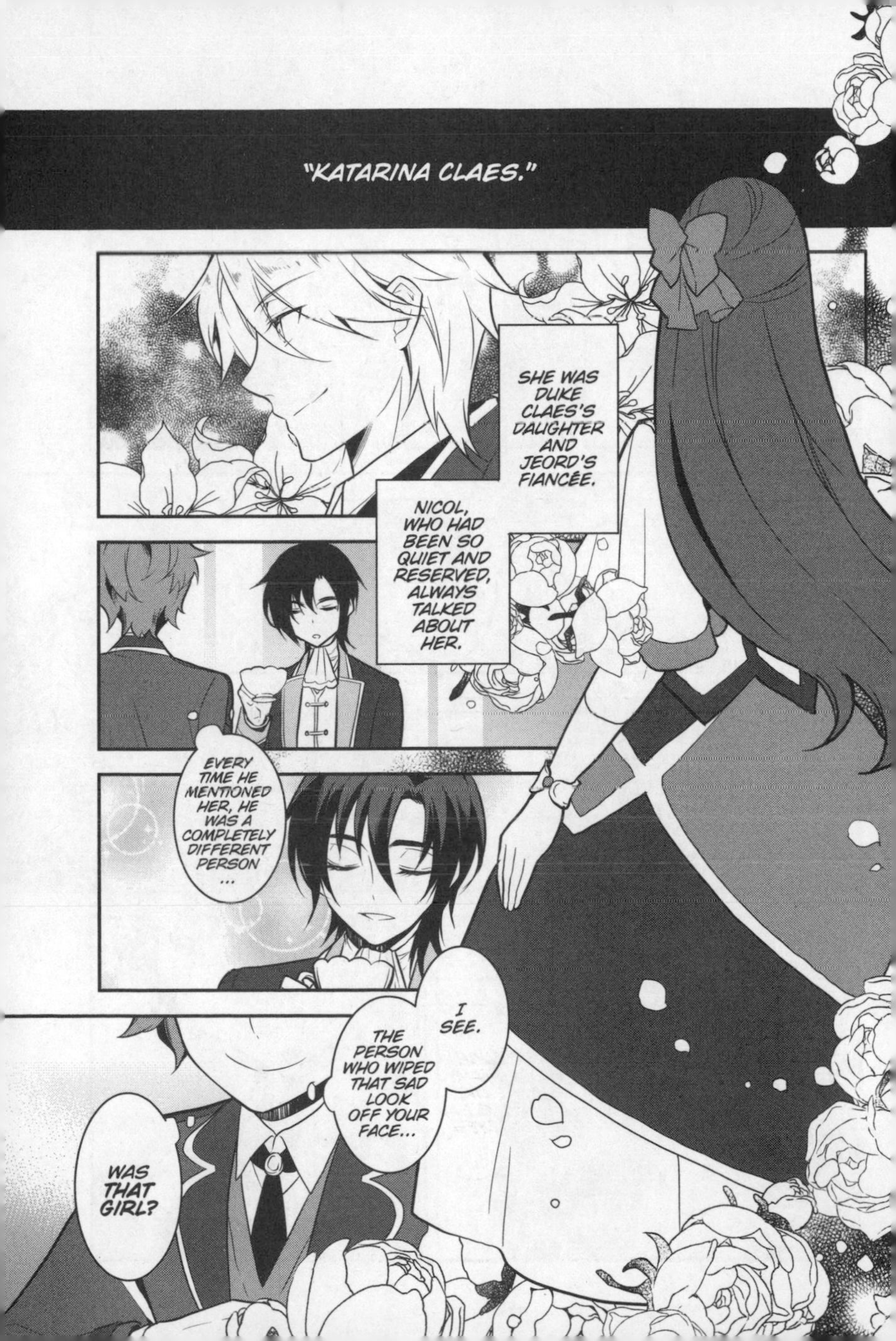
"KATARINA CLAES."
SHE WAS DUKE CLAES'S DAUGHTER AND JEORD'S FIANCÉE.
NICOL, WHO HAD BEEN SO QUIET AND RESERVED, ALWAYS TALKED ABOUT HER.
EVERY TIME HE MENTIONED HER, HE WAS A COMPLETELY DIFFERENT PERSON ...
I SEE.
THE PERSON WHO WIPED THAT SAD LOOK OFF YOUR FACE...
WAS THAT GIRL?

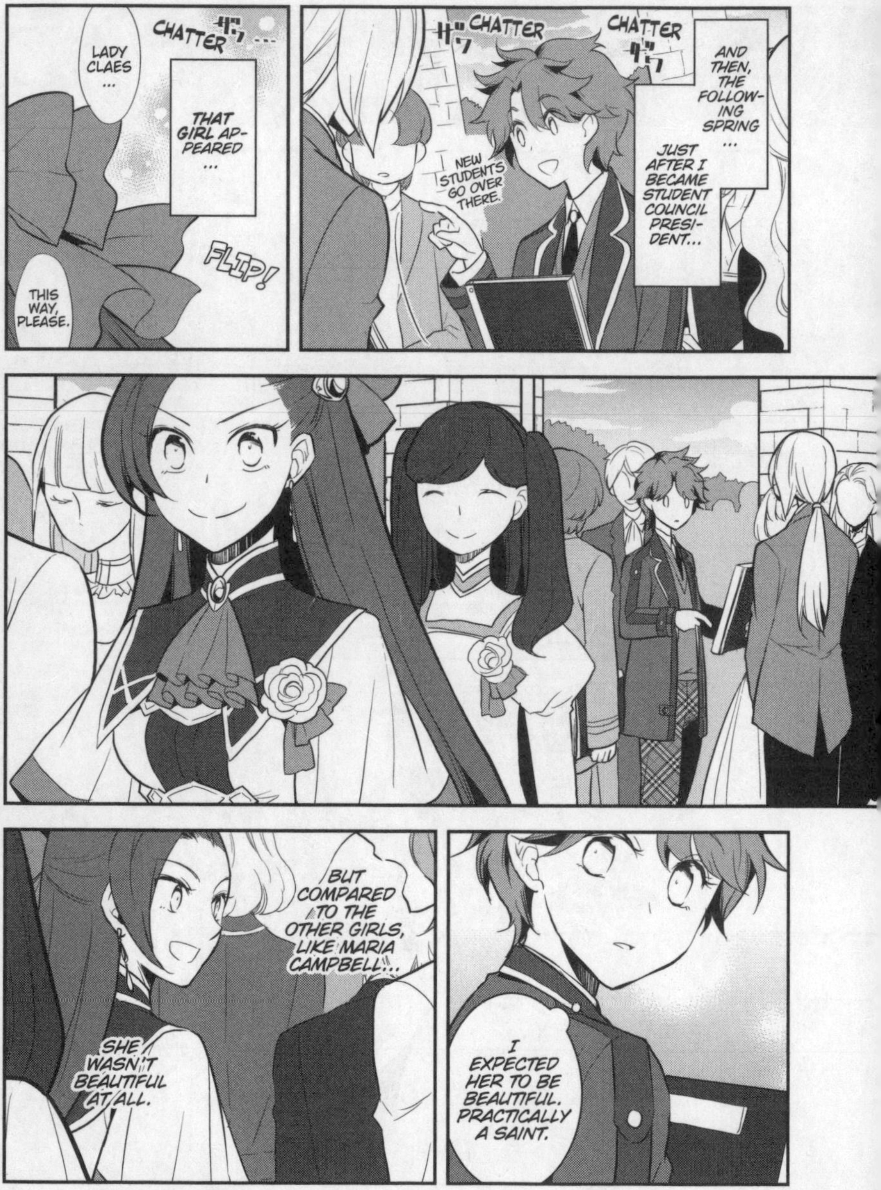
CHATTER
CHATTER
AND THEN, THE FOLLOWING SPRING...
JUST AFTER I BECAME STUDENT COUNCIL PRESIDENT...
NEW STUDENTS GO OVER THERE.
CHATTER...
LADY CLAES...
THAT GIRL APPEARED...
FLIP!
THIS WAY, PLEASE.
I EXPECTED HER TO BE BEAUTIFUL. PRACTICALLY A SAINT.
BUT COMPARED TO THE OTHER GIRLS, LIKE MARIA CAMPBELL...
SHE WASN'T BEAUTIFUL AT ALL.

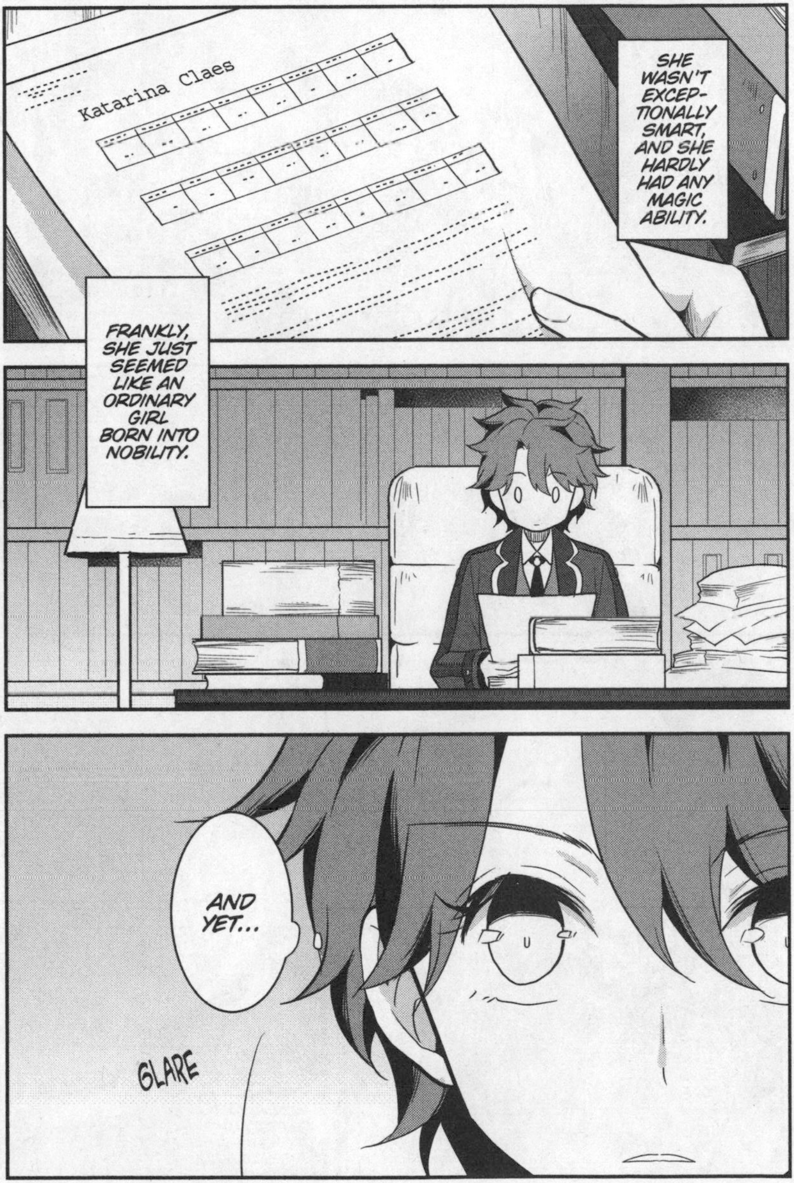
Katarina Claes
SHE WASN'T EXCEP-TIONALLY SMART, AND SHE HARDLY HAD ANY MAGIC ABILITY.
FRANKLY, SHE JUST SEEMED LIKE AN ORDINARY GIRL BORN INTO NOBILITY.
AND YET...
GLARE

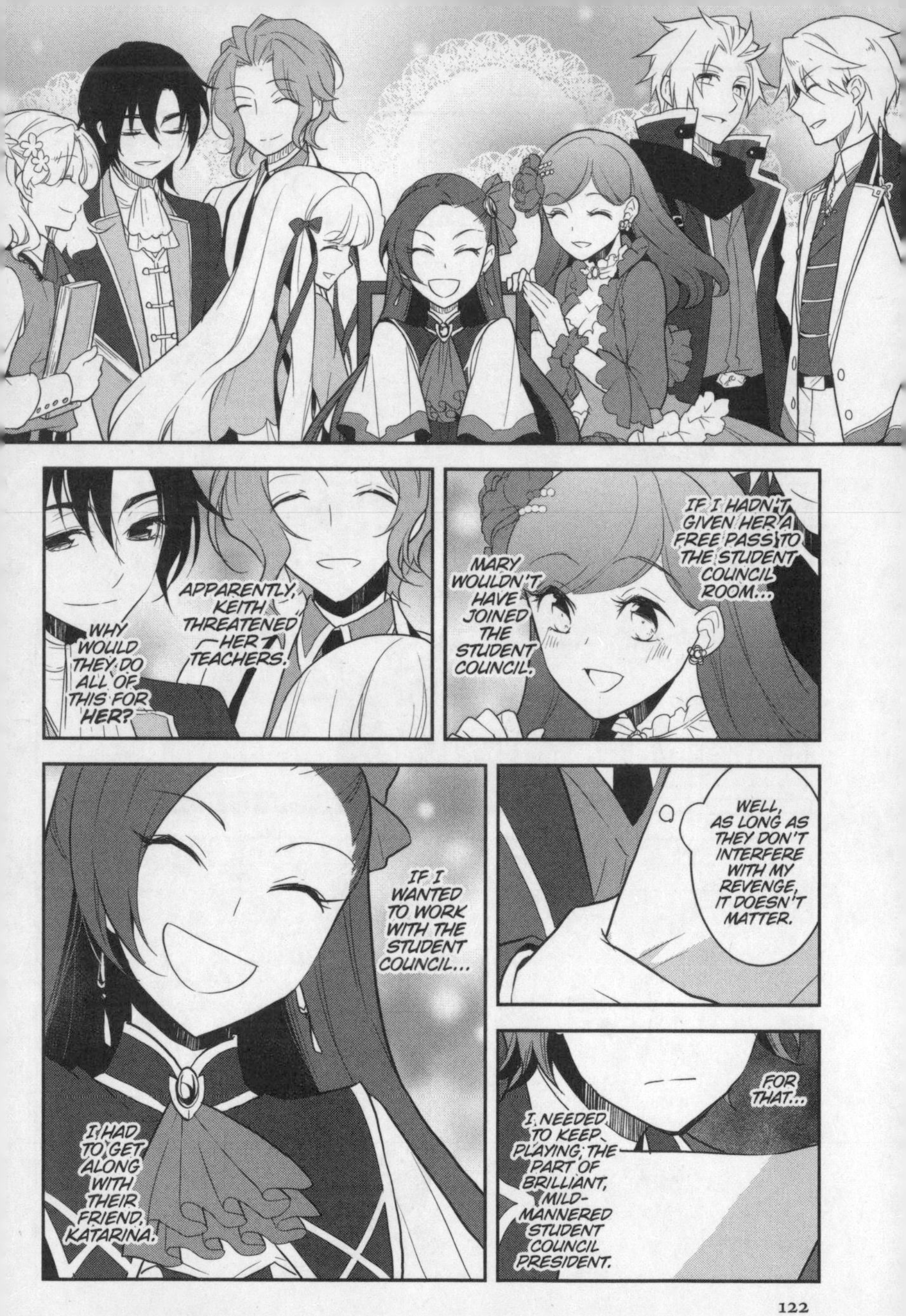
IF I HADN'T GIVEN HER A FREE PASS TO THE STUDENT COUNCIL ROOM...
MARY WOULDN'T HAVE JOINED THE STUDENT COUNCIL.
APPARENTLY, KEITH THREATENED HER TEACHERS.
WHY WOULD THEY DO ALL OF THIS FOR HER?
WELL, AS LONG AS THEY DON'T INTERFERE WITH MY REVENGE, IT DOESN'T MATTER.
FOR THAT...
I NEEDED TO KEEP PLAYING THE PART OF BRILLIANT, MILD-MANNERED STUDENT COUNCIL PRESIDENT.
IF I WANTED TO WORK WITH THE STUDENT COUNCIL...
I HAD TO GET ALONG WITH THEIR FRIEND, KATARINA.

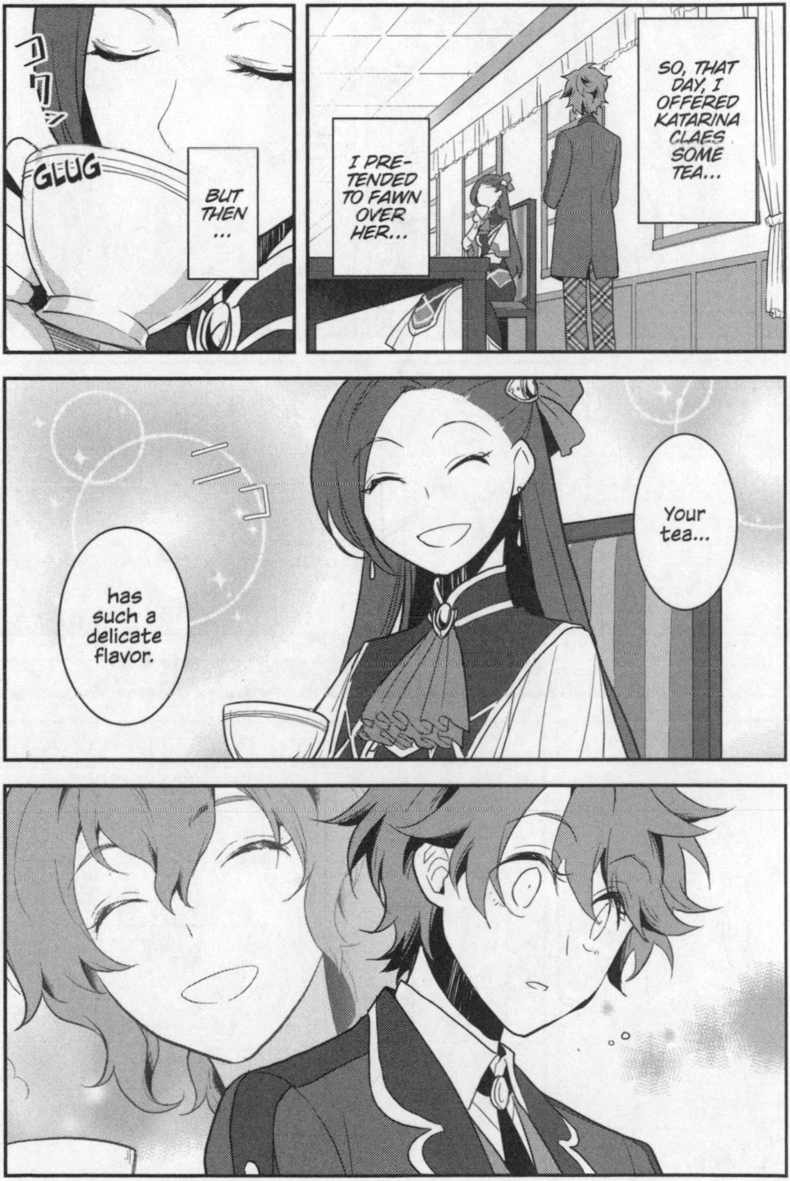
SO, THAT DAY, I OFFERED KATARINA CLAES SOME TEA...
I PRE-TENDED TO FAWN OVER HER...
BUT THEN...
GLUG
Your tea...
has such a delicate flavor.

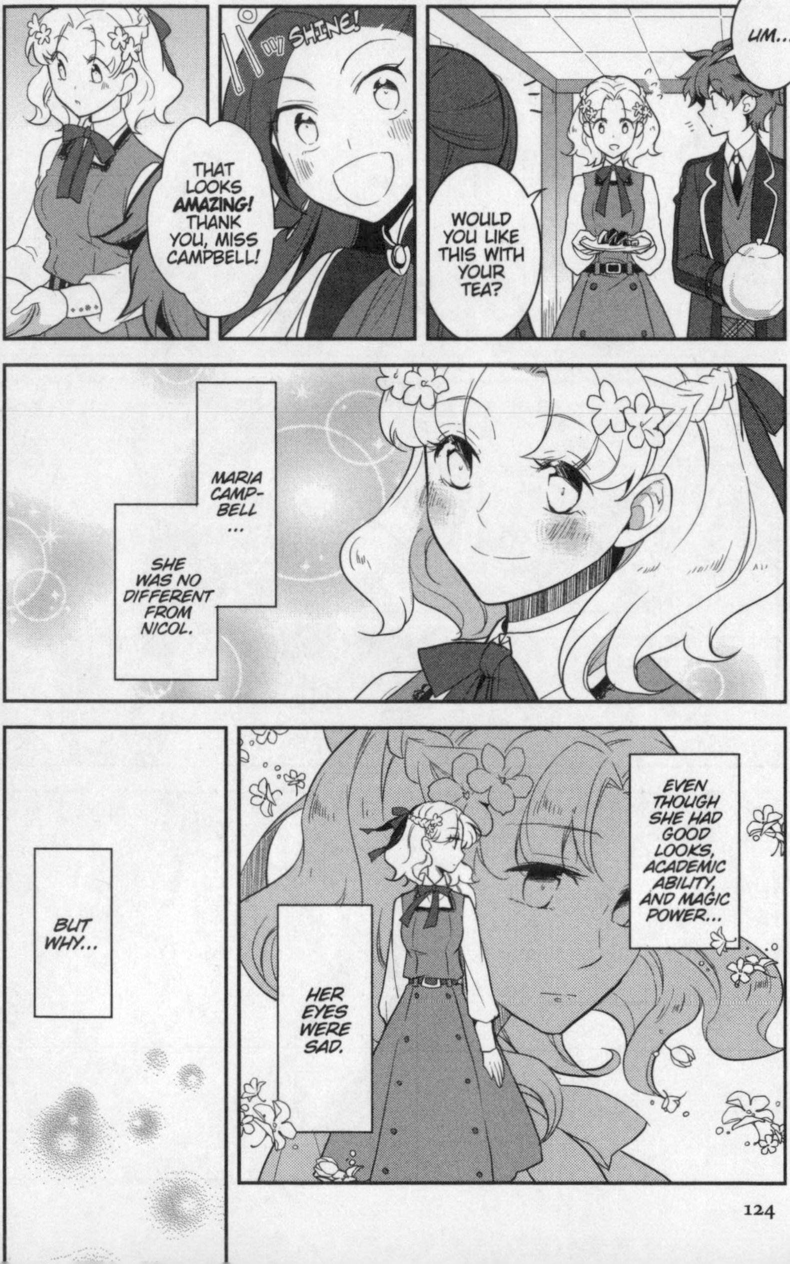
UM...
WOULD YOU LIKE THIS WITH YOUR TEA?
SHINE!
THAT LOOKS AMAZING! THANK YOU, MISS CAMPBELL!
MARIA CAMPBELL...
SHE WAS NO DIFFERENT FROM NICOL.
EVEN THOUGH SHE HAD GOOD LOOKS, ACADEMIC ABILITY, AND MAGIC POWER...
HER EYES WERE SAD.
BUT WHY...

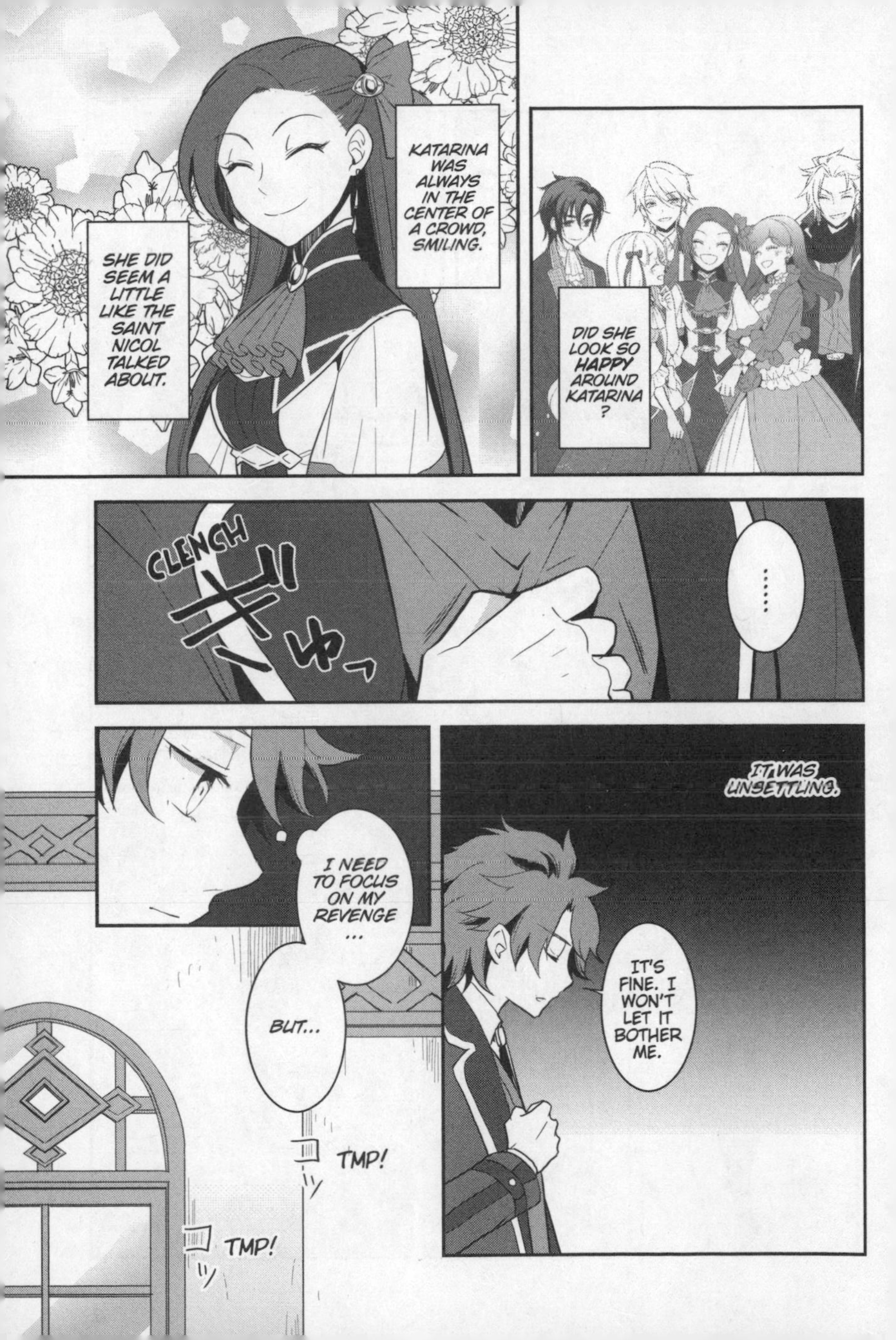
DID SHE LOOK SO HAPPY AROUND KATARINA?
KATARINA WAS ALWAYS IN THE CENTER OF A CROWD, SMILING.
SHE DID SEEM A LITTLE LIKE THE SAINT NICOL TALKED ABOUT.
......
CLENCH
ぎゅっ
IT WAS UNSETTLING.
IT'S FINE. I WON'T LET IT BOTHER ME.
I NEED TO FOCUS ON MY REVENGE...
BUT...
コツ
TMP!
コツ
TMP!

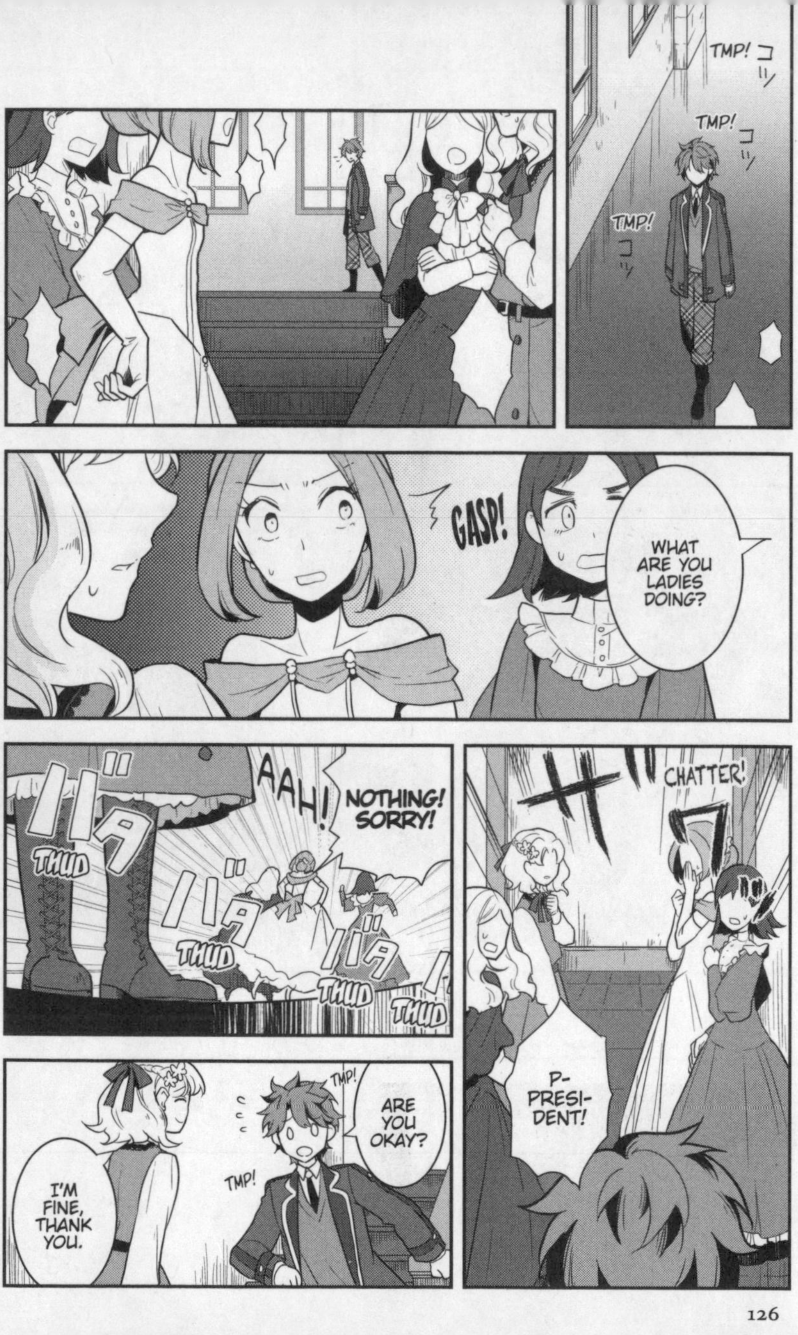
TMP!
コッ
TMP!
コッ
TMP!
コッ
WHAT ARE YOU LADIES DOING?
GASP!
CHATTER!
P-PRESIDENT!
AAH!
NOTHING! SORRY!
THUD
THUD
THUD
THUD
TMP!
ARE YOU OKAY?
TMP!
I'M FINE, THANK YOU.

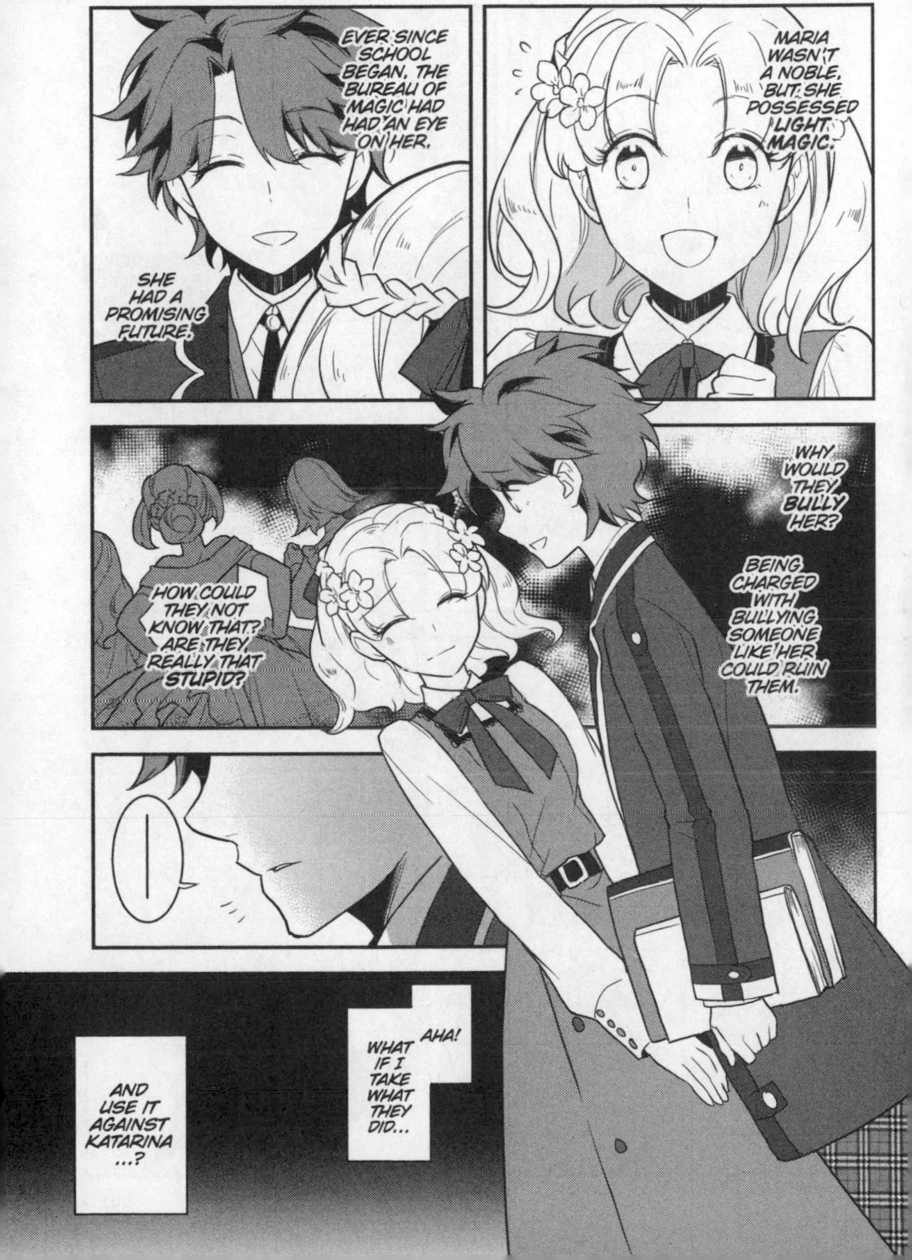
MARIA WASN'T A NOBLE, BUT SHE POSSESSED LIGHT MAGIC.
EVER SINCE SCHOOL BEGAN, THE BUREAU OF MAGIC HAD HAD AN EYE ON HER.
SHE HAD A PROMISING FUTURE.
WHY WOULD THEY BULLY HER?
BEING CHARGED WITH BULLYING SOMEONE LIKE HER COULD RUIN THEM.
HOW COULD THEY NOT KNOW THAT? ARE THEY REALLY THAT STUPID?
—
AHA! WHAT IF I TAKE WHAT THEY DID...
AND USE IT AGAINST KATARINA...?

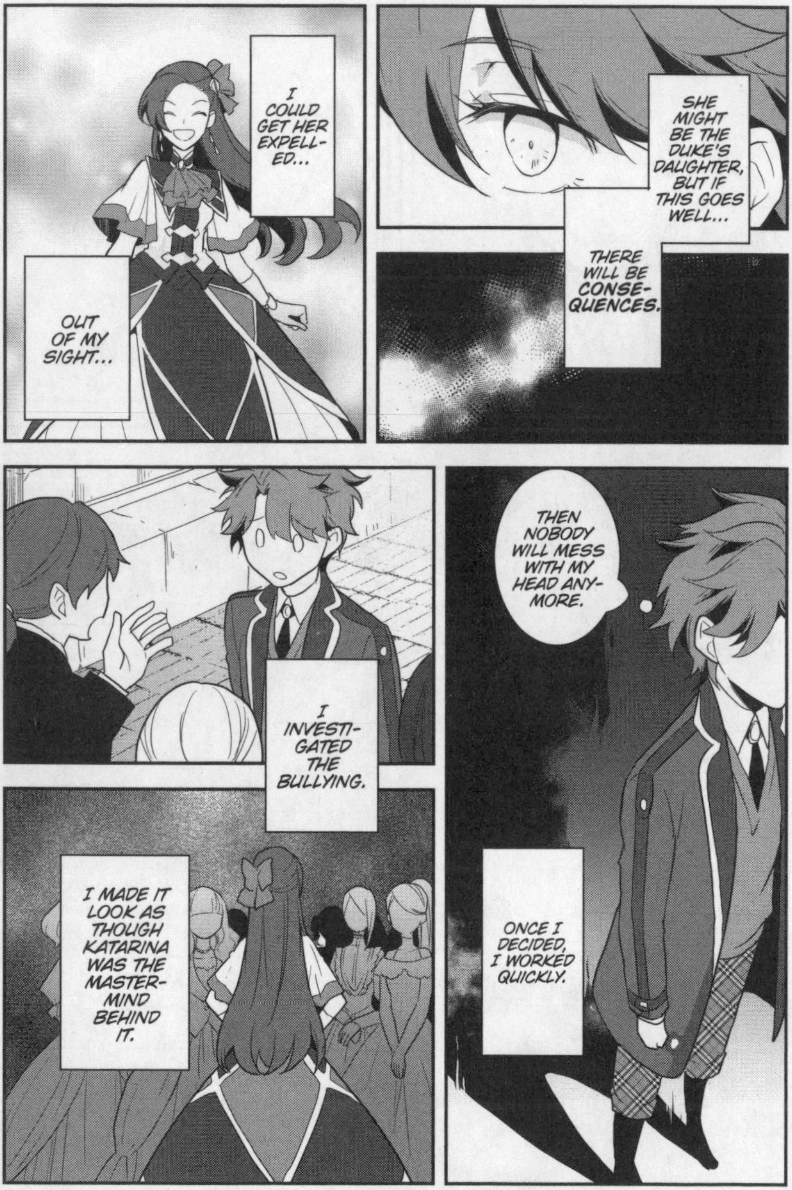
SHE MIGHT BE THE DUKE'S DAUGHTER, BUT IF THIS GOES WELL...
THERE WILL BE CONSEQUENCES.
I COULD GET HER EXPELLED...
OUT OF MY SIGHT...
THEN NOBODY WILL MESS WITH MY HEAD ANYMORE.
ONCE I DECIDED, I WORKED QUICKLY.
I INVESTIGATED THE BULLYING.
I MADE IT LOOK AS THOUGH KATARINA WAS THE MASTERMIND BEHIND IT.

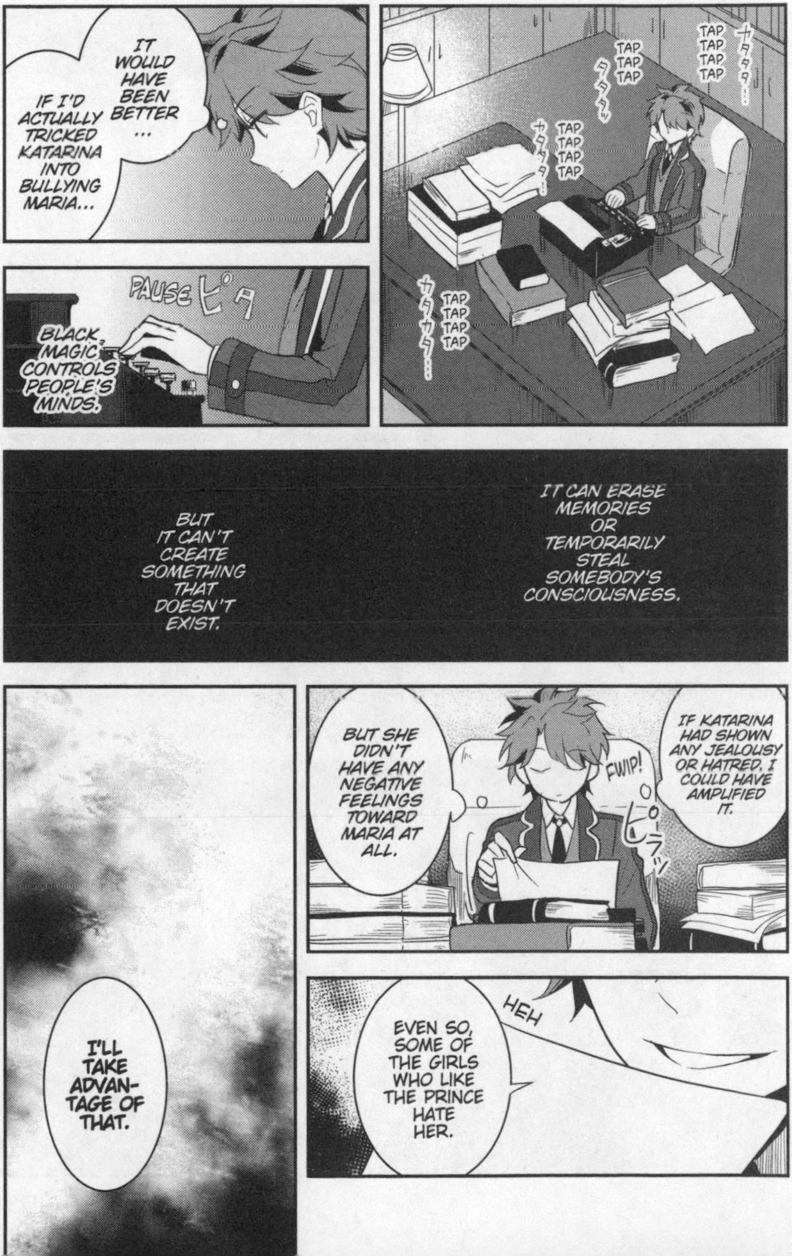
TAP TAP TAP TAP
TAP TAP TAP
TAP TAP TAP TAP
TAP TAP TAP TAP
IT WOULD HAVE BEEN BETTER...
IF I'D ACTUALLY TRICKED KATARINA INTO BULLYING MARIA...
PAUSE
BLACK MAGIC CONTROLS PEOPLE'S MINDS.
IT CAN ERASE MEMORIES OR TEMPORARILY STEAL SOMEBODY'S CONSCIOUSNESS.
BUT IT CAN'T CREATE SOMETHING THAT DOESN'T EXIST.
IF KATARINA HAD SHOWN ANY JEALOUSY OR HATRED, I COULD HAVE AMPLIFIED IT.
FWIP!
BUT SHE DIDN'T HAVE ANY NEGATIVE FEELINGS TOWARD MARIA AT ALL.
HEH
EVEN SO, SOME OF THE GIRLS WHO LIKE THE PRINCE HATE HER.
I'LL TAKE ADVANTAGE OF THAT.

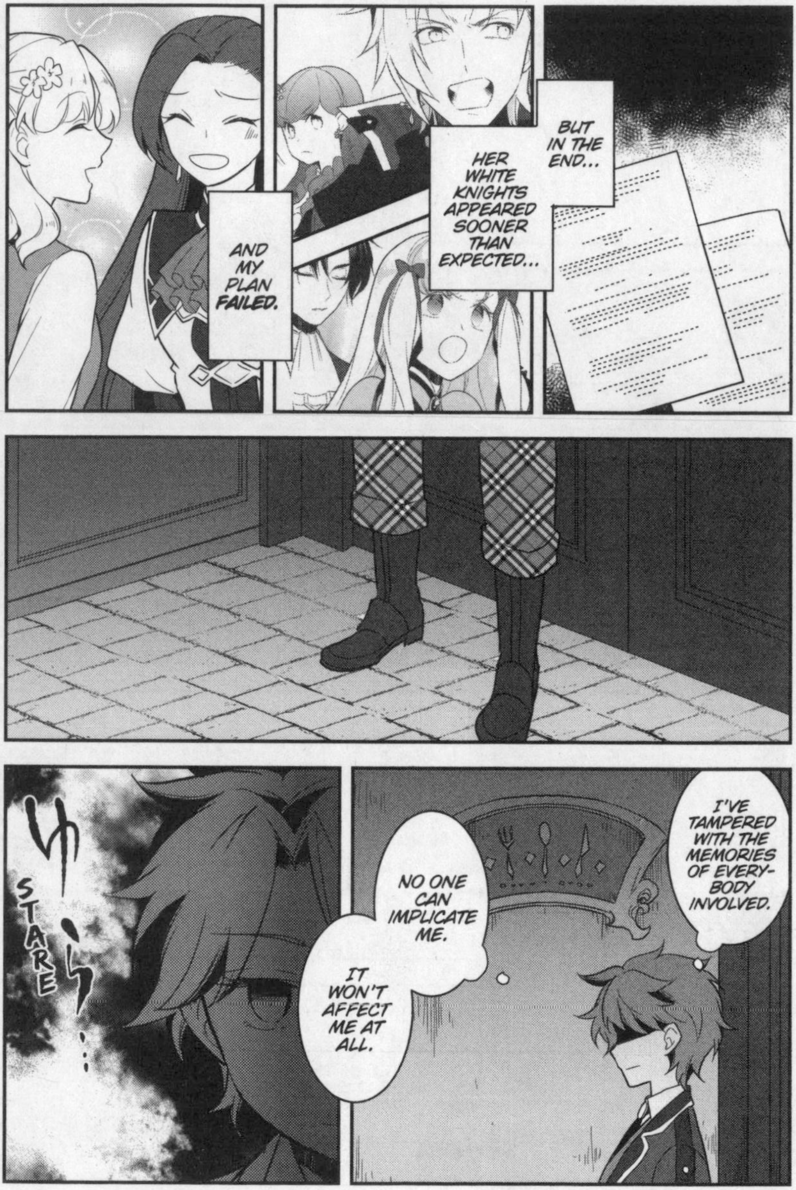
BUT IN THE END...
HER WHITE KNIGHTS APPEARED SOONER THAN EXPECTED...
AND MY PLAN FAILED.
I'VE TAMPERED WITH THE MEMORIES OF EVERY-BODY INVOLVED.
NO ONE CAN IMPLICATE ME.
IT WON'T AFFECT ME AT ALL.
ゆら
STARE...

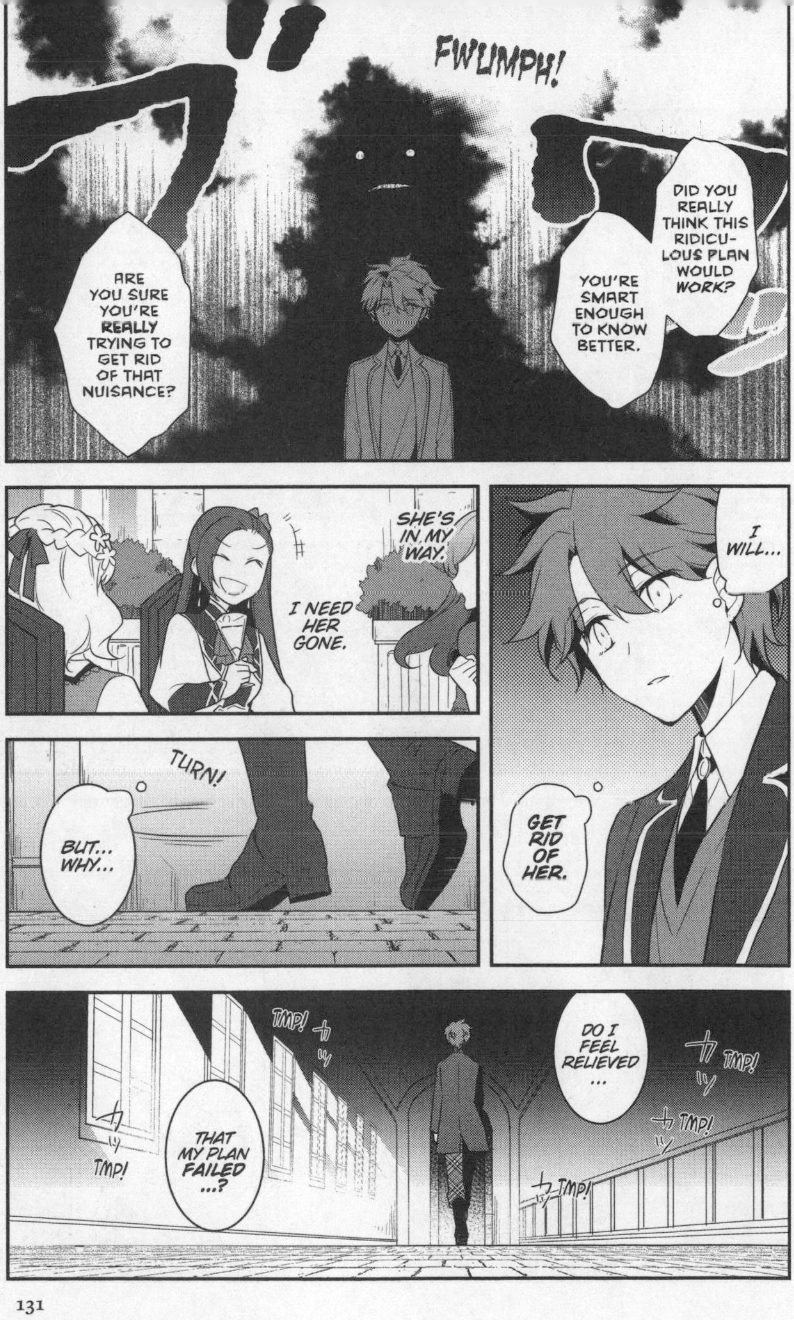
FWUMPH!
DID YOU REALLY THINK THIS RIDICU-LOUS PLAN WOULD WORK?
YOU'RE SMART ENOUGH TO KNOW BETTER.
ARE YOU SURE YOU'RE REALLY TRYING TO GET RID OF THAT NUISANCE?
I WILL...
GET RID OF HER.
SHE'S IN MY WAY.
I NEED HER GONE.
TURN!
BUT... WHY...
TMP!
DO I FEEL RELIEVED ...
TMP!
TMP!
TMP!
THAT MY PLAN FAILED ...?
TMP!

STUDENT
COUNCIL

THE INCIDENT SHOULD HAVE ENDED THEN AND THERE.

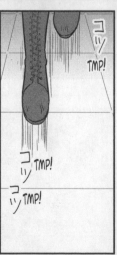

コツ TMP!

コツ TMP!

コツ TMP!

TMP!
コツ

KA-
CHAK!

PRESIDENT, MAY I HAVE A WORD WITH YOU?

WHAT IS IT, MISS MARIA?

LUNCH BREAK IS ALMOST OV--

I SAW YOU GLARING AT MISS KATARINA.

. . . . .

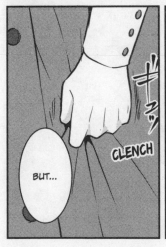

CLENCH

BUT...

I ASSUMED I HAD IMAGINED IT...

BUT DURING TODAY'S INCIDENT, I REMEMBERED.

I DIDN'T WANT TO BELIEVE YOU WERE INVOLVED...

SO I WANTED TO BE CERTAIN.

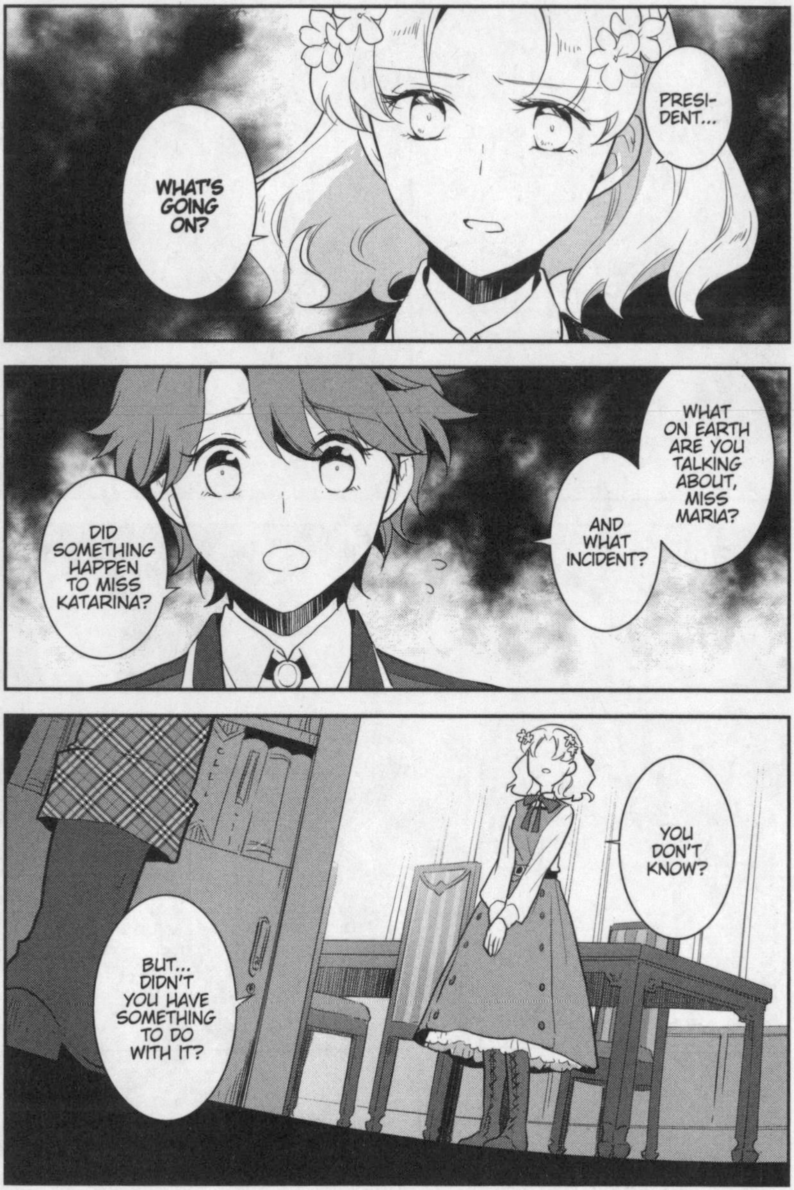
PRESIDENT...
WHAT'S GOING ON?
WHAT ON EARTH ARE YOU TALKING ABOUT, MISS MARIA?
AND WHAT INCIDENT?
DID SOMETHING HAPPEN TO MISS KATARINA?
YOU DON'T KNOW?
BUT... DIDN'T YOU HAVE SOMETHING TO DO WITH IT?

DOOM
THE SAME DARK PRESENCE...
THAT WAS BEHIND THE PEOPLE WHO CONDEMNED MISS KATARINA...
IS ALL AROUND YOU!
?!
WHAT...?!

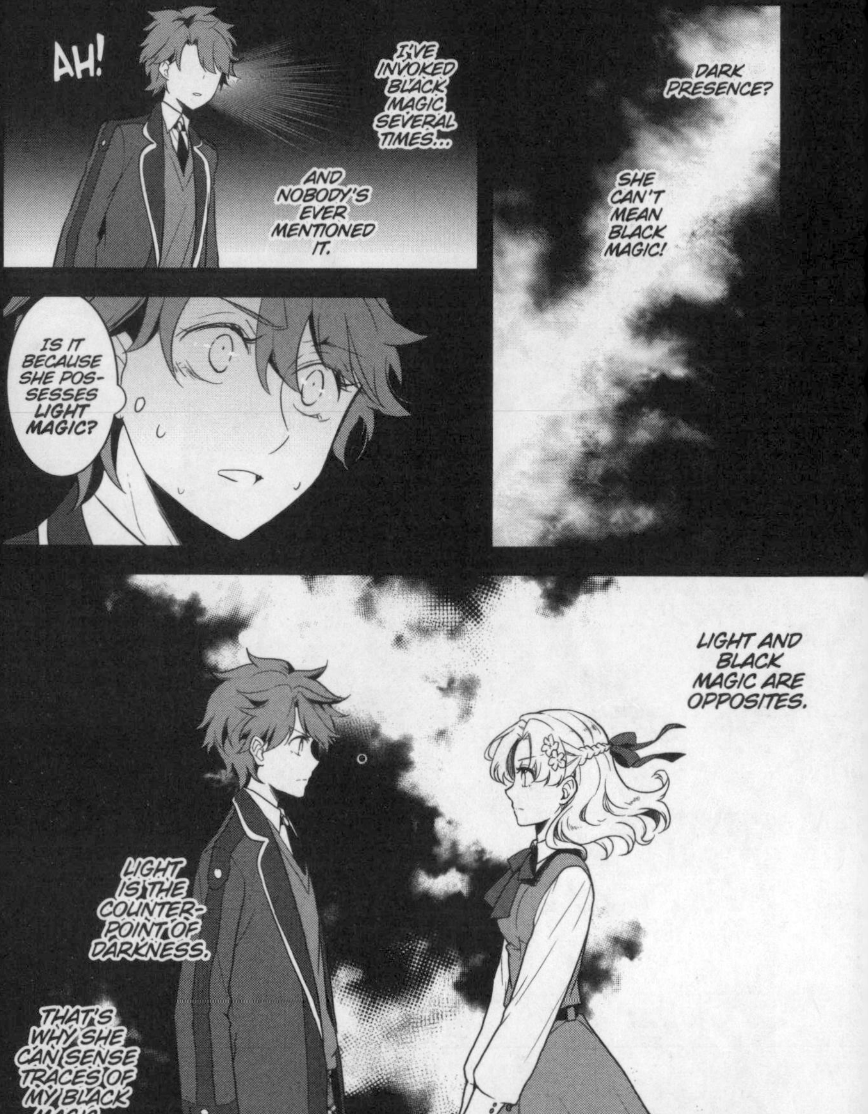
DARK PRESENCE?
SHE CAN'T MEAN BLACK MAGIC!
I'VE INVOKED BLACK MAGIC SEVERAL TIMES...
AND NOBODY'S EVER MENTIONED IT.
AH!
IS IT BECAUSE SHE POS-SESSES LIGHT MAGIC?
LIGHT AND BLACK MAGIC ARE OPPOSITES.
LIGHT IS THE COUNTER-POINT OF DARKNESS.
THAT'S WHY SHE CAN SENSE TRACES OF MY BLACK MAGIC...

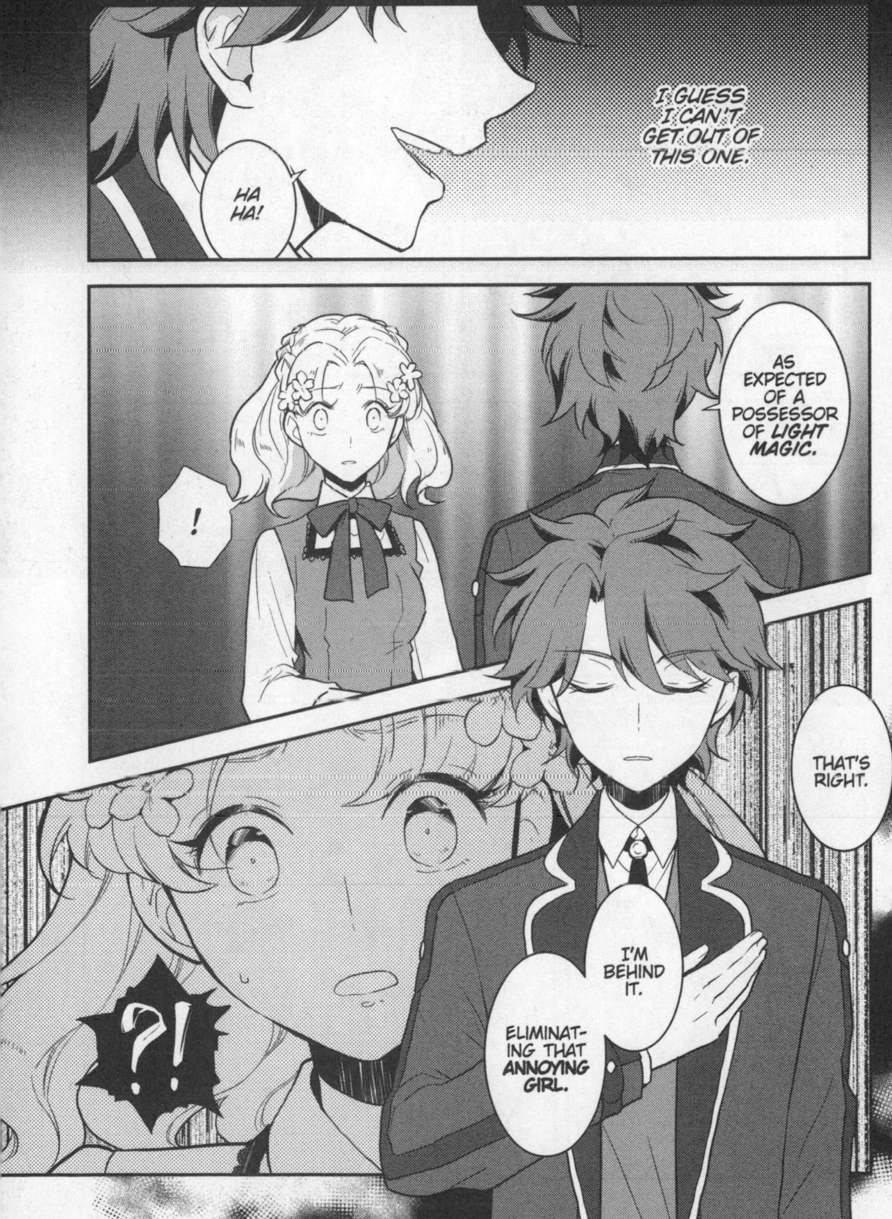
I GUESS I CAN'T GET OUT OF THIS ONE.
HA HA!
AS EXPECTED OF A POSSESSOR OF **LIGHT MAGIC.**
!
THAT'S RIGHT.
I'M BEHIND IT.
ELIMINATING THAT **ANNOYING GIRL.**
?!

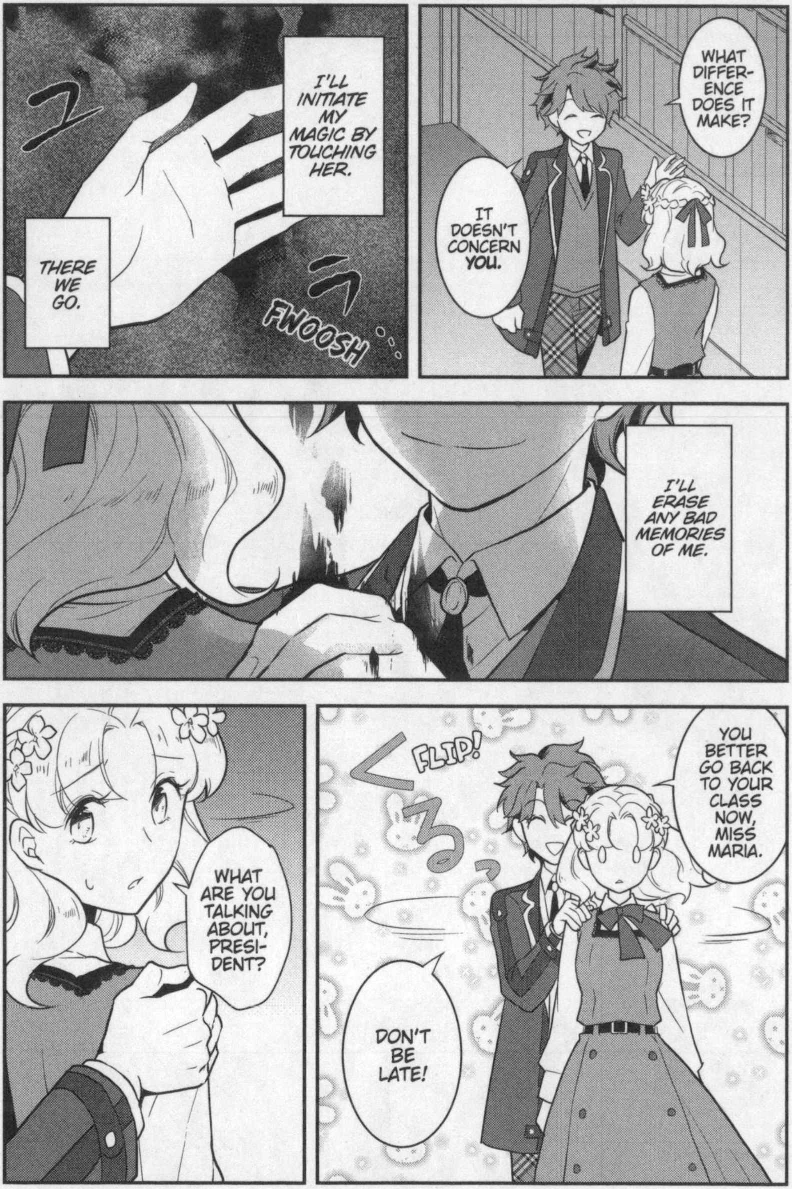
WHAT DIFFERENCE DOES IT MAKE?
IT DOESN'T CONCERN YOU.
I'LL INITIATE MY MAGIC BY TOUCHING HER.
FWOOSH
THERE WE GO.
I'LL ERASE ANY BAD MEMORIES OF ME.
FLIP!
YOU BETTER GO BACK TO YOUR CLASS NOW, MISS MARIA.
DON'T BE LATE!
WHAT ARE YOU TALKING ABOUT, PRESIDENT?

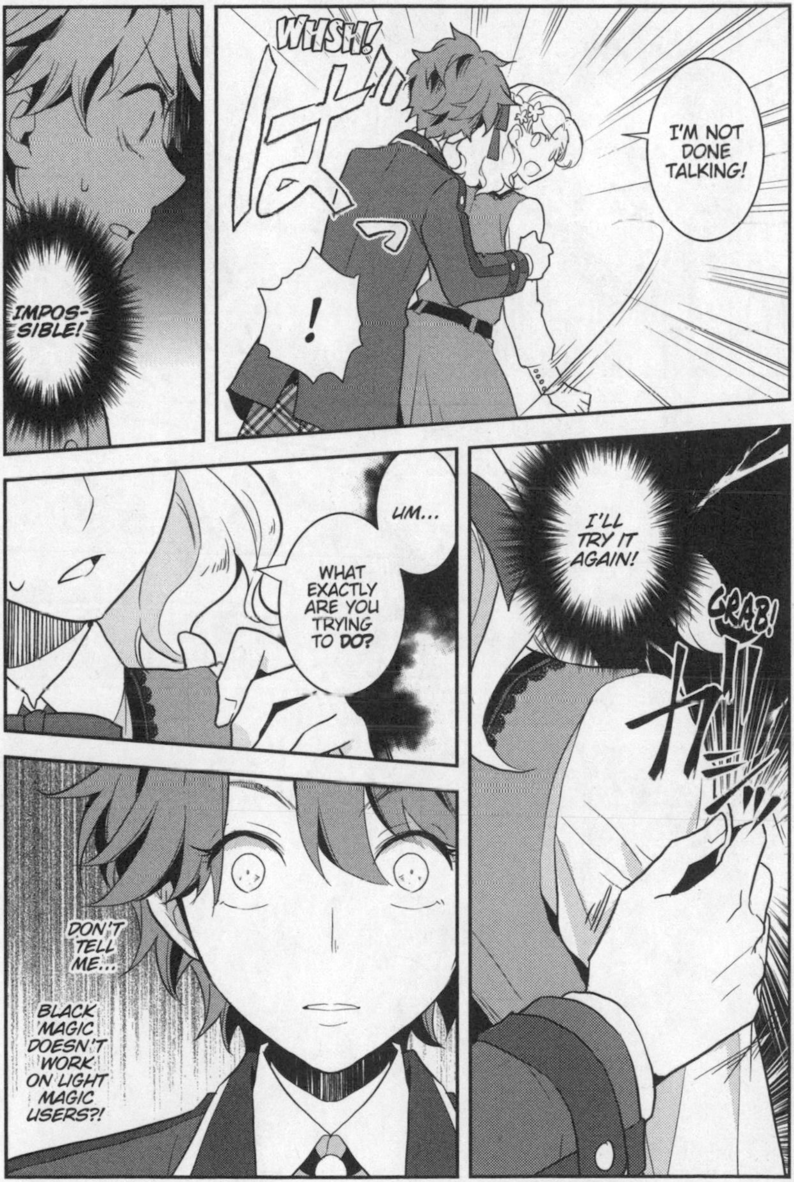
WHSH!
I'M NOT DONE TALKING!
!
IMPOS-SIBLE!
I'LL TRY IT AGAIN!
GRAB!
UM...
WHAT EXACTLY ARE YOU TRYING TO DO?
DON'T TELL ME...
BLACK MAGIC DOESN'T WORK ON LIGHT MAGIC USERS?!

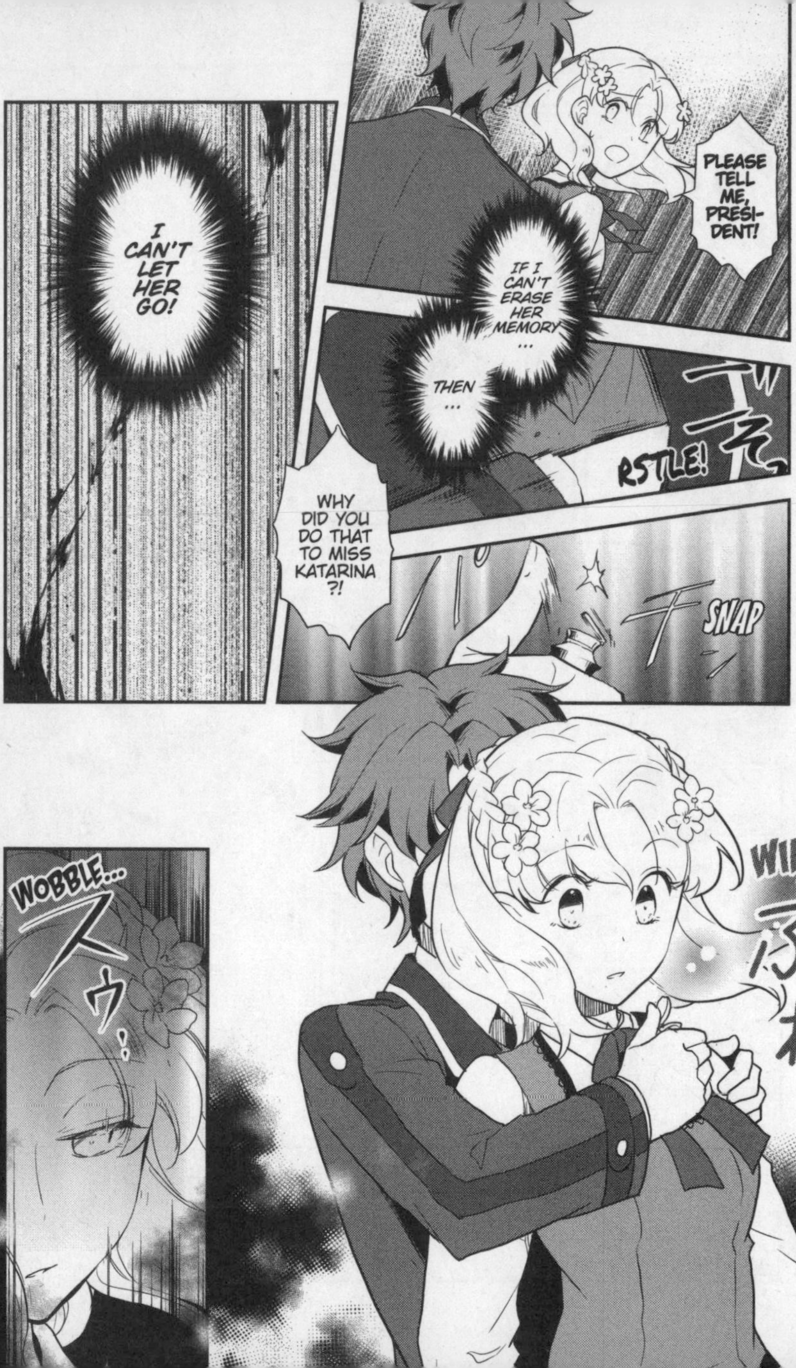
PLEASE TELL ME, PRESIDENT!
IF I CAN'T ERASE HER MEMORY...
THEN...
RSTLE!
WHY DID YOU DO THAT TO MISS KATARINA?!
SNAP
I CAN'T LET HER GO!
WIFF!
ふわっ
WOBBLE...
スゥ

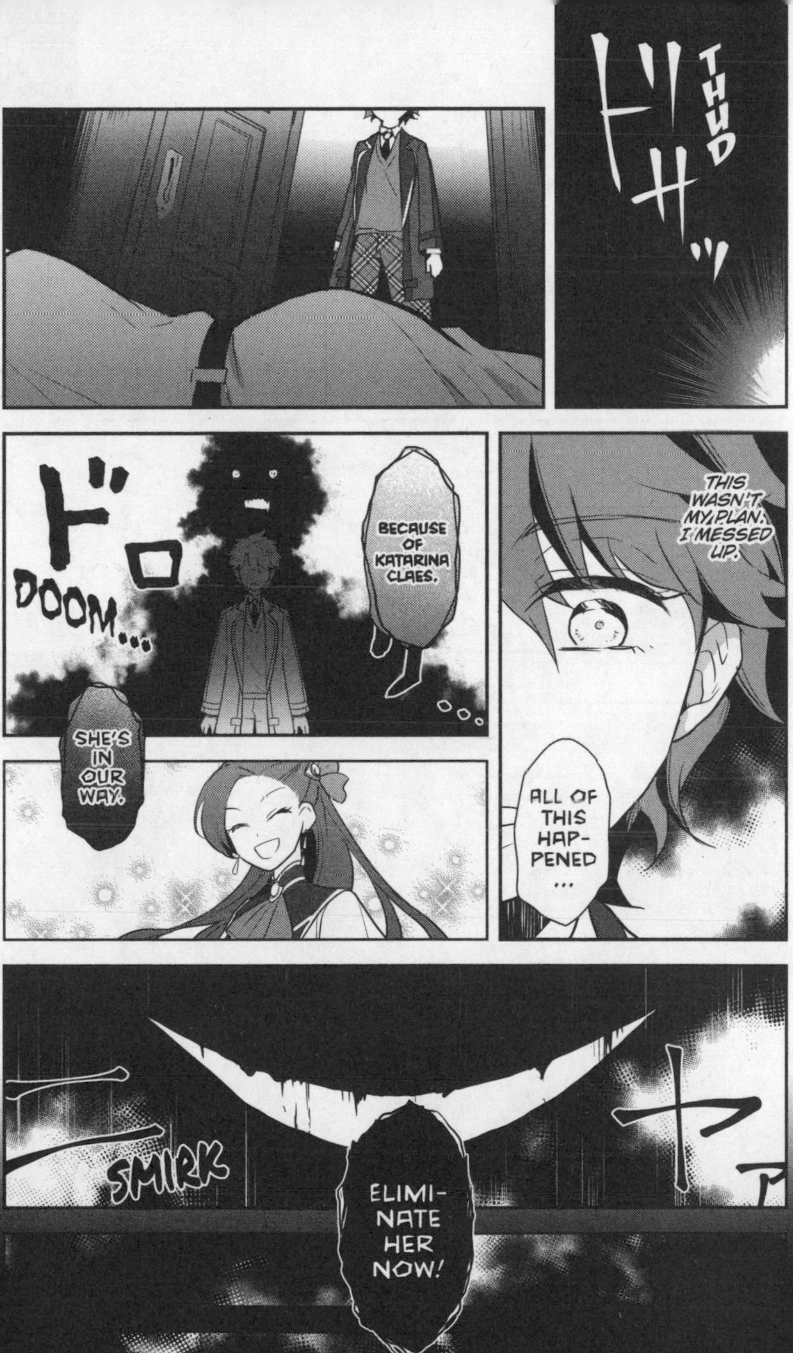

ドサッ
THUD
THIS WASN'T MY PLAN. I MESSED UP.
ALL OF THIS HAP-PENED...
BECAUSE OF KATARINA CLAES.
ドロ
DOOM...
SHE'S IN OUR WAY.
ニヤァ
SMIRK
ELIMI-NATE HER NOW!

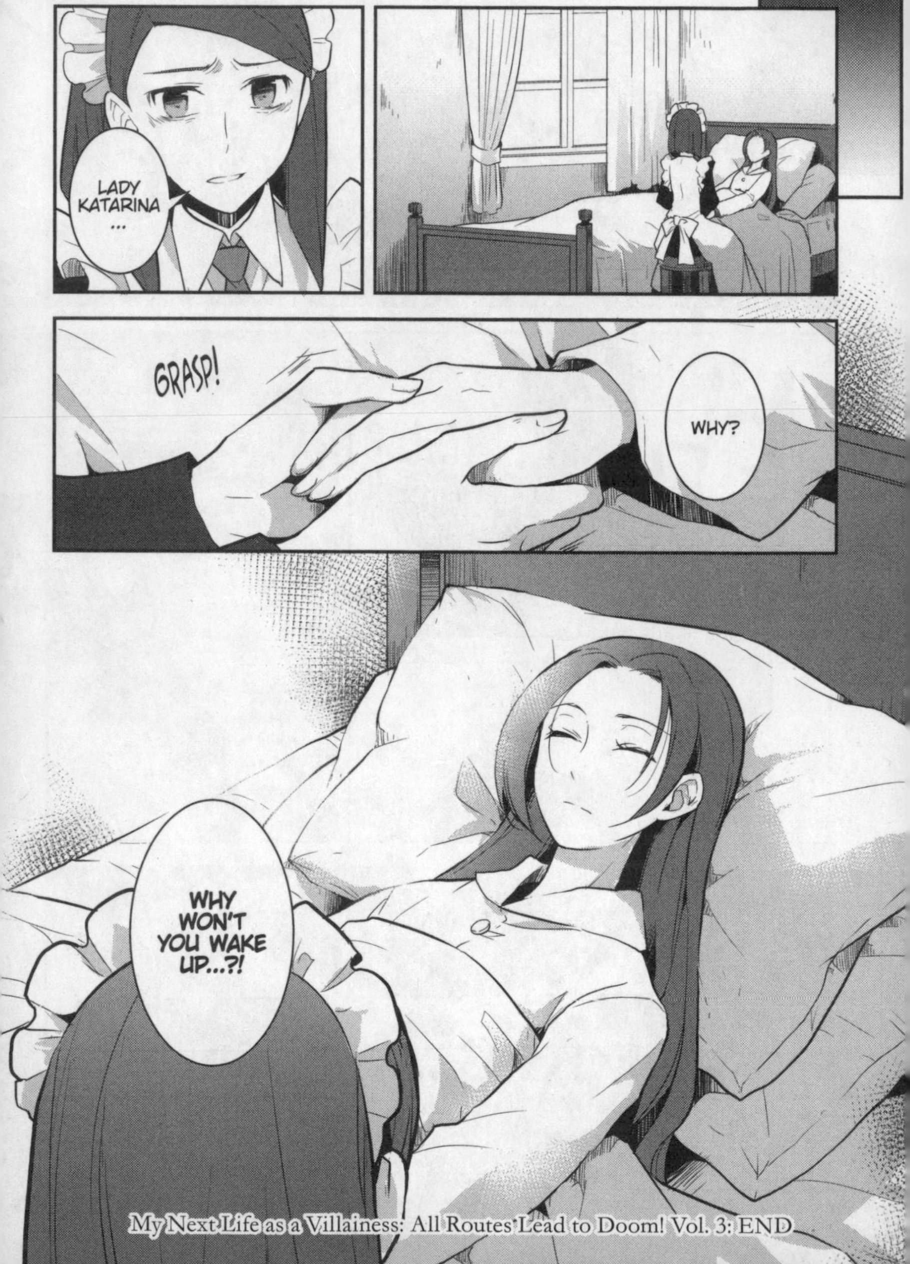
LADY KATARINA ...
GRASP!
WHY?
WHY WON'T YOU WAKE UP...?!

My Next Life as a Villainess: All Routes Lead to Doom! Vol. 3: END

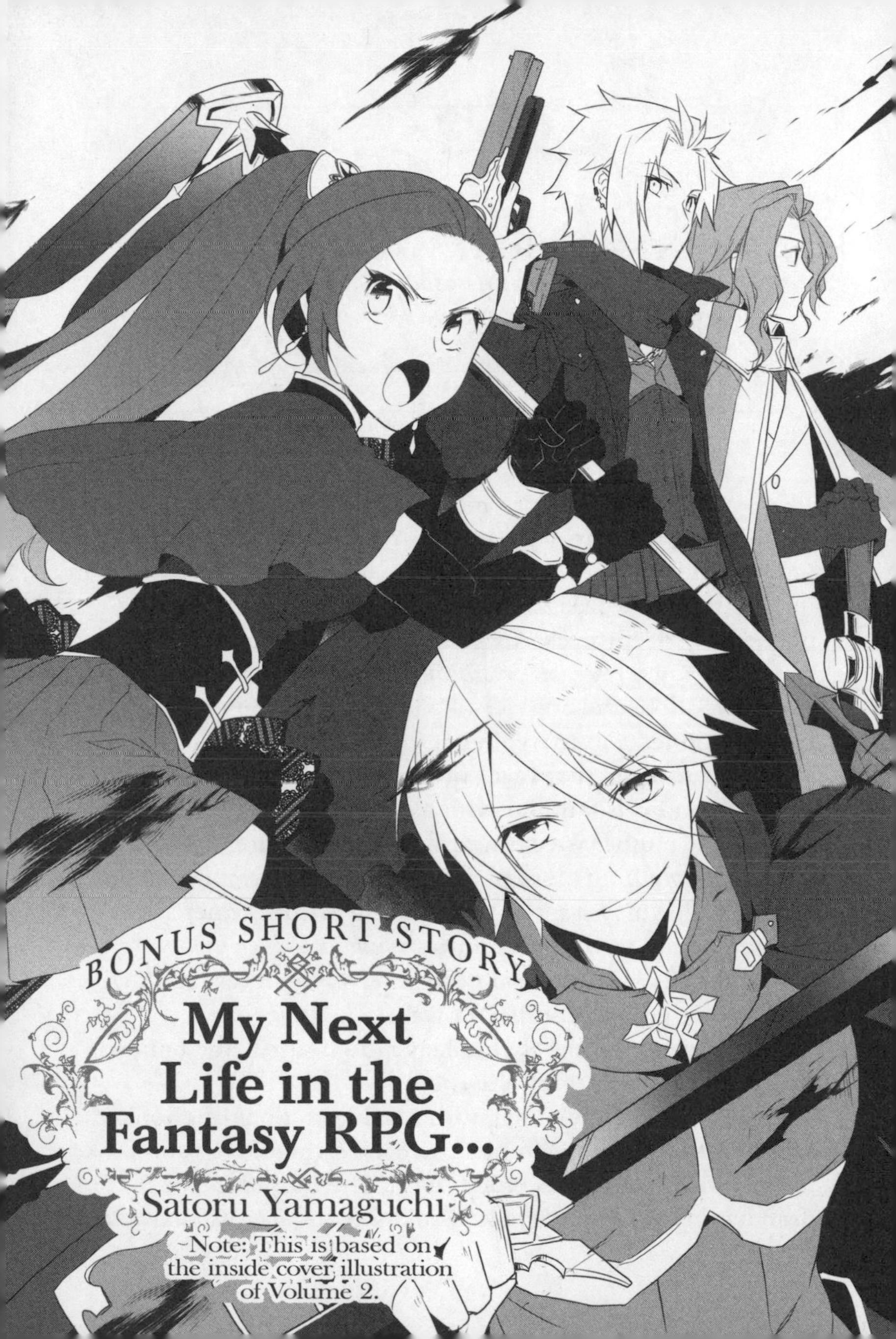
BONUS SHORT STORY
My Next Life in the Fantasy RPG...
Satoru Yamaguchi
Note: This is based on the inside cover illustration of Volume 2.

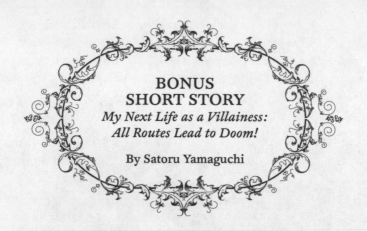

BONUS
SHORT STORY
My Next Life as a Villainess:
All Routes Lead to Doom!

By Satoru Yamaguchi

"Katarina. Katarina, wake up. You're going on your journey today."

With these words from my mother, I woke up and opened my sleepy eyes. Another ordinary day had begun.

Hm? Why is my mother waking me up? Usually, my maid, Anne, would be the one to wake me. And had my mother just mentioned a journey? What journey? When I got out of my bed, I realized that I was in a modest little room instead of the room I was familiar with at the Claes Estate. On top of that, my mother wasn't wearing her usual dress. She was wearing something more plain-looking than even our maid's uniform. I'd compare it to the clothing of the farmer's wife I'd met when I went to the countryside.

Wait. What? What is going on here? My mother didn't seem to notice how confused I was.

"Hurry up. Get dressed to leave the house." She handed me some clothes and left the room.

I decided to follow my mother's instructions and looked at the clothes she'd given me. I expected them to be similar to her outfit...until I unfolded them. The outfit had a cute design with a short cape, like you'd see on an RPG character.

Hey, this is cute! I got a little excited. After I changed, I posed in front of the mirror in my room. *Yeah, this looks great on me.* I could picture myself using cool magic or a weapon. As I did a fashion show by myself, my door opened, and my mother entered the room.

"Stop playing around. If you're done getting dressed, come out and have your breakfast," she said, raising her eyebrows.

"Okay." I obediently followed her out of my room.

I found myself in another room that looked like both a kitchen and dining area. There weren't any large hallways like in the Claes Estate. It reminded me of the little Japanese house from my previous life.

My father sat at what seemed to be a dining table, dressed in a plain outfit similar to my mother's. The moment he saw me, his beautiful expression softened, as it always did.

"Good morning, my sweet Katarina," he greeted me in his doting-parent voice.

I offered him a "good morning" in return, and took the seat he was pointing to.

"Now, hurry up and eat your breakfast," said my mother, as she brought my plate to the table. On the plate was a piece of golden-brown toast, a fried egg, and some salad—a simple meal, rarely served at the Claes Estate.

It's like a Japanese breakfast from my previous life! As I grew nostalgic and choked up, my mother chided me again.

"Don't take your time. Hurry up and eat. Keith already finished his breakfast and went to do a final check on his things."

"Huh? Final check on his things? For what?" When I asked, looking confused, my mother held her head and sighed.

"You're going on a journey today. When you're done

eating, go wash your face and check your things, too." Still unable to understand what was happening, I scarfed down my food, washed my face, grabbed my things, and went to what looked like a foyer.

As I stood in a daze after doing everything my mother had instructed, the door opened and a familiar face appeared.

"Good morning, Big Sister. I'm ready to go, too," said Keith. He came up to me with a smile, wearing an outfit commonly seen in RPGs. The way his long white cape flapped made him look just like a knight in shining armor.

As I stood in awe of Keith's fabulous appearance, our parents showed up.

"Have a safe journey. Promise you'll come back," they said, looking wistful. Then the front door opened, and a short elderly man with gray hair and a long gray beard appeared. He raised a staff that seemed like it was meant for a wizard.

"Become the chosen heroes. Save our world from the demon lord!" the elderly man shouted. We were seen off by villagers, who seemed like extras, clapping and cheering. I had no idea what was going on, but I waved at them with a smile and left the village I'd probably grown up in.

* * * * * * * * *

I'm Katarina Claes, and I'm sixteen years old. I apparently grew up as the eldest daughter of a distinguished farmer from a small village. I had planned to follow my father's footsteps and take over the farm with my adopted brother, Keith...however, one day, a demon lord appeared in my world! The demon lord led his monsters to start conquering this realm, putting us in a desperate situation!

Amidst all of this, the search for heroes began, and my

brother and I were chosen from our village. We were setting off on our journey today...

Wait, what's all this about? What demon lord? What hero? I reincarnated in the world of an otome game, didn't I? It wasn't a fantasy world of adventure like this! Keith, who probably hadn't expected me to scream this inside, made a remark.

"Come on, Big Sister. Our ride is here. Get inside." He threw me into a stagecoach. It wasn't the gorgeous one with the Claes family crest. It was a wagon used for transporting goods. The difference made me fidget.

"Big Sister, I know you're nervous, but you need to calm down," warned Keith. As we exchanged words, our stagecoach began to move. The ride was very bumpy, and not as comfortable as the Claes family carriage. However, it let us see the tranquil countryside, which made it enjoyable... *Oops, I'm getting too settled. What am I doing in this alternate universe?*

I was a Japanese high school girl in my previous life, and I reincarnated into another world, which was that of an otome game. It wasn't in an RPG where I would have to defeat a demon lord at all. And my role was a villainess, not a heroine. I would have much preferred to be a heroine, but that could never happen. *I was the villainess of an otome game just yesterday, and now I'm the heroine of an RPG. I must be dreaming. Reading an RPG-type story before bed must have caused this dream. I'm sure of it.*

After convincing myself, I was ready to enjoy my role as a heroine in this world. *Yeah, let's beat this demon lord, or whatever comes our way!*

* * * * * * * * *

"Big Sister, wake up. We're here." I was startled awake at Keith's voice. We seemed to have reached our destination while I was lost in thought. I must have given Keith the impression that I was asleep.

"*Unh*, we're already at the demon lord's place?" I asked.

Keith replied with a sigh. "Why would we go see the demon lord? We're at the castle."

"What? Why are we at the castle?"

"Big Sister, are you still asleep? We came here for the hero selection."

"Hero selection?"

"Get yourself together. We need to hurry!"

With Keith pulling my arm, I crossed a suspension bridge to the castle.

Past the large, sturdy-looking bridge was a fort-like castle, standing tall. After walking for a while, we found a line of people waiting to go through the checkpoint at the gate. It was pretty long.

"I wonder if all these people are here for the hero selection. There's quite a lot of them," said Keith.

After conversing with Keith for a while as we waited in line, I finally began to understand what the hero selection was about. It appeared that heroes from every village would be screened for the selection at the castle, and true heroes would be chosen out of those few. It was like an interview, from what I understood. The first interview was for the selections within a village, and the second interview was given at the castle, where we'd be selected to become real heroes.

Come to think of it, that old man said, "Become the chosen heroes." That must mean I'm just a candidate at the moment. But these interviews remind me of job hunting in my previous life. I guess the world of heroes isn't easy to live in, either.

While I was thinking about this, we reached the gate. We showed the certificates from our village to an official. Once we were approved, we entered the castle grounds.

There were a lot of people in the large hall that the official guided us to. Men and women of all ages and races were here. They were dressed in lovely RPG-style outfits. *Wow, this world is amazing! It's spectacular!*

"This is incredible!" I blurted.

"Yes, this is an incredible number of people," Keith replied.

I was more impressed by the fantasy-type world than the size of the crowd, but it was too much trouble to explain it to him. There were certainly a lot of people. There must have been over a hundred.

"How many people out of this crowd will be chosen?"

Keith paused to think before he responded. "Well, we've never had a hero selection before. No one really knows how many will be needed."

I see. They decided to hold a hero selection because the demon lord has appeared. No wonder no one has any idea.

"I doubt that everyone here will be selected," Keith continued. "It's rumored only a chosen few will make it."

"A chosen few." With that small of a group, I was less likely to be picked. There were many candidates who looked like powerful warriors or magic users, but I was just a peasant.

"If we don't pass, are we going to be sent back to our village?"

Keith sighed. "Well, probably, but don't talk about failing before the selection has even started."

"Y-you're right." *I still can't see us passing if they're only picking a few out of this many people.* "Hey, Keith. What do you think they're going make us do?"

"It hasn't been announced, so I have no idea."

That's right. None of this has ever been done before.

In RPGs, we might see a high priest raise a staff and declare, "I choose thee to be the hero!"

"Uh, Keith. Why were we chosen to represent our village?"

Keith's face was unreadable. "What? How could you forget it? They ran a lottery for young people and you won it."

I can't believe they used a lottery. Is it appropriate to choose a hero by lottery? Are they sure about this? This is a hero who has to defeat the demon lord!

"It seems larger towns and cities ran a legitimate selection process, but we were in a small village full of old people..." Keith seemed to have some opinions about the process, too.

Now it became clear. We probably wouldn't pass this selection. No one would pick a hero by lottery. We'd be sent home right off the bat. But I didn't have the nerve to go home after getting such a grand farewell from our village. What if we did some sightseeing before we left? As I began to think of beaches, mountains, or wherever we could have fun, I heard a voice echo through the hall.

"The hero selection will now begin." The announcement came from a podium set in the middle of the hall. It silenced the commotion in the room instantly. As the crowd turned its attention, the details of the hero selection were announced. It was quite different from the selection I'd pictured.

"Who would have expected to be hunting monsters?" I muttered with a sigh.

The hero selection process wasn't done by a high priest or through interviews or testing. It was an actual monster hunt. We were sent out to hunt monsters that appeared in the forest near the castle.

Everyone in the hall was to be randomly assigned to several small groups and sent to areas that monsters occupied. We went to the forest with a few other people and an official who would follow us for assessment.

"But it's an appropriate way to assess our abilities in defeating monsters," said Keith, who heard my grumbling.

He's right, but I don't stand a chance against a monster.

I may be dressed like an RPG character, but, in actuality, I'm just a peasant. And the weapon I'm carrying, which I pulled from a box, is a hoe. I'm accustomed to using it, but not as a weapon to kill monsters. Keith was given a sword, so how come I got a hoe? According to Keith, most candidates receive their weapons at temples, but they're unable to choose them. This isn't fair.

A monster probably can't be killed with a hoe. A hoe is used for plowing a field, not for killing monsters. If a monster appears when we reach the forest, Keith and the other candidates will probably defeat it. It'll end with me just watching them. However, I'll be in deep trouble if it attacks me.

"Um, what is a monster, exactly?" I asked the official who was with us. I had no intention of fighting, but I needed the information to defend myself.

"It has the appearance of a ferocious beast. You need to act very carefully." I couldn't see the official's expression behind his armored helmet, but he sounded serious.

"What kind of beast does it look like?"

"I'm sorry. We don't have all the details."

"I see." There was too little information. This might end with us being killed by the monster. In that case...

"Excuse me. I don't mind being eliminated from the selection. Can I watch from afar?"

I decided to take a chance on asking to be excused. Keith, who was standing next to me, looked shocked. I didn't know what kind of expression the official was making, but he seemed surprised, too.

"Didn't you come here to be selected as a hero?" he asked, in a puzzled tone.

"Well, um...the thing is, there weren't that many young people in our village. I lost the lottery—I mean, I won it—so I didn't come here by choice. I'm not really looking to become a hero."

I explained honestly. However, Keith held his head, as if to say, "How can you admit such a thing?"

The official's body began to tremble. *Uh-oh. I must have upset him when I told him that I didn't want to become a hero!* I began to panic.

"You're very interesting." He didn't seem particularly angry, which made me feel relieved. "If you're ever in danger, I'll protect you."

What a nice guy. His voice and the way he spoke sounded familiar. Could it have been my imagination?

I was given permission to sit out the battle, and I proceeded to the forest without any worries.

When our team reached the forest, we decided to go to the west side, where a monster had been seen. There were several monsters that occupied separate parts of the forest, and we headed out to where one of them had been reported.

It happened after we'd walked around for a little while. Just as we thought we heard something growling, a large, black wolf-like monster appeared.

"It's a monster!" the official shouted. The candidates took out their weapons and prepared for an attack.

A brawny swordsman lunged at the black wolf with his sword, but the monster dodged. I was in awe at the battle before me as I hid behind everyone and watched them fight.

The monster wasn't that large and didn't seem undefeatable. However, it moved too fast for anyone to strike it, which was frustrating them. I watched them worriedly, but I soon noticed something strange. I could hear something else growling along with the wolf.

Wait. Could it be?! I stared at the wolf. It looked very

agitated, but... I quietly pulled a treat out of my pocket that I'd been saving for later. I felt the wolf watching me. *Hm, maybe this monster is...* I tossed the treat at the monster. It dove, caught it brilliantly, and began munching away.

That's what I'd thought. This monster was hungry. An empty stomach could make anyone cranky. I threw another treat, and before I knew it, the wolf came and sat next to me. *What? It got friendly with me! But all dogs hated me in my previous life!* When I went to pat it, it whimpered and rubbed its face against my hand. This made me so happy.

"So cute!" I said.

Keith called out to me. "Big Sister!" When I realized what had happened and looked around, I found the other candidates staring at me in amazement. The official was trembling. I felt as if I'd done something wrong.

* * * * * * * * *

When I returned to the castle with the monster wolf, who'd become completely attached to me, I was chosen to be one of the heroes. I received a title, Monster Tamer, for befriending a monster. And that wasn't all.

"Please, let me join your team," said the official.

It turned out that the armored official was actually the prince, Jeord, who'd observed the selection in disguise, and so he joined our team. No wonder his voice and the way he'd spoken sounded familiar.

Jeord was dressed as a black knight when he revealed himself as the prince, which made him look hot. And so, Keith, who was also selected as a hero, Jeord, and I set out on a journey to defeat the demon lord.

When we started our adventure, we first traveled to a wasteland that looked like a field. After a while, we heard a voice say, "*Ee hee hee hee hee!*" A woman dressed like a witch appeared in front of us.

Oh, my God! There's a monster! I thought. I braced myself for an attack.

The witch spoke up. "Katarina, stop playing. Go practice your manners!"

The witch was my mother. Her eyebrows were raised, and she was holding a book on manners in her hand. I gasped in horror.

* * * * * * * * *

"Lady Katarina. Lady Katarina, please wake up. It's morning." I opened my eyes at the sound of Anne's voice. I was back in my familiar room, and my witch mom wasn't there. I sighed with relief.

It was an interesting dream, but it had a very frightful end. I'm glad I was dreaming! It was scary to have my witch mom telling me to study.

"Oh, by the way, Lady Katarina, it's your day off. Madam has instructed you to study some manners." Anne showed me a stack of books on my desk.

"*Eep!*" I gasped, just like I had in my dream.

It sucks to have predictive dreams.

AFTERWORD

Good morning, good afternoon, and good evening. This is Nami Hidaka. Thank you for your continued support! Because of it, I was able to bring you Volume 3.

Get this. Because of everyone's help, a decision has been made on an anime adaptation. An anime! Isn't that incredible? Katarina and the others are going to move and talk. As a professional and an anime lover, I'm really looking forward to it. It's going to be exciting to enjoy Yamaguchi-sensei's fun, powerful story animated.

If you could read or watch the original light novel, anime, and manga of this series, that would be great. Please continue your support! As the artist of this series, I will work hard to show you how wonderful *My Next Life as a Villainess* is! I hope you'll continue to follow it!

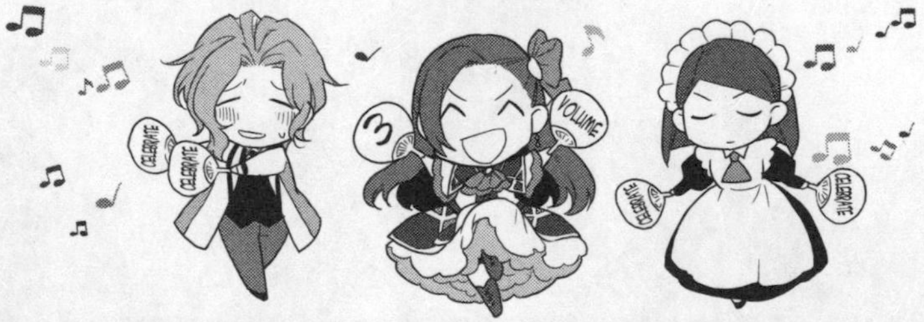
CELEBRATE
CELEBRATE
3
VOLUME
CELEBRATE
CELEBRATE

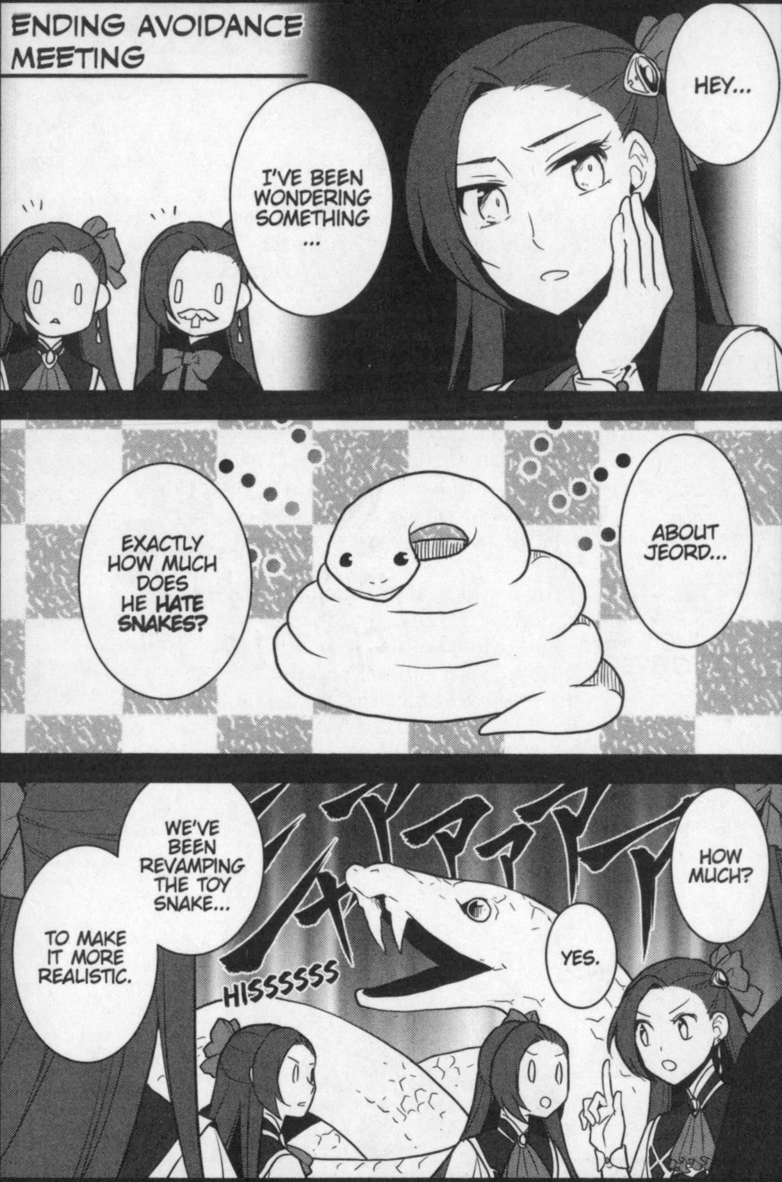
ENDING AVOIDANCE MEETING
HEY...
I'VE BEEN WONDERING SOMETHING ...
ABOUT JEORD...
EXACTLY HOW MUCH DOES HE HATE SNAKES?
HOW MUCH?
YES.
WE'VE BEEN REVAMPING THE TOY SNAKE...
TO MAKE IT MORE REALISTIC.
HISSSSSS

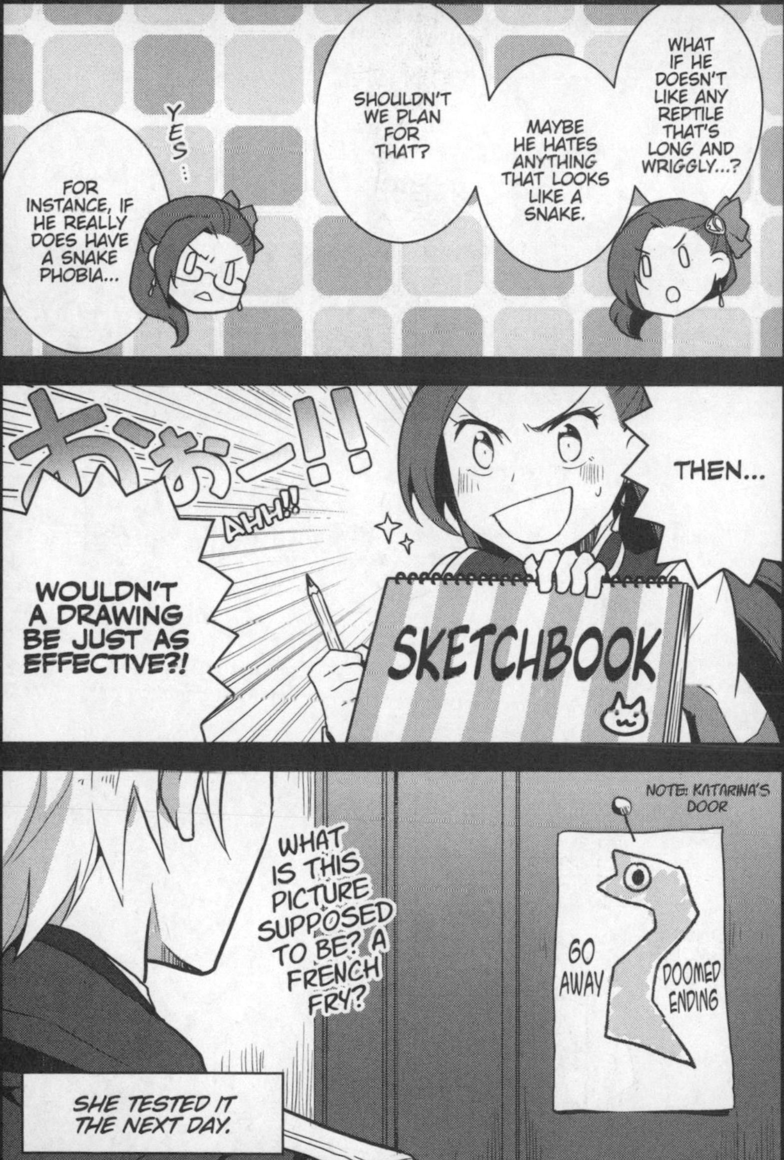
WHAT IF HE DOESN'T LIKE ANY REPTILE THAT'S LONG AND WRIGGLY...?
MAYBE HE HATES ANYTHING THAT LOOKS LIKE A SNAKE.
SHOULDN'T WE PLAN FOR THAT?
YES...
FOR INSTANCE, IF HE REALLY DOES HAVE A SNAKE PHOBIA...
THEN...
おおー!!
AHH!!
WOULDN'T A DRAWING BE JUST AS EFFECTIVE?!
SKETCHBOOK
NOTE: KATARINA'S DOOR
DOOMED ENDING
GO AWAY
WHAT IS THIS PICTURE SUPPOSED TO BE? A FRENCH FRY?
SHE TESTED IT THE NEXT DAY.

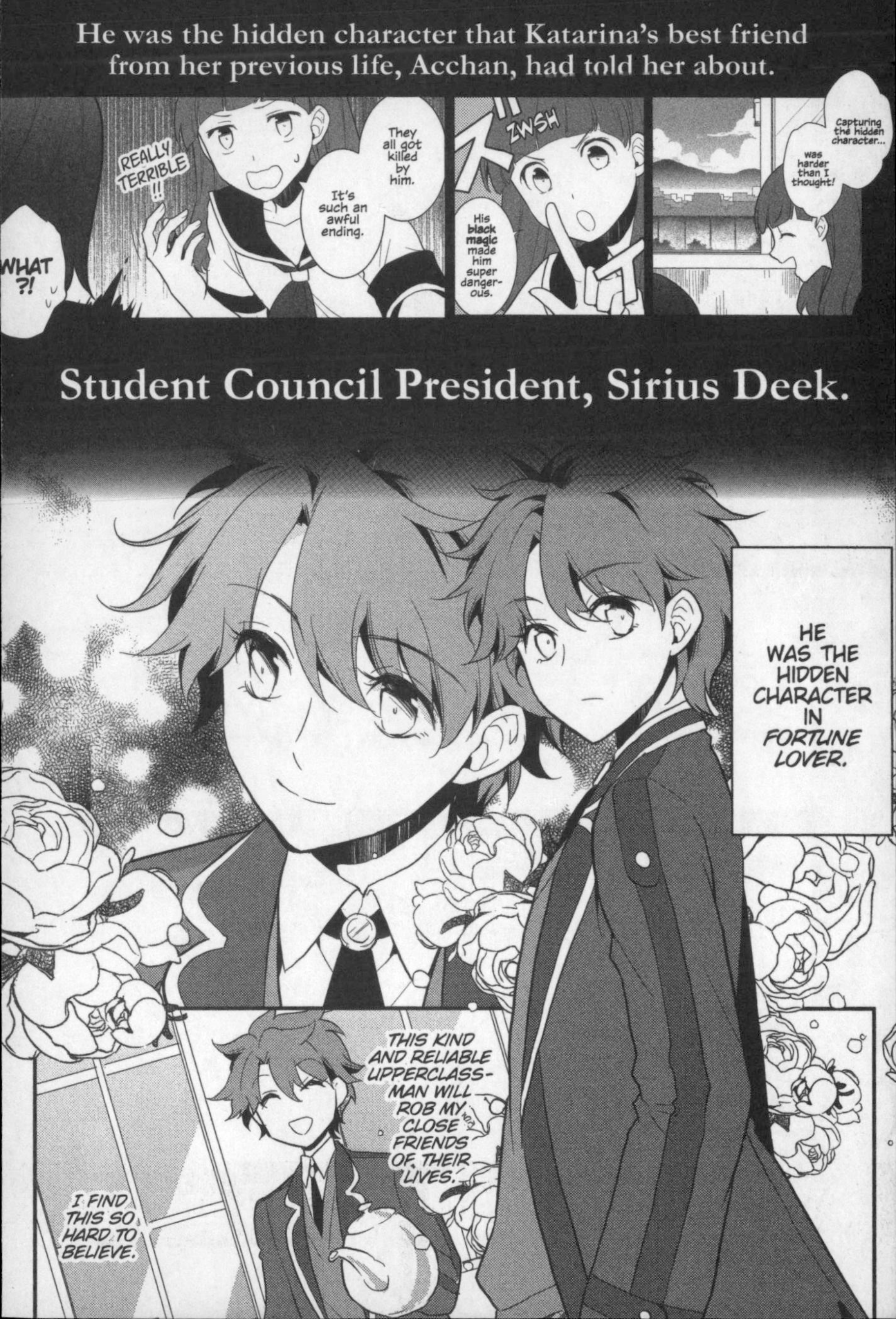
He was the hidden character that Katarina's best friend from her previous life, Acchan, had told her about.
Capturing the hidden character...
was harder than I thought!
ZWSH
His black magic made him super danger-ous.
They all got killed by him.
It's such an awful ending.
REALLY TERRIBLE!!
WHAT?!
Student Council President, Sirius Deek.
HE WAS THE HIDDEN CHARACTER IN FORTUNE LOVER.
THIS KIND AND RELIABLE UPPERCLASS-MAN WILL ROB MY CLOSE FRIENDS OF THEIR LIVES.
I FIND THIS SO HARD TO BELIEVE.

Katarina realizes Sirius's true identity, but...

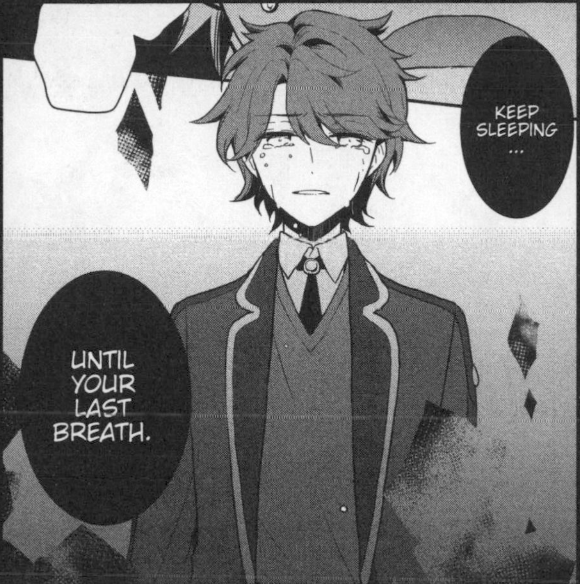
KEEP SLEEPING ...
UNTIL YOUR LAST BREATH.

she is put into a deep sleep by his black magic.

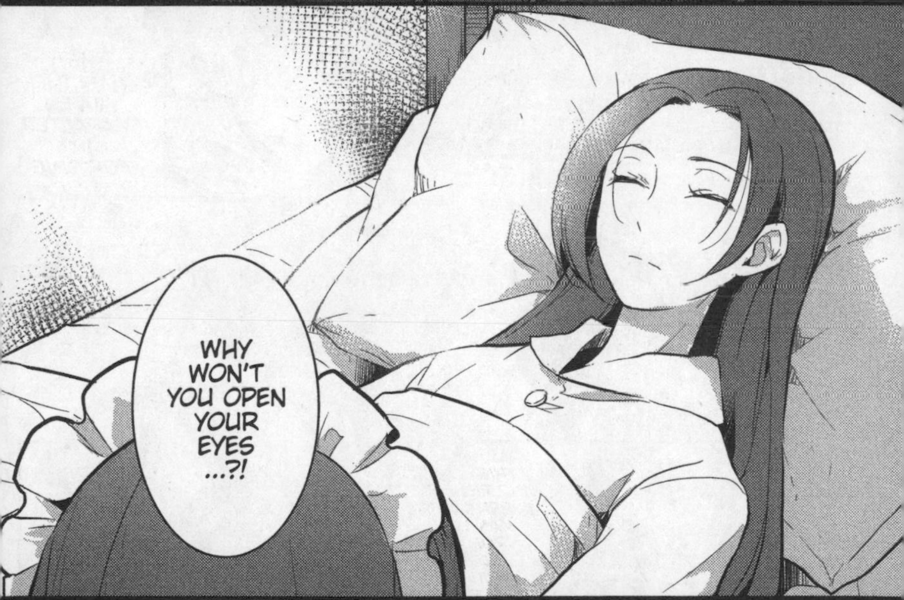
WHY WON'T YOU OPEN YOUR EYES ...?!

Will Katarina avoid this bad ending?

FIND OUT IN VOLUME 4!

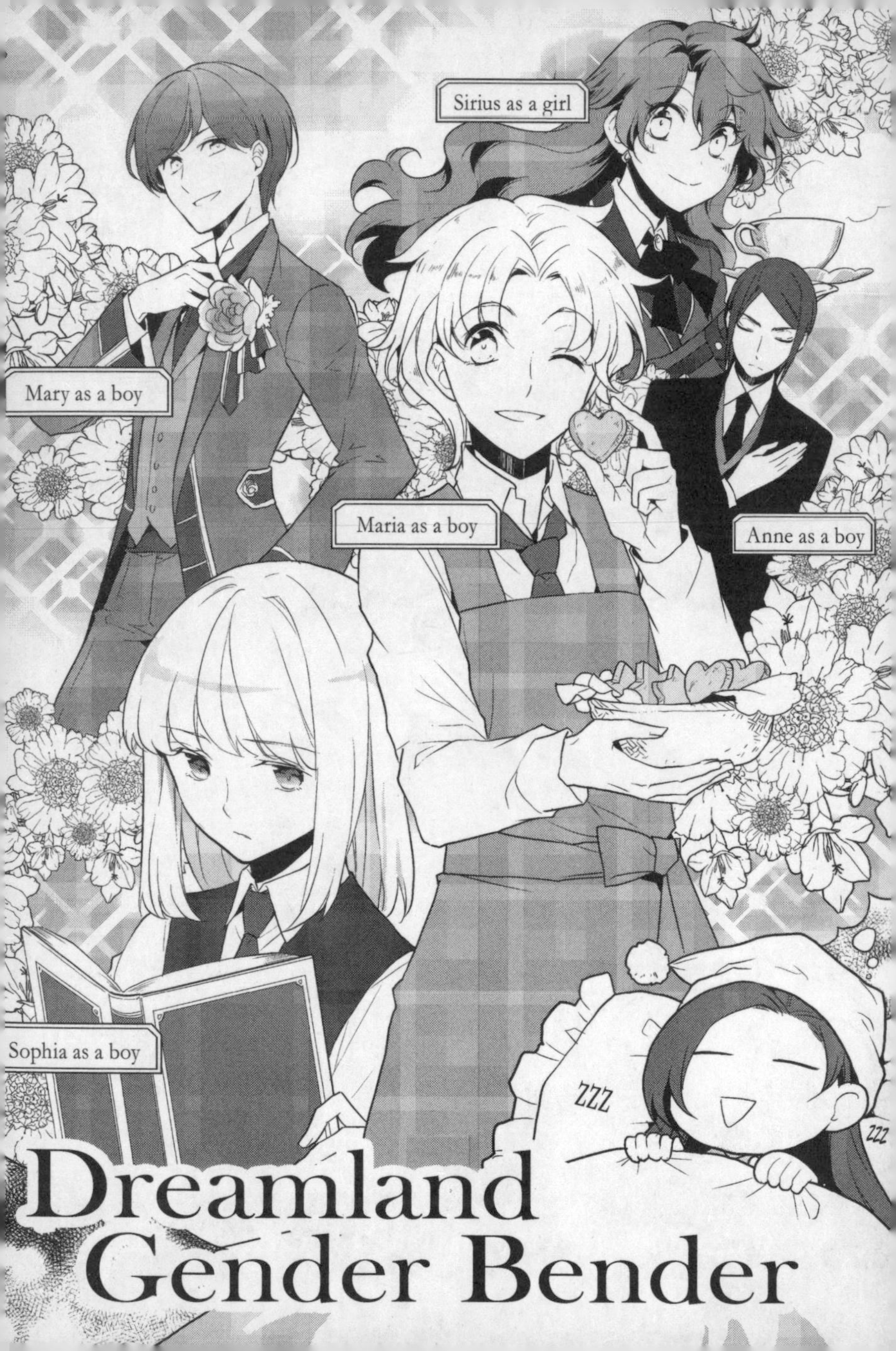
Sirius as a girl
Anne as a boy
Maria as a boy
Mary as a boy
Sophia as a boy
ZZZ
ZZZ
Dreamland
Gender Bender

SEVEN SEAS ENTERTAINMENT PRESENTS

My Next Life as a Villainess: All Routes Lead to Doom!

art by **NAMI HIDAKA**   story by **SATORU YAMAGUCHI**   **VOLUME 3**

TRANSLATION
Elina Ishikawa-Curran

ADAPTATION
Lora Gray

LETTERING AND RETOUCH
Rina Mapa

COVER DESIGN
KC Fabellon

PROOFREADER
Kurestin Armada

EDITOR
Peter Adrian Behravesh

PREPRESS TECHNICIAN
Rhiannon Rasmussen-Silverstein

PRODUCTION MANAGER
Lissa Pattillo

MANAGING EDITOR
Julie Davis

ASSOCIATE PUBLISHER
Adam Arnold

PUBLISHER
Jason DeAngelis

MY NEXT LIFE AS A VILLAINESS: ALL ROUTES LEAD TO DOOM! VOL. 3
© Nami Hidaka 2019, Satoru Yamaguchi 2019
First published in Japan in 2019 by ICHIJINSHA Inc., Tokyo.
Publication rights for this English edition arranged through Kodansha Ltd., Tokyo.

Seven Seas press and purchase enquiries can be sent to Marketing Manager
Lianne Sentar at press@gomanga.com. Information regarding the distribution
and purchase of digital editions is available from Digital Manager CK Russell
at digital@gomanga.com.

Seven Seas and the Seven Seas logo are trademarks of
Seven Seas Entertainment, LLC. All rights reserved.

ISBN: 978-1-64505-230-2

Printed in Canada

First Printing: April 2020

10 9 8 7 6 5 4 3 2 1

FOLLOW US ONLINE: *www.sevenseasentertainment.com*

READING DIRECTIONS

This book reads from *right to left*, Japanese style.
If this is your first time reading manga, you start
reading from the top right panel on each page and
take it from there. If you get lost, just follow the
numbered diagram here. It may seem backwards at
first, but you'll get the hang of it! Have fun!!

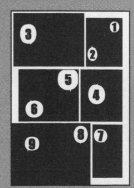

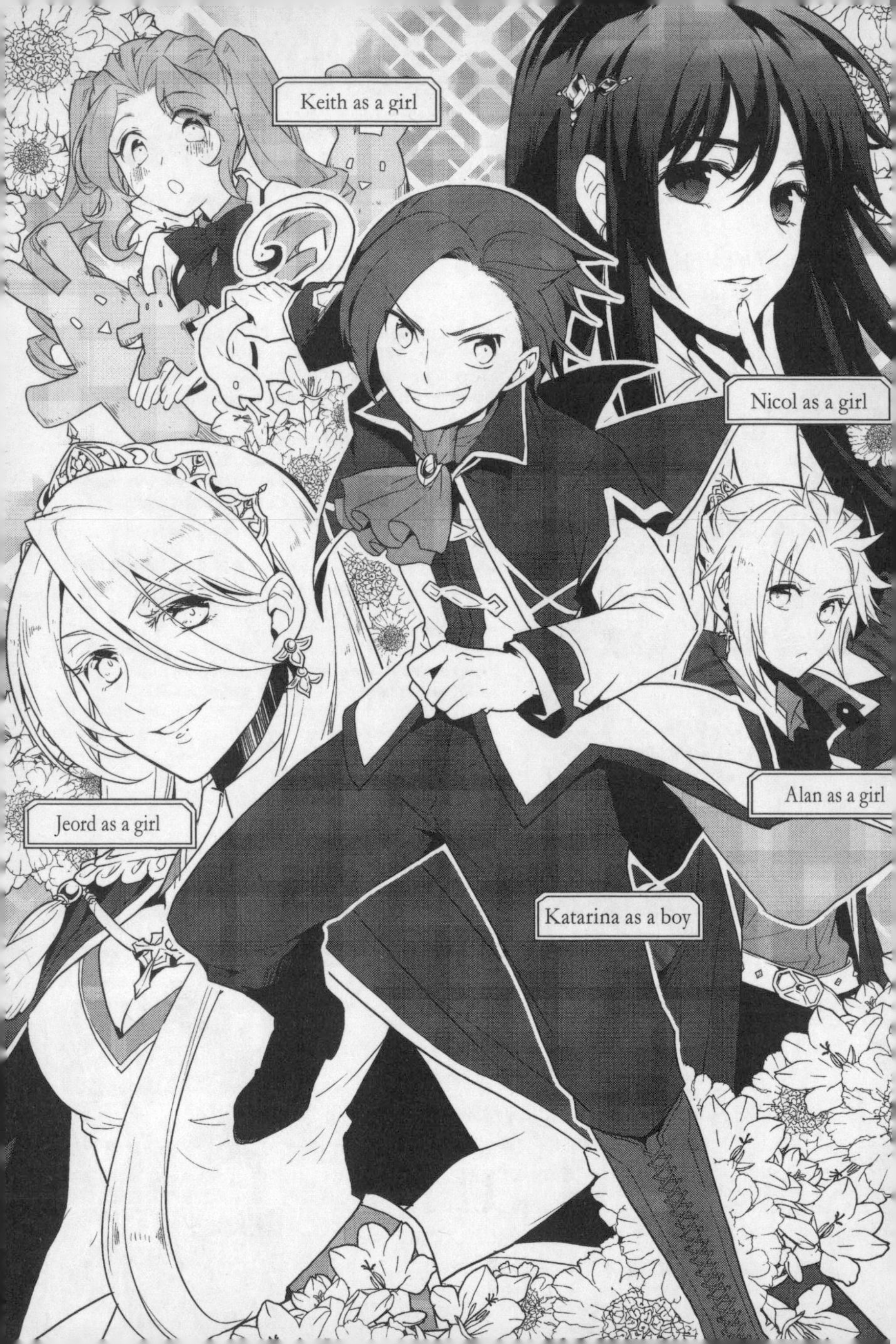
Keith as a girl
Nicol as a girl
Alan as a girl
Jeord as a girl
Katarina as a boy